Music Through Topics

an activity resource

Veronica Clark

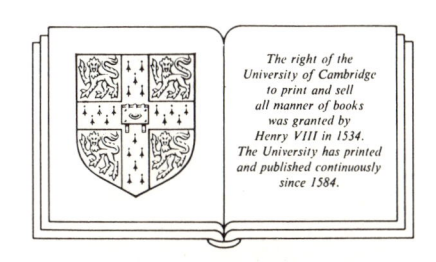

*The right of the
University of Cambridge
to print and sell
all manner of books
was granted by
Henry VIII in 1534.
The University has printed
and published continuously
since 1584.*

Cambridge University Press
Cambridge
New York   Port Chester   Melbourne   Sydney

Published by the Press Syndicate of the University of Cambridge
The Pitt Building, Trumpington Street, Cambridge CB2 1RP
40 West 20th Street, New York, NY 10011, USA
10 Stamford Road, Oakleigh, Melbourne 3166, Australia

© Cambridge University Press 1990

First published 1990

Printed in Great Britain by Bell & Bain Ltd, Glasgow

British Library cataloguing in publication data
Clark, Veronica
Music through topics: an activity resource.
1. Music. For schools
I. Title
780

ISBN 0 521 34842 0

Book design by Anne Colwell
Cover and text illustrations by Daryl Harding

Acknowledgements

The author and publishers wish to thank the following for permission to reproduce copyright material.

'I went for a walk in the park today' (p.17) and 'Dring! Dring! Telephone' (p.114) from *Over and Over Again*, eds Barbara Ireson and Christopher Rowe, Beaver Books 1978; extract from 'Oliphaunt' (p.18) by J.R.R. Tolkien, in *Man and Beast*, Unwin Hyman; 'Hi! said the elephant' (p.22), words and music by Sandra Kerr, from *Birds & Beasts, Animal Songs, Games and Activities*, chosen by Sheena Roberts, © 1987 A & C Black (Publishers) Ltd; 'Marching through the jungle' (p.26), originally entitled 'The prehistoric animal brigade' music by Muriel Reeve, from *Okki-Tokki-Unga, Action Songs for Children*, chosen by Beatrice Harrop, Linda Friend and David Godsby, © 1976 A & C Black Ltd; 'A long-haired Griggle from the land of Grunch' (p.42), Alice Gilbert, Doubleday, New York; 'The sounds in the evening' (p.45) from *Seeing and Doing*, Eleanor Farjeon, Methuen and Co. Ltd; 'What happiness' (p.50), arranged and adapted by June Tillman; 'Eggs are laid by turkeys' (p.67) reprinted by permission of Gina Macoby Literary Agency © 1974 by Mary Ann Hoberman; 'Egg thoughts' (p.69) from 'Soft-boiled egg' by Russell Hoban in *Egg Thoughts and other Frances songs*, Faber & Faber 1973; 'Chicks grow into chickens' (p.76), David Moses of Tinderbox, 93 Stradella Road, London SE24; 'Woodland fairies' (p.116) Rose Needham; 'Lullaby' (p.122), Pauline Apps; 'Flicker-flicker-flack' (p.140), Jan Betts; 'Look out!' (p.140) from *Rhythmic Tunes and Songs for Children*, Paul Edmonds, Pitman Publishing; 'Ace!' (p.144) from *Hot Dog and Other Poems*, Kit Wright, Kestrel Books 1981, © 1981 Kit Wright; 'Fog' (p.146), from the Scunthorpe and District Teachers' Centre book *Foundations of Music 5–7: Religious Education*.

Every effort has been made to reach copyright holders; the publishers would be glad to hear from anyone whose rights they have unknowingly infringed.

denotes items on the cassette (ISBN 0 521 35630 X) which accompanies this book. The cassette can be ordered through a bookshop or, in case of difficulty, direct from the Educational Sales Department, Cambridge University Press.

Other song books and musical activity books published by Cambridge University Press

Seasonal Songs by Dot Paxton
A collection of easy-to-learn songs for each season of the year with ideas for 'spin-off' work
ISBN 0 521 33668 6

Story, song and dance compiled by Jean Gilbert
For the young, a collection of ideas for improvised drama with music
Book   ISBN 0 521 33967 7
Cassette   ISBN 0 521 32758 X

Light the Candles! by June Tillman
Songs of praise and ceremony from around the world, for use with multicultural groups
ISBN 0 521 33969 3

Titles in the *Cambridge Young Musicals* series

The Bells of Lyonesse
ISBN 0 521 33590 6

Seaspell
Piano/Conductor edition   ISBN 0 521 33588 4
Performers' edition   ISBN 0 521 33589 2

Duffy and the devil
Piano/Conductor edition   ISBN 0 521 33592 2
Performers' edition   ISBN 0 521 33593 0

In preparation
African Madonna
ISBN 0 521 37880 X

SE

Contents

Introduction **4**

Summary of topics **8**

Notes on the activities **9**

Elephants **13**

At home **41**

Hens and chicks **65**

Trains **91**

Bells **113**

In town **139**

Introduction

Listening, discussion and experimentation, singly and in groups, are central to the music-making activities described in this book. These learning processes, plus the development of cross-curricular themes, reflect the ethos of the National Curriculum.

This book is for . . .
. . . those teachers who find class music difficult. It should also be helpful to student teachers. Teachers with some knowledge of music will feel at home here too, and will find plenty of new material to supplement their repertoire.

The book aims to dispel the myth that music can only be taught by teachers with a formal music training, although it does help if you are able to sing in tune. The spoken word is often the starting point of a musical activity, so the ability to recite jingles and poems with a feeling for the rhythm is an asset. A sense of humour, enthusiasm and confidence are important extras. If you lack the last of these attributes, *Music Through Topics* may help you to gain it.

The book contains . . .
. . . six topics: *Elephants*, *At home*, *Hens and chicks*, *Trains*, *Bells* and *In town*. The topics have been chosen not just because of their appeal to young children, but because they lend themselves to the teaching and expression of one or more specific musical skills. *Elephants*, for example, introduces a slow, heavy beat and explores the lower range of sound. Quick, light and high sounds are practised in *Hens and chicks*. The more elementary skills receive attention in the earlier topics. The chart on pages 6–7 shows at a glance how the skills are distributed across the topics and how they progress.

Each topic contains the following activities:
 speech rhymes
 action rhymes and songs
 poems
 songs
 dancing and singing games
 sound story
 games and exercises
 music corner activities
 ideas for making simple percussion instruments

Each of these activities is helpful in the training and development of several aspects of musicianship. Speech rhymes, for example, encourage clear diction, help to establish a feeling for the beat or pulse, and introduce rhythmic patterns which can be interpreted by body sounds and on instruments. In addition, there are ideas for taking the topic across the curriculum, and a list of resources.

A detailed summary of each topic and general notes on the activities follow on pages 8–12.

How to use this book

Most of the material is accompanied by teaching notes. There are usually several suggestions for each item. They are numbered or bulleted to make the notes easier to follow. Each suggestion leads gently and logically to the next so that you can adapt the musical treatment to suit the age and ability of the children. Don't, however, follow the notes too slavishly. Add your own and your children's ideas and you will end up with some original and exciting sounds. Always encourage the children to experiment and think for themselves, and welcome alternative suggestions.

You won't achieve satisfactory results first time. Musical skills, like any other, need to be practised. Learn with the children and be generous with your praise.

Music and the school day

Music, like number and language activities, is something which should form an integral part of the school day. There are usually several times during the school day when a teacher can find a few minutes for songs or stories or poems or number and language games. It is during moments like these that many of the activities described in the book can be practised. Encourage the children to sing as they model or paint or sew, especially if the songs are relevant to what they are doing. As well as these informal, maybe impromptu music sessions, there should be one or two occasions during the week when a period of about 20 minutes is set aside for music. If the hall or any relatively large area is available at such times, movement and games can be incorporated into the sessions.

The **short music sessions** are valuable for practising items learnt on a previous occasion, and maybe for developing them. They can also be used to introduce new songs or poems. These moments are ideal for playing listening games and exercises. These games often help to settle children down or to bring them together after a period of varied activities.

Unless musical instruments are readily accessible it is unlikely that they will be used, especially for these short music sessions. A small selection of percussion instruments should, therefore, always be set out ready for use. A useful set of instruments would include one or two tambourines, one or two tambours, a few jingles, woodblocks, a range of beaters, a largish cymbal and some good maracas. An octave of chimes and one more tuned percussion instrument, e.g. a xylophone, are useful. Train the children to fetch instruments when requested and to put them away again. One instrument that is always available is the body, and that includes the voice. Use body sounds to accompany stories, poems and songs.

The **longer music session** requires preparation. It's a good idea to keep a record of these sessions so that development and progress can be monitored.

Involve the children in getting ready for the music lesson. Train them to carry the instruments in a safe way – safe for themselves, for others and for the instruments. Dispatch a door-holder with the instrument carriers to ensure a safe passage through doorways. It is helpful for all concerned if the pool of school percussion instruments is kept in an area not generally used for teaching purposes. It is a deterrent to using the instruments if you know that you'll have to disturb another class in order to assemble them.

If the children are seated in a large semi-circle or horseshoe you'll be able to keep track of who has 'had a go' on the instruments. Reassure the children that, subject to good behaviour, everyone will have the opportunity to play an instrument at least once during the session. Contrary to the expectations of many teachers, discipline in these longer, instrument oriented lessons is no problem. You have at your disposal lots of incentives for good behaviour. It can't be denied, however, that such lessons require a concentrated teacher input of both physical and mental energy. Teacher and children need to be fresh – the end of the school day isn't usually the best time to make music.

Finally, don't worry if a music session doesn't go as planned. If you are doing your job properly – that is, allowing for experimentation and individual interpretation – the music making could become – dare I say it – noisy! Always encourage the children to listen to what they are creating and to discuss the effect of the sounds they produce.

Musical skills developed by topic

	Dynamics	Tempo Beat
elephants	• strong, heavy elephant footsteps • loud trumpeting	• slow, steady elephant movements • introducing the **beat**
at home	• loud – noisy people and machinery • quiet – bedtime • introducing *f* and *p*	• ticking clocks } various • dripping taps } speeds
hens and chicks	• quiet *cheep*s and taps	• rapid running and flapping movements of chicks
trains	• trains approaching • trains moving off	• fast and slow trains • trains speeding up/ slowing down for hills, stations, signals
bells	• loud (near) } bells • quiet (far) }	• steady, slow tolling bells • fast, pealing bells • chiming clocks
in town	• town sounds near (*f*) and far off (*p*) • moving traffic < and >	• windscreen wipers • people marching, walking, running, etc. • traffic speeding up/ slowing down

Rhythm	Pitch / Melody / Harmony	Environmental sounds	Instruments
• the crotchet ♩ • animal rhythms ♫ ♩ e-le-phant	• low and deep • ascending/descending scale • elephants climbing up/ going down hill • tunes with E and G	• water • jungle • storm • wild animals	drums tambours xylophone
• quaver pairs ♫ • rhythm of things found in the house ♫♫♩. knock at the door ♫♫♩ bub-ble bub-ble • rhythm of various types of dwelling	• contrasts of high/low household sounds • ascending scale – going upstairs • tunes with E and G	• water • machines • clocks • people • pets • utensils	claves woodblocks tuned glasses tuned bottles
• the rest 𝄽 • egg and bird rhythms ♩𝄽 hen ♫♩ chi-cken ♫♫ tip-per tip-per tap	• high-pitched *cheeps* • tunes with E G A	• beach and sea • chickens • eggs • birds • farm animals	jingles tambourines claves

• train rhythms
♫♫♩ ready steady go
	• ascending/descending scale trains going up and down hill
	• harmony based on major chord: [G/E/C]
	• tunes with E G A
		• trains – steam
		  – electric
		  – whistles
		• crowds
			maracas
			slither boxes
			sandpaper blocks
			rasps
			guiros

• the minim 𝅗𝅥 • bell rhythms ♫♩ te-le-phone ♩♩ ding dong • instrument rhythms	• high and low bells • descending scale – pealing bells • bell harmony based on major chord: [G/E/C] • tunes with C E G A	• bells indoors and out • stars • frost and snow • Christmas and other festivals • fairies and magic	gongs and cymbals Indian bells triangles chime bars glockenspiel metallophone wind chimes plant pot bells
• vehicle rhythms	• car horn harmony based on major chord: [G/E/C] • tunes with C E G A	• crowds talking and walking • vehicle noises • park sounds	tubular woodblocks coconut shells

Summary of topics

Elephants

The slow, deliberate movement of elephants is described in rhymes, poems and songs and imitated by the children with voices, actions and on instruments. The activities introduce contrasts of tempo, volume and touch. The lower range of notes is explored. The principal percussion instruments used are the drums and tambours, and ideas are given for making these. The children are encouraged to compose simple tunes based on E and G. The rhythmic pattern ♫ ♩ is practised. The crotchet (or walking note) ♩ is described. The beat or pulse is explained.

At home

This topic draws the children's attention to the sounds they hear daily in their homes. Most of the activities are designed to develop aural discrimination and to extend the children's sound vocabulary. Water, tools and machinery are imitated with voices and on instruments. 'Instruments' made from glasses and milk bottles are described. Melodic composition still centres around E and G. The rhythmic patterns ♫ ♫ and ♫♫ ♩. are introduced. The children play an ascending octave in imitation of climbing stairs. Pairs of quavers describe a ticking clock and a dripping tap.

Hens and chicks

In contrast to the slow, heavy and deep associations of elephants, *Hens and chicks* introduces high, light and quick sounds and movements. The children are shown how to make jingles, jingle sticks and tambourines. This time the rhythmic pattern ♫ ♫ ♩ receives most attention. The note A is added to E and G for melodic composition. In the sound story the children imitate the sounds of the sea and jungle.

Trains

This topic is primarily concerned with tempo or speed. Some of the games and exercises are about getting faster and getting slower, getting louder and getting quieter. Maracas are used for sound-effect work and the children are shown how to make shakers, rasps, guiros, sandpaper blocks and slither boxes. Compositions involving E G and A are encouraged. Quavers, crotchets and minims (not necessarily identified as such) are practised in some of the exercises. Harmony based on a major chord is included.

Bells

This topic is suitable for the weeks leading up to Christmas. It introduces the ringing and chiming instruments. Descending peals of bells are imitated on tuned percussion, and more two- and three-part harmony is introduced. Bells in the environment – bicycle, telephone, door and alarm – are used in sound-effect work. The children are shown how to make wind chimes, plantpot bells and simple tubular bells. Middle C is added to E G and A for melodic composition. The minim is explained and practised in conjunction with crotchets.

In town

Here the children move outdoors to explore the sounds made by traffic, weather, machines and animals. They are told how to use simple materials to make realistic sound effects. More melodic work incorporating C E G and A is encouraged. Several rhythmic patterns familiar to the children are presented and harmony based on a major chord is sung once again.

Notes on the activities

Speech rhymes

Speech rhymes are traditionally brief, regular and simple. Many of those selected for the topics contain funny and unusual words. Speech rhymes are intended for speaking aloud. Encourage the children to think about speed, pitch and expression. Clear diction is important. Pay attention to word endings and repeated letter sounds. Talk about the vocabulary. Why are some of the words 'good'? A lot of the words are onomatopoeic and the notes suggest ways of interpreting these sounds on instruments.

Most of the speech rhymes require a steady pulse or beat. This can be sustained by controlled speaking. Give a strong lead. The beat can be clapped or tapped or shaken. The short rhythmic patterns made by some of the words introduce the children to the concept of long and short sounds. Help the children to copy these rhythmic patterns with their bodies and on instruments. The teaching notes describe how simple tunes can be given to the rhythmic patterns using a limited range of notes.

Children should be encouraged to find their own methods of recording their rhythms and tunes. Traditional notation is introduced where relevant.

Many of the skills developed through chanting and singing these simple rhymes can be taken to the music corner and practised. Some of the rhymes are suitable for drama and movement, and some, because of their simplicity, make good material for handwriting and word-building activities.

Action rhymes and songs

Much of what has been said for speech rhymes also applies here. The simple actions which accompany action rhymes and songs help physical co-ordination and memory. As far as possible the actions should fit in with the beat and rhythm of the rhyme or song. The children should aim to speak and move together. Take the rhymes and songs slowly to begin with. Ideas for instrumental accompaniment are given in the teaching notes. The speed (**tempo**) should be fairly flexible to accommodate the actions and match the sense of the words.

Poems

The main function of the poems is to encourage the children to think and talk about sound quality (**timbre**). Here pulse and rhythm are often secondary to the general mood or feeling of the poem. Voices, instruments and body sounds are used to create a suitable background sound. Involve the children in experimentation and decision making. Some of the poems, because of their length and/or complexity, are best spoken by the teacher. Others can be spoken by individual children, large groups of children or small groups of children – or combinations of all these.

Songs

Some of the songs have simple piano accompaniment. Most have guitar chords.

Most of the songs fall within the range of one octave – middle C to the C above. Some of the songs are **pentatonic** – that is, they have no semitone intervals. This makes them especially suitable for younger children.

Just as some of the words in the rhymes are isolated because of their rhythmic interest, fragments of some of the tunes are given special attention. These mini-tunes can be sung to their original words, to *la*, or they can be given new words. Children enjoy making up new words to familiar tunes. Repetition of short sung phrases helps to train the voice and the ear, and is especially helpful for children who find it difficult to sing in tune.

The notes which accompany the songs contain suggestions for simple accompaniments. These accompaniments are repetitive and usually take the form of a **drone** (repeated single note or notes played together), or an **ostinato** (repeated pattern on notes). Try them. After a few attempts you'll be amazed how effective they sound.

Singing is a lovely and natural form of expression and is enjoyed by most young children. The songs in the topics can be sung at any convenient moment of the day, *with or without accompaniment.*

The songs appear in a variety of forms. There are 'straight' songs, action songs, dancing and singing games, and short singing exercises.

Dancing and singing games

Most of the dancing and singing games require more space than is usually available in the classroom. Some of the games are cumulative – that is, they gradually draw in all the children – while others do the reverse. Some of the games are designed to improve listening skills.

The singing games can be accompanied by the teacher on guitar or piano. However, the dances often require a lot of co-operation and co-ordination and will benefit from the direct involvement of one or more adults. Be prepared, therefore, to abandon piano or guitar, and join in the games and dances. Take the games and dances out into the playground and encourage the children to play them at playtime.

Sound stories

The stories in the topics are built around a range of interesting environmental sounds. These can be imitated with voices and other body sounds, on instruments and with all sorts of odds and ends. As with most of the activities in the book, several short practice sessions will be needed before the desired effect is achieved. Encourage experimentation and discussion. Pay attention to volume, pitch and tempo. Talk about starting the sounds and stopping them. Would they be better 'faded' in and out? Sometimes a sudden entry is more appropriate.

Try to involve all the children in making the sound effects. All the time they are waiting to make their sound they will pay attention. When the stories have been rehearsed, a special performance can be given, preferably before an invited audience. Tape it so that it can be enjoyed again and again.

Pictures are good stimuli for sound-effect work. Make a collection of pictures and posters suitable for sound effects. Help the children to make their own sound picture, the bigger the better. Point to the picture to indicate the sound that is to be made.

Games and exercises

Here the children practise all sorts of skills – copying the beat, playing rhythms, singing tunes, experimenting on the instruments, etc. Some of the games teach correct handling and playing of percussion instruments. As far as possible the exercises have been arranged in order of difficulty, beginning with the simplest. The musical skills which are being practised in each game are stated under the game title.

Several of the games require a screen. A tipped-up table will serve the purpose, but a simple screen can be made by threading a piece of material onto a long garden cane. The cane can be lowered and raised as required. A screen adds a bit of drama to the music session.

Most of the games only take a few minutes. They can be played at any convenient time of the day (assuming that you have easy access to instruments). Some of them, after a few practices, can be played by small groups of children in the music corner.

Music corner activities

What is a **music corner**? A music corner is generally understood to describe a small, screened-off area where a limited number of children can experiment with sound. As significant as the physical setting, however, is the nature of the activity which takes place there.

Each topic contains several suggestions for music corner activities. They are marked with the screen symbol . The activities include games and exercises which help to develop one or a combination of the following musical skills: sustaining a beat or pulse, playing rhythms, making up tunes, imitating environmental sounds, and so on. Some of the activities are for one child, others involve two or more. *All the work designed for the music corner is based on activities which have already been practised in other sections of the topic.*

The question of where to place the music corner and how to organise it can be a problem. There are times when the relentless tapping of a tambourine threatens to be the straw that breaks the camel's back! A large stock cupboard or a screened-off area in the cloakroom or corridor may be more acceptable than the classroom. Ideally the music corner should be movable. I have a small table with a quiet, solo music activity permanently on display in the classroom, and move the noisier activities out of the classroom. As long as the children involved know that they must respect the conditions which this type of music-making demands, there should be little disturbance to other teachers or children.

The following guidelines may be helpful:

1. Make sure that the children understand fully what is expected of them. As the activity will be an extension of something initiated in a class lesson, this should not be a problem.
2. Teach the children to transport, pick up and put down the instruments in a sensible way. Emphasise that all playing, singing and speaking should be quiet, and explain why. Any child who disregards the conditions should be withdrawn from the music corner.
3. Keep a regular check on the children in the music corner.
4. Limit the time available in the music corner – use a timer. If the children know that time is precious they will be more inclined to get on with the matter in hand.
5. Listen to and talk about the end product. If possible, let the whole class hear what has been practised. The children will quickly learn from each other.
6. Keep a record of which children use the music corner and make sure that every child who wants to is able to use it. By judicious grouping, even reluctant musicians will be persuaded to have a go, although the problem is more likely to be one of over-demand.

A parent interested in music could be asked to come into school to supervise music corner activities. Make sure that she or he is as well briefed as the children.

Ideas for making simple percussion instruments

In each topic one or more percussion instruments receive particular attention. Instructions for the construction of simplified versions of these are given. Don't forget to use them in music sessions.

Curricular links

This section is headed with a list of themes which relate to the topic. Thus the teacher can move from the rather narrow confines of some of the topics to a wider field of reference, and vice versa.

This section also takes the topic theme into other areas of the curriculum – into language (spoken and written), number work, environmental and physical science, art and craft, movement and drama. Thus music is prevented from becoming a separate 'subject' and can be seen as being an integral part of the infant school experience. Where one of the rhymes, poems, songs or stories used in another section lends itself to development in a wider context, the link is made 'on the spot'.

Resource list
(*including notes on the use of the tape-recorder*)

Here are details of more rhymes, poems, songs, stories and information about each topic. Information about recorded music is included.

Although young children have a short listening span, most enjoy hearing short extracts of music, especially if the music is offered with obvious enthusiasm. It is usually the teacher's own favourites which go down best. It is recommended that teachers make their own tapes of musical extracts. As long as the quality of the recording is good, and a note is made of what has been taped (to facilitate location), it is well worth the effort involved. The music can be used for listening, movement, singing, drama, games, for art and as a stimulus for spoken and written work.

It is important to have access to equipment which will allow for tape dubbing – that is, direct recording from one tape to another without the use of a separate microphone. County music advisers might be able to help in this matter. Most authorities offer a cassette and record lending service to their teachers.

Tape-recorders which operate both from batteries and from the mains are useful as you can't always guarantee to be near a plug when the tape-recorder is required.

When the extract to be taped is in the middle of a longer piece of music, it sounds better if it is faded in. This is done by starting with a low volume and gradually increasing it to the required strength. The reverse procedure is followed at the end of the extract. Tape a longer extract than is likely to hold the attention of the children, as you may wish to use it for another type of activity – painting or movement, for example. Also, the children's listening span will increase with age and experience.

Don't always insist on complete stillness and silence for listening. The children should be allowed to express their enjoyment by 'conducting' or clapping or singing, or by pretending to play an instrument. However, the participation should not be allowed to be disruptive, and now and then it is enjoyable to listen in complete quietness.

When you are introducing a new piece of music, play it several times on successive days after its first airing. The children need to know music well before they can really appreciate it – rather like a new story.

Children like to hear themselves on tape. Whenever possible and appropriate, record the children singing, playing and speaking. Teach them how to use the tape-recorder so that they can make their own recordings. Use the tape-recorder too for listening games. The teaching notes include suggestions for several sound lotto games. There are also some commercially produced cassettes which aim to develop aural discrimination. The children will enjoy the cassette which accompanies this book, and the ▭ symbol indicates a song which can be heard on the *Music Through Topics* cassette.

elephants

speech rhymes
Elephant, elephant *14*
Trumpety-trump *14*
Curly-whirly *15*

action rhymes
As high as a hill *15*
An elephant goes like this and that *16*

poems
I went for a walk in the park today *17*
The elephant is a graceful bird *17*
Sometimes he's slow *18*
From 'Oliphaunt' *18*

songs
The six blind men and the elephant *19*
Hey, hey, hey Mister Elephant *21*
Hi! said the elephant *22*
Un éléphant *24*
One elephant came out to play *25*
Marching through the jungle *26*

sound story
Tosca the baby elephant *28*

games and exercises *31*

instruments to make and play
Tambours, drums and beaters *36*

curricular links *38*

list of resources *40*

speech rhymes

Elephant, elephant

Elephant, elephant,
Saw you on the telly-phant.

Elephant, elephant,
Wibble-wobble jelly-phant.

Elephant, elephant,
Hope you're very welly-phant.

v.c.

1 Chant and enjoy the humour of the words. Encourage clear diction – put *t* on the end of *elephant*. Keep a steady pulse.

2 Add actions to lines 2, 4 and 6: in line 2 draw a box (television) shape in the air, wobble around in line 4 and shake hands with self or partner in line 6.

3 Clap, slap and knock the rhythm to *Elephant, elephant*. Display a rhythm card and talk about it – how many claps, how many notes? Transfer the rhythm to instruments and accompany the word *elephant* whenever it appears in the rhyme. Put rhythm card and instrument in the music corner – let the children choose the instrument.

4 Play four 'solid' beats on a tambour or drum as an introduction. These four beats can be played as a link in between stanzas and as an ending. If you like, continue playing the beat throughout the speaking but at a reduced volume.

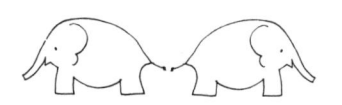

Trumpety - trump

Trumpety - trump,
Bumpety - bump,
E - le - phant.

Snippety - snap
Flippety - flap,
Croc - o - dile.

Hippety - hop,
Bippety - bop,
Kang - a - roo.

v.c.

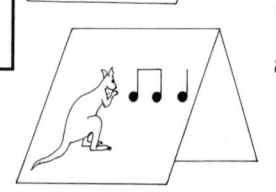

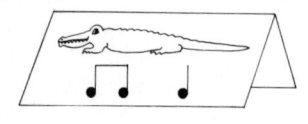

1 Get to know the rhyme. Talk about each animal – its appearance and movement.

2 Practise chanting each stanza. Encourage the children to use their lips and mouth to produce clear sounds. Aim for a heavy sound in the first stanza, a snapping sound in 2 and a bouncy sound in 3. When the children know the words, adapt the tempo to match the animal.

3 Clap, slap, knock and chant the rhythm of each animal name. Display the three rhythm cards. Choose an instrument for each – allow time for experimentation. Accompany the chanting with instruments.

4 Display cards and instruments in the music corner. Encourage the children to chant (or sing) as they play.

speech rhymes

Curly-whirly

Curly-whirly
Lazy-wavy
Loopy-scoopy,
Tug-a-lug.

Gripper-ripper,
Lusty-dusty,
Power-shower,
LONG STRONG TRUNK.

v.c.

1 Talk about the rhyme. Match voice to words. Make a contrast between the smooth, languorous sound of the first stanza and the strong mood of the second. Aim for a crescendo in the last line. Display the word card.

long strong trunk

2 Accompany the last three words with three heavy taps on a drum or tambour.

3 Wave imaginary trunks around, matching the quality of the arm movement to the timbre and speed of the voice.

action rhymes

As high as a hill

As high as a hill,
As wide as a whale,
As strong as an ox,
But – what a small tail!

v.c.

1 Talk about the size of an elephant. Collect 'large' words – huge, enormous, massive, etc. Talk about *high* and *wide*. Make up new similes – as high as a wardrobe, as wide as the playground, etc.

2 ACTIONS
- line 1 Lift both arms high (stand up)
- line 2 Stretch both arms wide
- line 3 Flex biceps
- line 4 Bring hands together to indicate a small size, or point to own posterior

3 Let the voice reflect the words – the voices can rise up the hill, mouths can stretch to accommodate the words *wide* and *whale*. Use strong voices for line 3 and whisper the last line.

action rhymes

An elephant goes like this and that

An elephant goes
Like this and that.
He's terrible tall
And he's terrible fat.
He has no fingers
He has no toes,
But – GOODNESS GRACIOUS
WHAT A NOSE . . .

ANON

1 Learn the poem. Look carefully at a picture of an elephant and in particular at the feet and trunk. Children love elephants' trunks. What can elephants do with their trunks? What can the children do with their noses? What would the children enjoy doing if they had trunks?

2 ACTIONS Slap knees with alternate hands in lines 1 and 2. Indicate great height in line 3 and great width in line 4. Either scrunch up or wiggle fingers then toes in lines 5 and 6. Raise arms in amazement in line 7, and mime a long trunk in the last line.

3 To help sustain a slow and steady beat, slap knees with alternate hands throughout the poem – two taps per line. Or walk round the room – don't bother to clear a space but ask the children to move carefully between tables placing feet firmly on the floor in time with the beat. Speak in deep, strong voices.

4 Play the beat on a large drum, a large tambour or a large cardboard box (or anything else the children might suggest). Slow down a bit in the last two lines, or stop the beat at the end of line 6.

5 Make the most of the last two lines – the amazement should know no bounds!

There are two main types of elephant – Asiatic and African. *Asiatic* elephants have smaller ears. They live in small herds and don't like bright sunlight. They spend a lot of time in the jungle. The females don't usually have tusks. The newborn elephant is covered in short grey fur, but this is soon shed. Elephants live for between 45 and 60 years. Twins are unusual. *African* elephants are similar in many ways to Asiatic elephants but they have larger ears and don't mind sunlight. The African elephant is the world's largest land animal. It can weigh the same as a London bus – that is, about 5,000 kilograms. Tosca, the baby elephant who features in the sound story on page 28, is an Asiatic elephant. What else can the children discover about elephants?

poems

I went for a walk in the park today

I went for a walk in the park today,
And what do you think I met on the way?
I met a lion, and what did he say?
ROAR! ROAR! ROAR!

I went for a walk in the park today,
And what do you think I met on the way?
I met an elephant, and what did he say?
TRUMPETY – TRUMPETY – TRUMP!

I went for a walk in the park today,
And what do you think I met on the way?
I met a snake, and what did he say?
S – s – s – s – s – s.

BARBARA IRESON

1 The children will need no prompting to make the animal sounds. Encourage a loud roar and a quiet hiss. Good luck with the trumpeting!

2 The animal sounds in the fourth line of each stanza can be represented by instruments of the children's choosing. Aim for a continuous sound, e.g. the roll of a drum for the roar, a gentle shake of the maraca for the hiss. Squeal down a cardboard tube for the trumpeting or hunt around for a toy trumpet. Try the instrumental sounds with the vocal sounds.

3 One wouldn't expect to meet a lion, an elephant or a snake in a park. Think of other unlikely rendezvous and substitute for *park*. Or match the animals to their correct environment.

The elephant is a graceful bird

The elephant is a graceful bird
It flits from twig to twig.
It builds its nest in a rhubarb tree,
And whistles like a pig.

ANON

This can be spoken straight, it can be spoken lightly to match the words, or it can be spoken with a heavy voice to bring out the nonsense. Let the children whistle at the end.

poems

> **Sometimes he's slow**
>
> Sometimes he's slow.
> Sometimes he's lazy,
> But sometimes he hurries
> And acts as though crazy.
>
> Sometimes he's strong
> And pushes down trees,
> Sometimes he's gentle
> And careful to please.
>
> V.C.

1 This poem brings out the contrasts between *slow* and *fast* and between *strong* and *gentle*. Read the poem to the children in such a way that these contrasts are evident. Talk about *slow* and *fast*. What animals move slowly/quickly? Slap hands on knees slowly, then quickly. Do the same with clapping, stamping, rubbing palms of hands together, shaking hands, etc. Talk about *strong* and *gentle*. Pretend to chop wood with strong movements. Now stroke a cat.

2 Make a collection of drums, real or improvised (see page 37). Table tops, cardboard boxes or plastic tubs will do. Tap them slowly then quickly. Tap them with strong taps then with gentle taps. Divide the class into two groups – one group listens while the other plays. Try to tap slowly and quietly/slowly and loudly. What about quietly and quickly, then loudly and quickly?

> **From 'Oliphaunt'**
>
> Grey as a mouse,
> Big as a house,
> Nose like a snake,
> I make the earth shake,
> As I tramp through the grass;
> Trees crack as I pass.
> With horns in my mouth
> I walk in the South,
> Flapping big ears.
> Beyond count of years
> I stump round and round,
> Never lie on the ground,
> Not even to die.
> Oliphaunt am I.
>
> (extract from 'Oliphaunt'
> by J.R.R. TOLKIEN)

1 Talk about the poem with special reference to the similes. Make up similes to describe the distinguishing features of other animals, e.g. with reference to an ant, 'small as a ......', or a cheetah, 'fast as a ......'.

2 Experiment with percussion instruments to produce an earth-shaking sound. Make the sound of a stampede of elephants, complete with snapping twigs (the real thing) and trumpeting. Read the first six lines against a background of noise, or give three children two lines each to shout in sequence. Try again, but ask the three children to shout their lines simultaneously. Any children not playing or speaking can slap the floor with their hands and make an ululating sound with their voices. Choose your time and place for this exercise!

The six blind men and the elephant

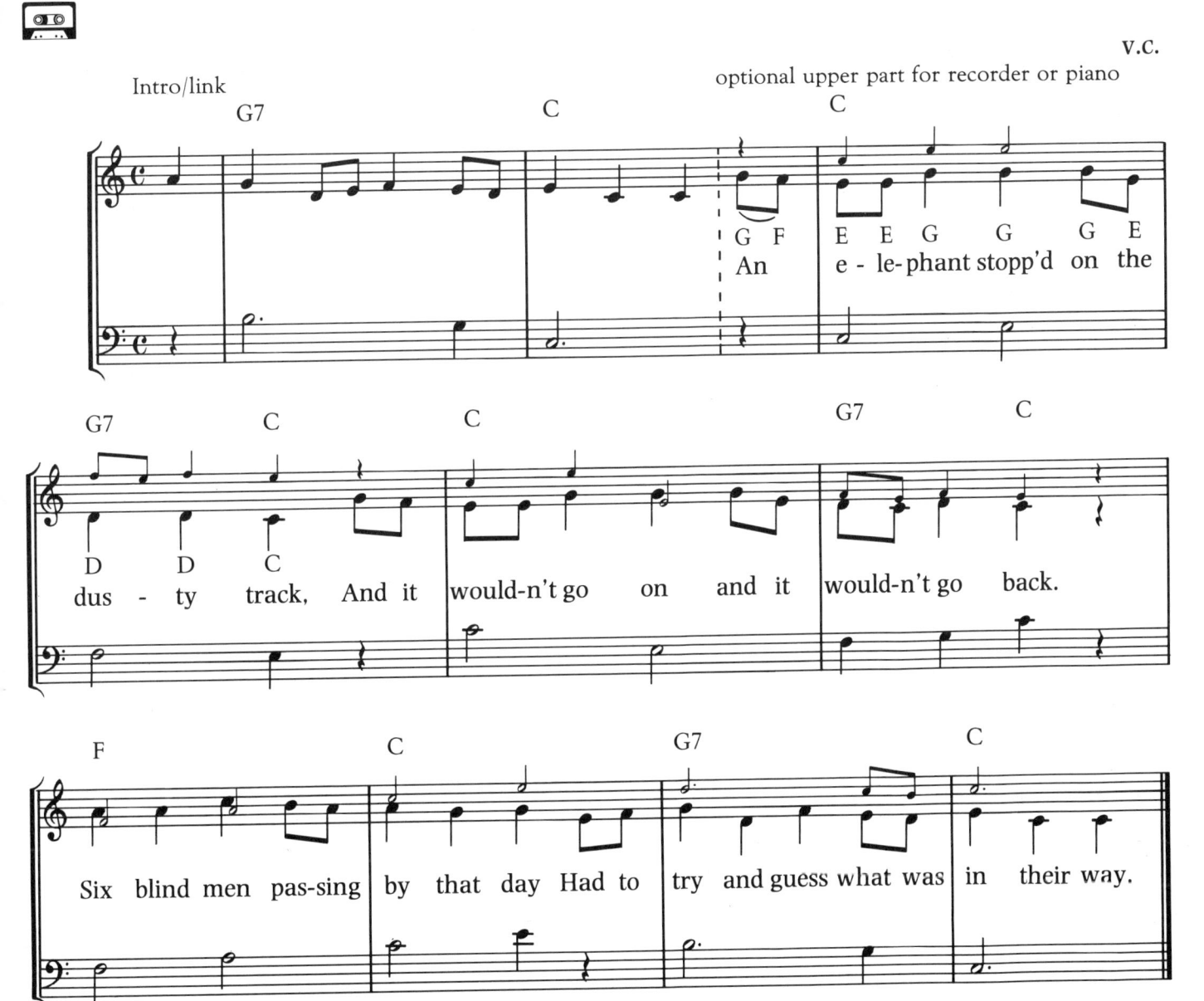

v.c.

Intro/link — optional upper part for recorder or piano

An e-le-phant stopp'd on the dus-ty track, And it would-n't go on and it would-n't go back. Six blind men pas-sing by that day Had to try and guess what was in their way.

And the first blind man felt the elephant's side.
It was hard and rough, it was tall and wide.
'That's a very funny place for a wall to be,
And dangerous too if you're blind like me.'

And the second blind man felt the elephant's tusk.
It was long and smooth with a pointed cusp.
'That's a very funny place for a spear to be,
And dangerous too if you're blind like me.'

And the third blind man felt the elephant's trunk.
It waved and curled, it stretched and shrunk.
'That's a very funny place for a snake to be,
And dangerous too if you're blind like me.'

songs

And the fourth blind man felt the elephant's leg.
It was thick and firm like a knocked-in peg.
'That's a very funny place for a tree to be,
And dangerous too if you're blind like me.'

And the fifth blind man felt the elephant's ear.
It flipped and flapped for the man to hear.
'That's a very funny place for a fan to be,
And dangerous too if you're blind like me.'

And the sixth blind man felt the elephant's tail.
It whisked around like a busy flail.
'That's a very funny place for a rope to be,
And dangerous too if you're blind like me.'

This song tells the traditional Indian tale of the six blind men and the elephant. Make sure that the children know the names of the various parts of the elephant mentioned in the song. *Cusp* and *flail* may need an explanation. The children will soon want to join in the last two lines of each verse. What might a blind person make of a rabbit's scut, a hedgehog's spines, a giraffe's neck?

1 Act out the story. Pretend to be blind and feel your way round the room. Half the children can stand still and be 'obstacles' while the rest move carefully round them. Swap over. Pretend to walk along a rough, stony track. Pretend to bump into a tree – feel it upwards and then around its trunk.

2 Move slowly along like the elephant. Stop and pull leaves off a tree.

3 Now pretend to be the elephant's owner. Push and tug at the huge creature in an attempt to get it to budge. Work in pairs – one child is the elephant, the other the owner. Try to achieve a contrast between the stubborn, solid beast and the agitated, heaving and shoving owner. Remember that it's a hot day.

4 Back to being blind men – mime feeling the various parts of the elephant's body (eyes closed). After each mime, shake head in a puzzled manner, walk round the elephant and move slowly on along the track.

5 Improvise dialogue between the six blind men – let each describe his experience in turn.

6 Sing the story with actions.

How do the children get on with identifying an unseen object? Put an unusual object into a large fabric bag and allow a few children to feel it. No peeping! Encourage them to talk about their discoveries. At the end of the exercise, do they all agree what the object is?

Through discussion and experimentation, select one instrument for each of the verses. Use the instruments as a stimulus for movement. For example, if a triangle is chosen to represent the pointed tusk, practise sharp, pointed movements. A large drum (the thick leg) might inspire heavy stamping movements. Use the instruments to accompany the singing.

songs

Hey, hey, hey Mister Elephant

WORDS V.C.
TUNE NICK CLARK
ACCOMPANIMENT JOHN PURCELL

Hey, hey, hey Mister E-le-phant Your trunk is real-ly long.

Hey, hey, hey Mister E-le-phant Your legs are ve-ry strong.

Hey hey, hey Mister Elephant
Your eyes are small and bright.
Hey, hey, hey Mister Elephant
Your tusks are shining white.

Hey, hey, hey Mister Elephant
Your ears go flip-flip-flap.
Hey, hey, hey Mister Elephant
You look a friendly chap.
HOW D'YOU DO!

1 When tune and words are familiar, ask the children to clap the beat as they sing, or place feet gently on the floor in time with the music.

2 Find an instrument for each part of the body mentioned in the song (e.g. jingles for the twinkly eyes) and play with the singing in the appropriate places. Don't insist on precise rhythmic accompaniment – let the children find their own style.

3 Another time, accompany all the sung *hey*s with claps and/or tambourines.

4 Set out chimes D G and B and encourage the children to search out and play the tune to the first three *hey*s. What about the second set of *hey*s? Put the chimes in the music corner.

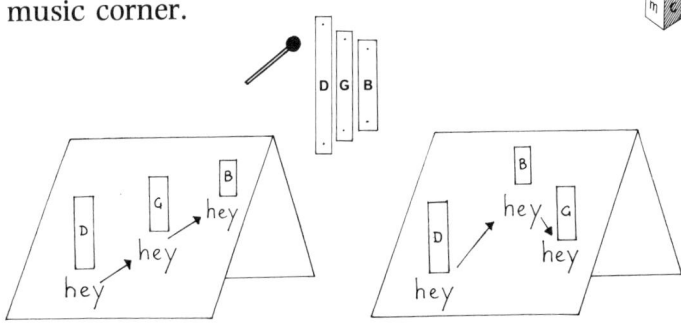

songs

Hi! said the elephant

SANDRA KERR

Hi! said the e-le-phant, look at me, I've got a long trunk, can you see? It's an arm, it's a leg, it's a hand, it's a nose: It pulls and it push-es and it sucks and it blows. Have you ev-er seen a long trunk

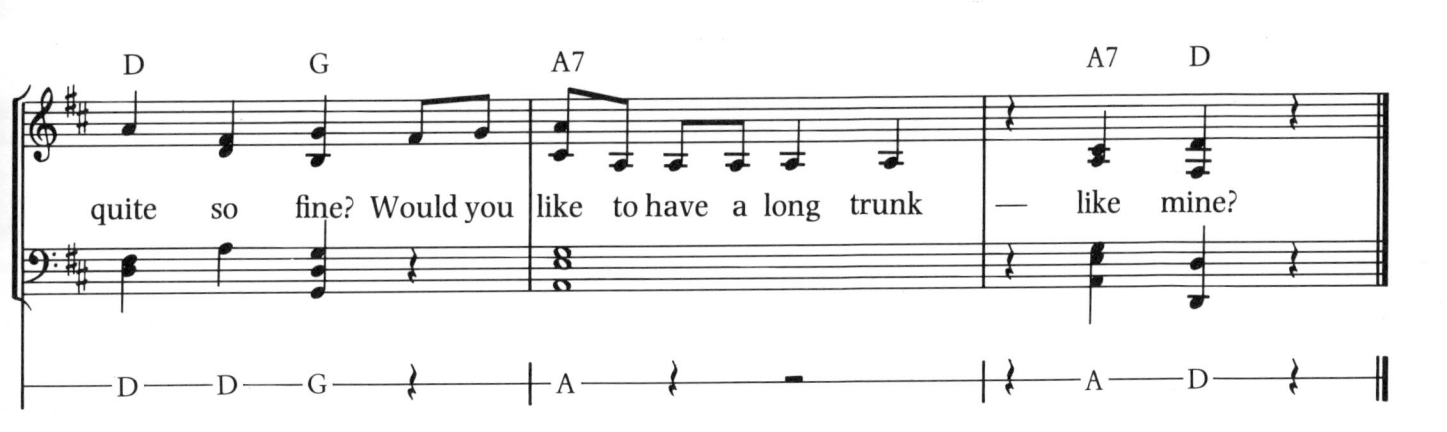

songs

[Music notation: D G A7 A7 D]

quite so fine? Would you like to have a long trunk — like mine?

[Chord tabs: D — D — G — A — A — D]

Hi! said the pussy cat, look at me.
I've got whiskers, can you see?
Long spiky hairs sticking out of my face:
They help me to feel if I can squeeze through a space.
Have you ever seen whiskers quite so fine?
Would you like to have whiskers – like mine?

Hi! said the rabbit, look at me.
I've got a white tail, can you see?
When I wobble my behind and it flashes up and down:
It's a signal to the other rabbits danger is around.
Have you ever seen a white tail quite so fine?
Would you like to have a white tail – like mine?

Hi! said the tortoise, look at me.
I've got a hard shell, can you see?
It's a nice suit of armour and wherever I may roam,
I'm safe from attack and I'm always at home.
Have you ever seen a hard shell quite so fine?
Would you like to have a hard shell – like mine?

1 This is a long song for the children to learn, but they'll soon start to join in the first and the last two lines. A clap on all the *Hi*'s and on *like mine* at the beginnings and endings makes an effective accompaniment. Transfer to instruments (untuned).

2 Talk about the four animals in the song and mime the actions described in the four stanzas. Find an instrument for each and tap lightly on the beat in the third and fourth lines of each verse.

songs

Un éléphant

• dancing and singing game •

TRADITIONAL FRENCH

Un é-lé-phant, ça trom-pe, ça trom-pe,
Un é-lé-phant, ça trompe é-nor-mé-ment!

Deux éléphants, ça trompe, ça trompe,
Deux éléphants, ça trompe énormément!

Trois éléphants, ça trompe, ça trompe,
Trois éléphants, ça trompe énormément!

Quatre éléphants, ça trompe, ça trompe,
Quatre éléphants, ça trompe énormément!

Cinq éléphants, ça trompe, ça trompe,
Cinq éléphants, ça trompe énormément!

Many young children can recite the numbers one to five in French, and this traditional French song provides them with the opportunity to show off their expertise. The rest of the French words will be quickly picked up.

ACCOMPANIMENT   A simple melodic accompaniment for xylophone is provided. If you have five tuned percussion instruments, let them enter cumulatively. Experiment with drums to make a trumpeting sound, and play the sound at the end of each stanza – the first time just one drum, then two, then three, and so on.

When the song is well known, make it into a dancing game. All the children except one walk round in a circle, moving in time with the slow beat if possible. The elephant stands in the centre of the circle waving a trunk. At the end of the first verse he/she lifts the trunk and trumpets as loudly as possible. He/she then chooses a friend to be elephant number 2, and so on.

One elephant came out to play
• dancing and singing game •

WORDS TRADITIONAL
TUNE AND ACCOMPANIMENT V.C.

One e-le-phant came out to play U-pon a spi-der's web one day. She found it such e-nor-mous fun That she called for a-no-ther e-le-phant to come.

songs

Two elephants came out to play
Upon a spider's web one day.
They found it such enormous fun
That they called for another elephant – to – come.

Four elephants . . .
Eight elephants . . .
Sixteen elephants . . .
Thirty-two elephants . . .

The better-known tune to these words has been replaced here by a simpler tune in order to avoid an octave leap. Teachers of older infants may prefer to stick to the familiar melody.

This is a cumulative ring game where the numbers double each time. One child takes the centre of a circle where she or he dances lightly around on an imaginary spider's web. The rest of the children walk round holding hands. They should try to step in time with their singing. After each verse each of the children in the middle chooses a partner and they dance together for the duration of the following stanza. Once you get beyond eight elephants in the centre, the children left in the circle will have to drop hands in order to make their circle larger to accommodate the gambolling elephants.

ACCOMPANIMENT   Find 8/16 real and/or improvised drums and allocate one each to 8/16 children. These children come in (on the beat) cumulatively to match the elephants in the ring – first one player, then two, then four, etc. Encourage careful, delicate playing. Older infants can have a go at the melodic accompaniment for glockenspiel(s) and xylophone(s). If you succeed in putting together the singing, actions, drumming and tuned percussion parts, you deserve a medal!

Marching through the jungle

● dancing and singing game ●

WORDS V.C.
TUNE MURIEL REEVE

Mar-ching through the jung - le, Mar-ching through the jung - le,

Mar-ching through the jung - le in an e - le-phant ring.

songs

Dip and suck up water,
Dip and suck up water,
Dip and suck up water
   and squirt it on your back.

Stop and scratch your bottom,
Stop and scratch your bottom,
Stop and scratch your bottom
   and flick your tail around.

Stretch and pull the green leaves,
Stretch and pull the green leaves,
Stretch and pull the green leaves
   and stuff them in your mouth.

Roly-poly in the mud,
Roly-poly in the mud,
Roly-poly in the mud
   and get back on your feet.

Time to go to bed now,
Time to go to bed now,
Time to go to bed now
   – goodnight.

Make an elephant ring. In verse 1 each child holds the 'tail' of the child in front (an arm) with its 'trunk' (the other arm). The elephants march round in time with the singing. Mime the actions in the rest of the verses. Slow down the tempo in verse 6 and sing in a sleepy voice.

The song sounds effective if the pitch is raised one semitone each verse (as demonstrated on the cassette). If you want to try this, you'll have to begin in the lower key of E major. The tune of verse 1 will therefore begin on the note E.

ACCOMPANIMENT Simply play a steady beat on a large tambour or drum, or ask several children to tap anything they like on real or improvised drums. Don't try this until the children know the song well. Aim to create a jungle sound. Add sound effects. To give the final chorus a carnival flavour, use whistles, rattles, squeakers, etc. (as demonstrated on the cassette).

If you are sticking to the one key, help a child or children to play the simple ostinato tune:

   G E D E

This skeleton melody can be sustained throughout the singing. Use as many tuned percussion instruments as you have.

Play the bass line of the piano accompaniment to the children. Let the children move round the room as you play it.

In a large space the elephant ring can be changed into an elephant *line*. Choose a leader. The leader must be followed wherever he or she goes, with no overtaking. Repeat verse 1 as often as you like.

sound story

Tosca the baby elephant
by Veronica Clark

Tosca was a baby Indian elephant. Although she was only a few months old she was much bigger than you. She was bigger even than me. Her mother was enormous. Do you know – Tosca could stand right underneath her mother's legs. It must have been rather like being in a bus shelter.

Tosca loved her great big mother. She was glad her mother was big and strong because, as you will soon find out, Tosca was an extremely timid baby elephant. All kinds of things frightened Tosca: sudden movement, loud noises, things that went bump in the night. (I expect you know the sort of things I mean.) Tosca always stayed close to her mother. She never strayed from the herd.

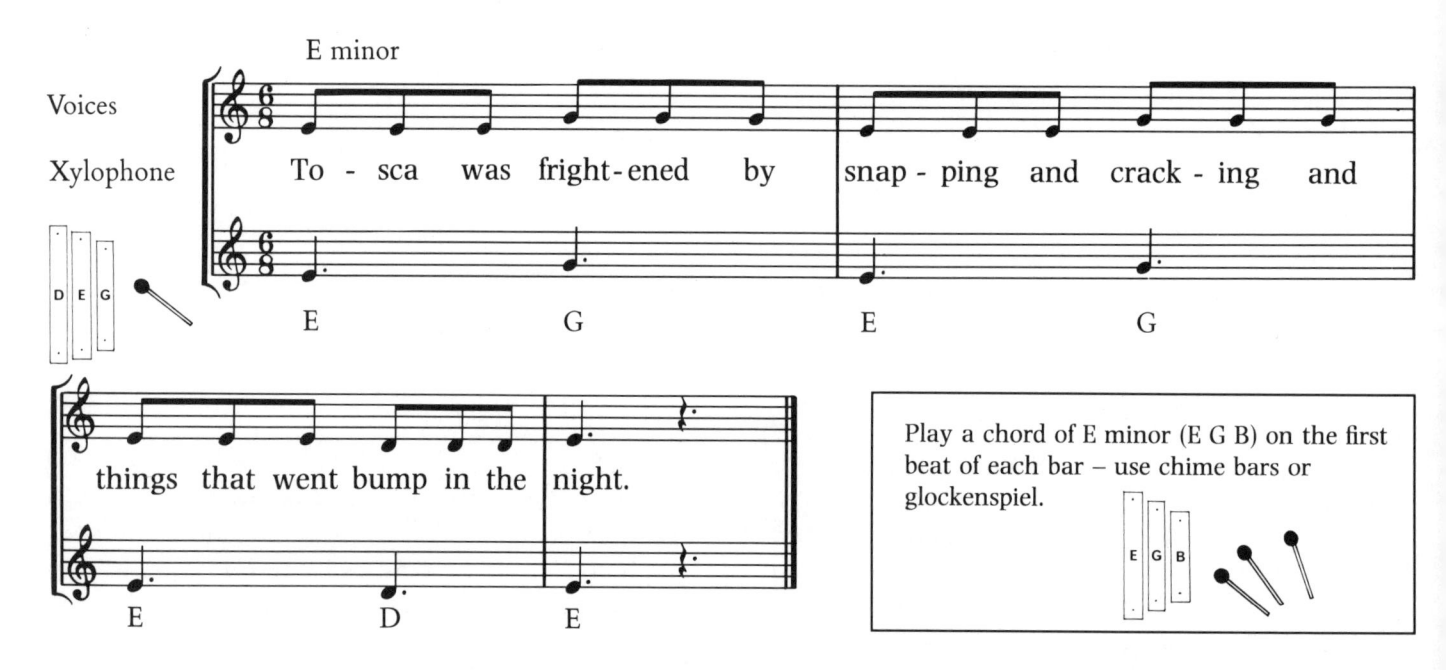

Voices / Xylophone:
E minor
To-sca was fright-ened by snap-ping and crack-ing and things that went bump in the night.

(E G E G E D E)

Play a chord of E minor (E G B) on the first beat of each bar – use chime bars or glockenspiel.

Every morning the elephants would lumber slowly along the jungle path to the waterhole [1]. Tosca had to trot quite fast in order to keep up with her mother [2]. Every now and then the elephants would pause and rip off branches of leaves to eat [3]. When the sun was hot the elephants would flap their leathery ears to keep cool [4].

sound story

When the elephants reached the waterhole the fun would begin. First they sucked the water up into their trunks ⑤, then they would curl their trunks under and up into their mouths and squirt ⑥. Later the elephants would give themselves cooling showers by showering water over their backs. Tosca loved it at the waterhole. She would have liked to stay there all day. The grownups, however, preferred the shady jungle. The jungle was cool and dark and full of strange noises. Tosca always stayed close to her mother's side in the jungle.

Repeat song

Once Tosca heard a loud snapping sound ⑦. She jumped and trumpeted, 'Crocodiles!'

'Not crocodiles dear,' said her mother, blowing gently down her ear with her soft trunk. 'Just a dry twig snapping under your feet.'

Another time Tosca heard a hissing sound ⑧. She jumped and trumpeted, 'Snakes!'

'Not snakes dear,' said her mother, nudging her gently with her huge grey flanks. 'Just the wind running through the grass.' Tosca did feel silly.

One hot, sticky day Tosca heard a far-off roar ⑨. 'Lions!' she whispered.

'Not lions dear,' said her mother, curling her long trunk round Tosca's trembling body. 'Just the thunder rolling round the hills. We shall have a storm today, just you wait and see.'

And there was a storm that very afternoon. The lightning flashed ⑩, the thunder rolled and grumbled (⑨ again), and the rain fell in sheets ⑪. Because Tosca loved water she quite forgot to be frightened and stood out in the rain and let it beat down on her hairy, grey back. She was a very clean little elephant that evening.

Song to the following words:
Tosca grew up and was no longer frightened
Of things that went bump in the night.

sound story

Read the story without sound effects and talk about it. What do the children learn about Indian elephants? What sort of things frighten the children? What used to frighten them when they were younger?

Most of the sound effects can be made with body sounds. Sounds which can be made by several children are marked +. Instruments and other items needed to make sound effects are emphasised for quick identification.

story sounds	body sounds	instrumental or other sounds
1 *elephants walking* +	hands slapped slowly on chest or covered thighs	assorted **drums** and **tambours** tapped slowly with hands
2 *Tosca running*	as above but solo and faster and lighter	two small **drums** or **tambours** tapped lightly and quickly with hands
3 *ripping leaves* +	tricky – try Donald Duck sounds with mouth	**guiros** or **scrapers**, or rip long lengths of **paper**
4 *flapping ears* +	tap cheeks very lightly at random with floppy hands	clappers sound a bit harsh – try **magazines** flapped in the air
5 *sucking water* +	suck inwards noisily	let a few children suck up **water** dregs from the bottom of a **beaker** using **straws**
6 *squirting water* +	either 'raspberry' or *psh* sounds	let a few children drink and slurp into **beakers of water**
7 *snapping sound*	clicks with mouth or random claps	**claves**, or **rulers** slapped down on table top – hold one end down firmly with palm of one hand and snap the other end against the table
8 *hissing sound*	*ssss* with mouth or rub hands over clothes	**maracas** filled with sand or salt, or **slither boxes** filled with same
9 *roaring sound* +	vocal roar, or beat cupped hands against thighs	either **drum** roll (large drum), or wobble a **stiff piece of card**
10 *lightning*	clap hands loudly	clash two **cymbals** together
11 *rain* +	rapid tapping of back of nails on hard surface	**maracas** shaken with continuous movement

+ sounds which can be made by several children

games and exercises

ALL JOIN IN — *beat*

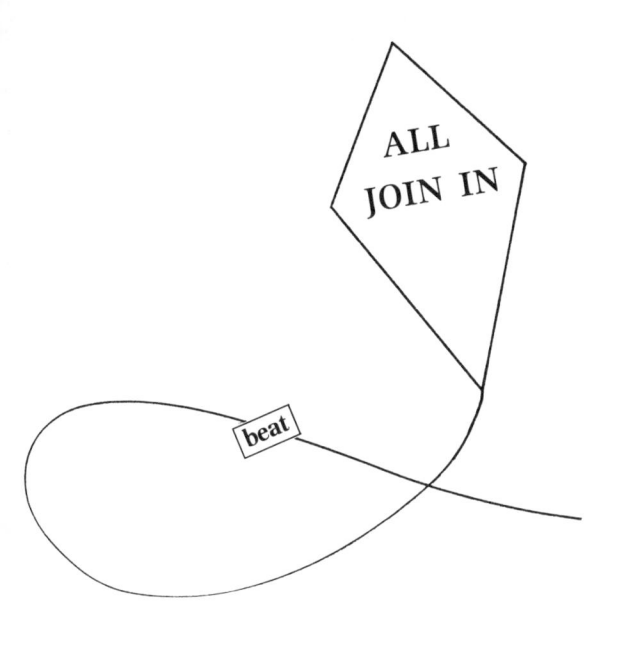

- Clap a steady beat at a 'walking' speed and invite the children to join in. Say *Listen to the beat and join in when you are ready. Stop when I stop.* Pause and try again but with a slower beat. Remind the children to listen to a few claps before they join in. Next time try a faster beat – but not too fast.

- Use a different body sound: shake, knock, rub (palms of hands together), or slap (hands on thighs) on the beat.

- Use instruments – one for each child if possible. (Build up a collection of 'homemade' shakers, drums and woodblocks to use for the games and exercises.)

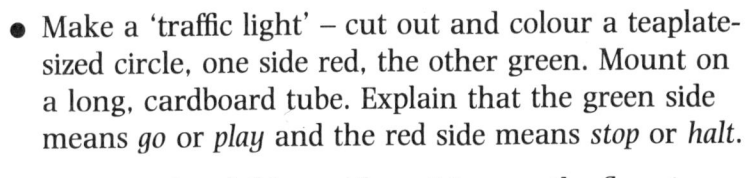

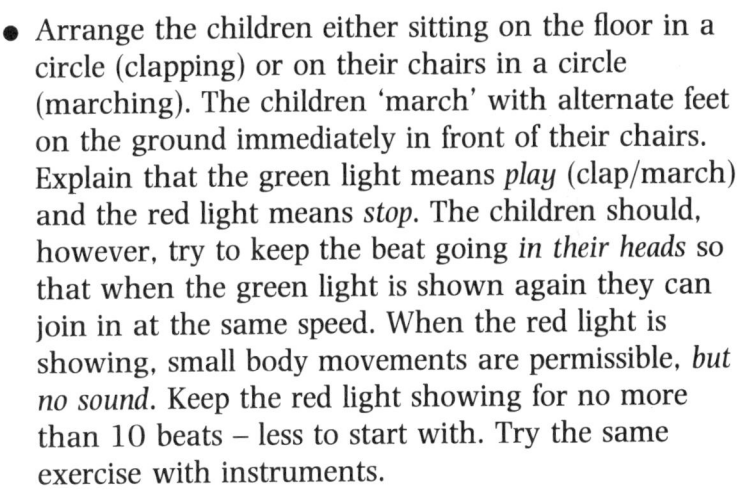

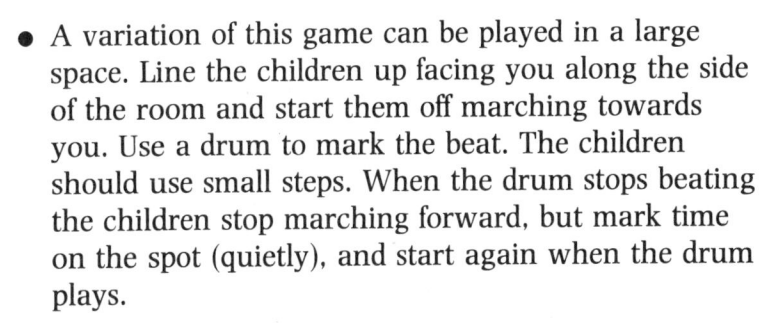

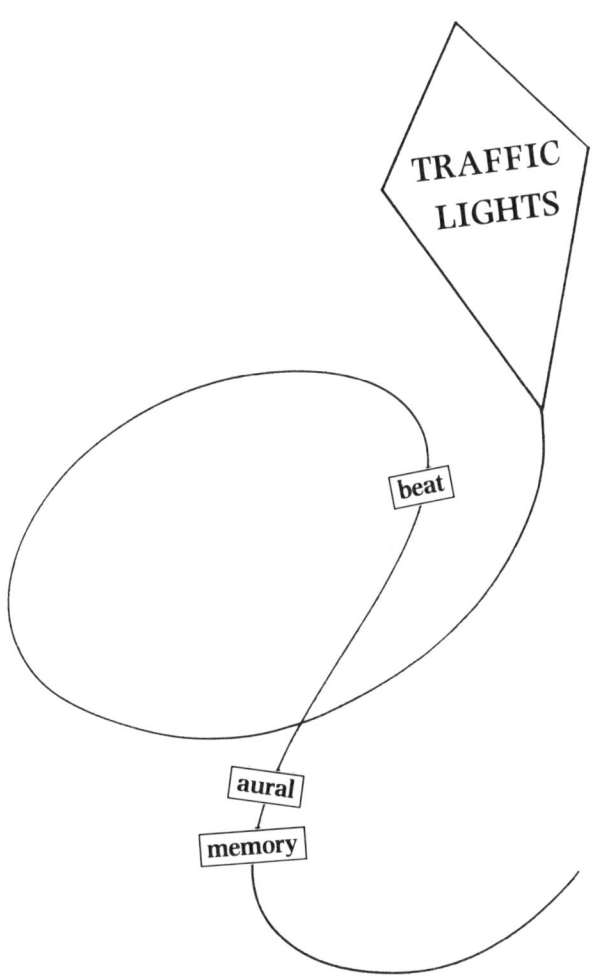

TRAFFIC LIGHTS — *beat, aural memory*

- Make a 'traffic light' – cut out and colour a teaplate-sized circle, one side red, the other green. Mount on a long, cardboard tube. Explain that the green side means *go* or *play* and the red side means *stop* or *halt*.

- Arrange the children either sitting on the floor in a circle (clapping) or on their chairs in a circle (marching). The children 'march' with alternate feet on the ground immediately in front of their chairs. Explain that the green light means *play* (clap/march) and the red light means *stop*. The children should, however, try to keep the beat going *in their heads* so that when the green light is shown again they can join in at the same speed. When the red light is showing, small body movements are permissible, *but no sound*. Keep the red light showing for no more than 10 beats – less to start with. Try the same exercise with instruments.

- A variation of this game can be played in a large space. Line the children up facing you along the side of the room and start them off marching towards you. Use a drum to mark the beat. The children should use small steps. When the drum stops beating the children stop marching forward, but mark time on the spot (quietly), and start again when the drum plays.

31

games and exercises

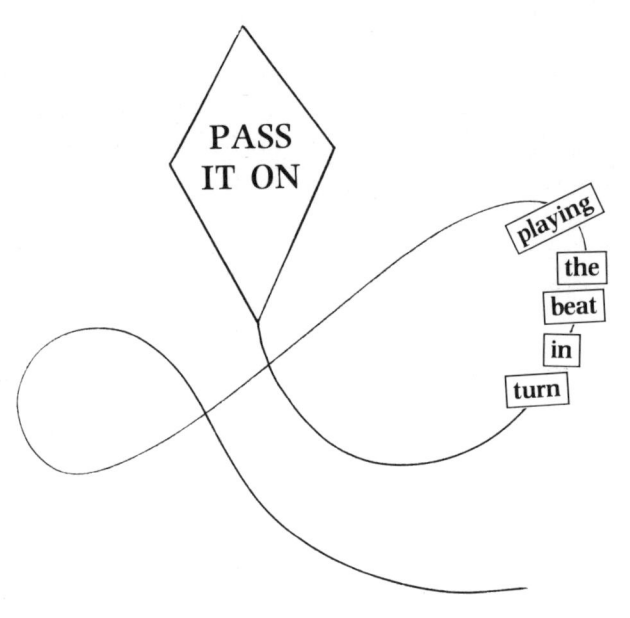

PASS IT ON — *playing the beat in turn*

- Clap a steady 'walking' beat together. Invite four children to come to the front. Line them up facing the class. Tell them they are each allowed four claps before the next person takes over. Start the first child off. Help to pass the four beats along the line.

- Change the children.
  Change the sound – rub hands together, stamp, shake, play instruments, etc.
  Change the number of beats in a group – 2/3/5/8.
  Change the tempo – though it should never be too fast. Have more beats in a group if the beat is brisk.

- Older children who are familiar with the game will be able to stress the first beat in the group.

CROTCHETS

- Don't introduce this teaching point until the children have tried *All join in* and *Traffic lights* (page 31).

> *Ask the children how they write down the spoken sounds* a *and* o. *Musical sounds can be written down too. You use NOTES not letters to write down musical sounds. Notoheads are either black ● or empty ○ and they usually have a stick going up or down: ♩ ♪. The black notes are shorter than empty notes. Black notes with stems are called crotchets: ♩*

- Play *All join in* using untuned percussion instruments, e.g. drums, shakers, woodblocks – one for each child if possible. Draw a long line of crotchets on the board and tell the children that that is what they have been playing. Play again, but this time point to the notes in turn:

  ♩ ♩ ♩ ♩ ♩ ♩ ♩

  The strokes show the *beat*.

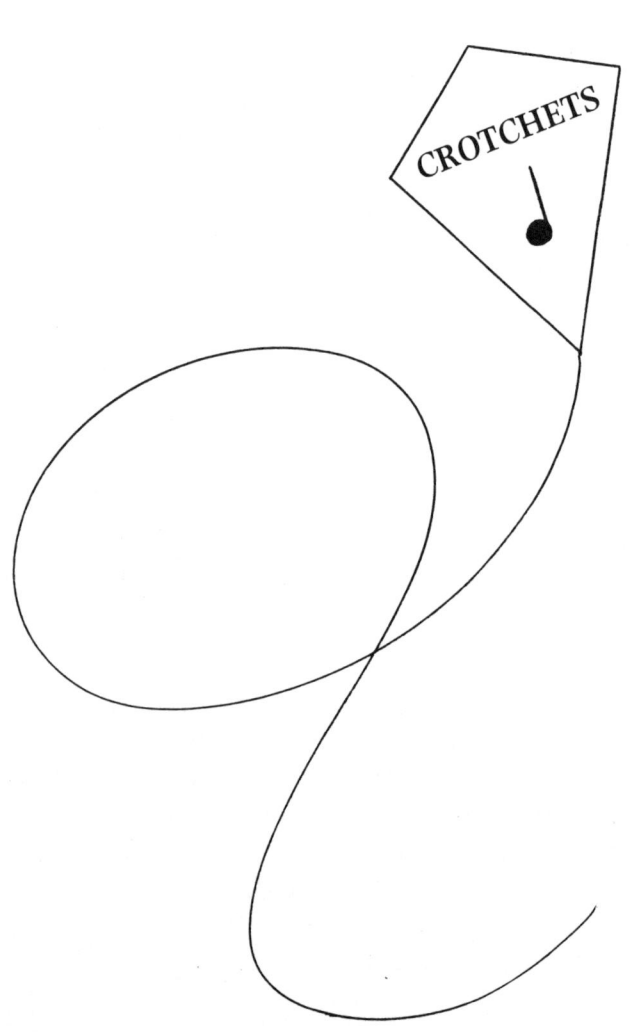

32

games and exercises

| 4 ♩♩♩♩ | 2 ♩♩ |

- Rub out all except four of the crotchets. Invite someone to play the new, short piece of music. All try it. Start together and stop together. Change the number of notes – 2/3/5/8. Encourage the children to make up, play and write down their own pieces of crotchet music.

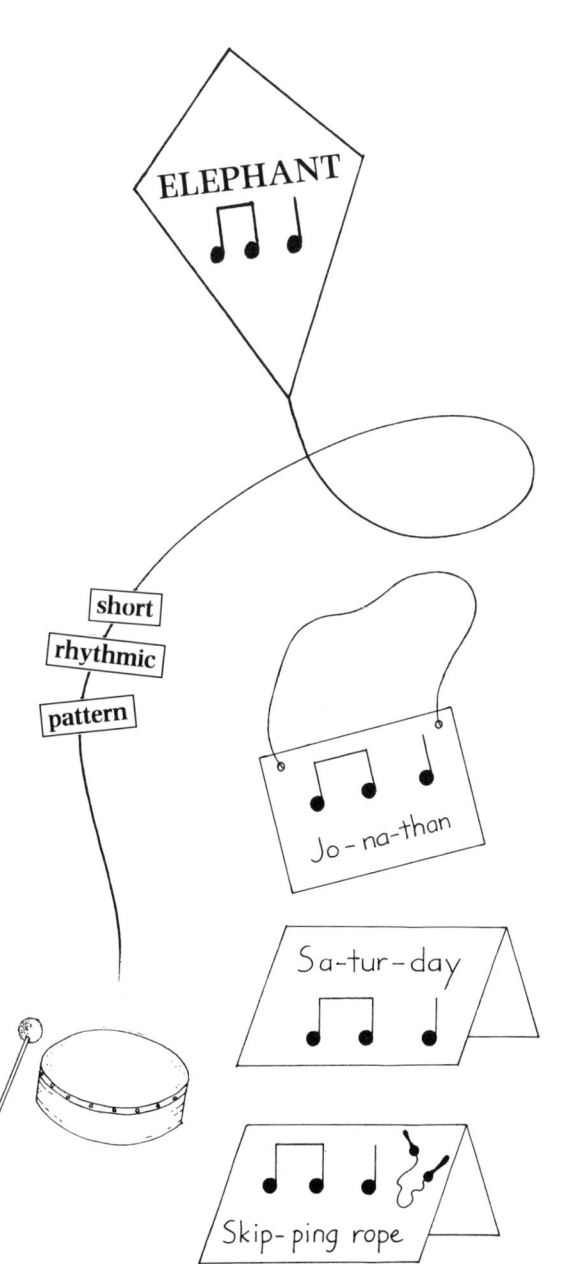

short rhythmic pattern

- Clap and chant the word *elephant* over and over again. Stop. Ask the children to listen while you clap it. Clap the rhythm once only. Ask *How many claps? Yes, three claps, so I'll write down three notes:* ♩ ♩ ♩ Say *But two of the claps are quick. Listen again and try to spot the quick claps.*

- At first the children will find it hard to pick out the quick notes (quavers), but it will come with practice. Explain that two quick notes are joined with a bridge: ♫ Draw the rhythm for *elephant*, and write the word underneath. Point to the notes as the children clap the rhythm again. Play on instruments.

♫ ♩

e-le-phant

- Ask the children to speak and clap their own names (quietly). Has anyone got a name with the same rhythm as *elephant*? These children should come to the front and chant and clap and play their names, several times each. Make a card to hang round their neck with their name and rhythm on one side.

- Keep an ear open for other words with the *elephant* rhythm – Saturday, xylophone, glockenspiel, tambourine, skipping rope, etc. Chant and play them and write their names and rhythms down.

33

games and exercises

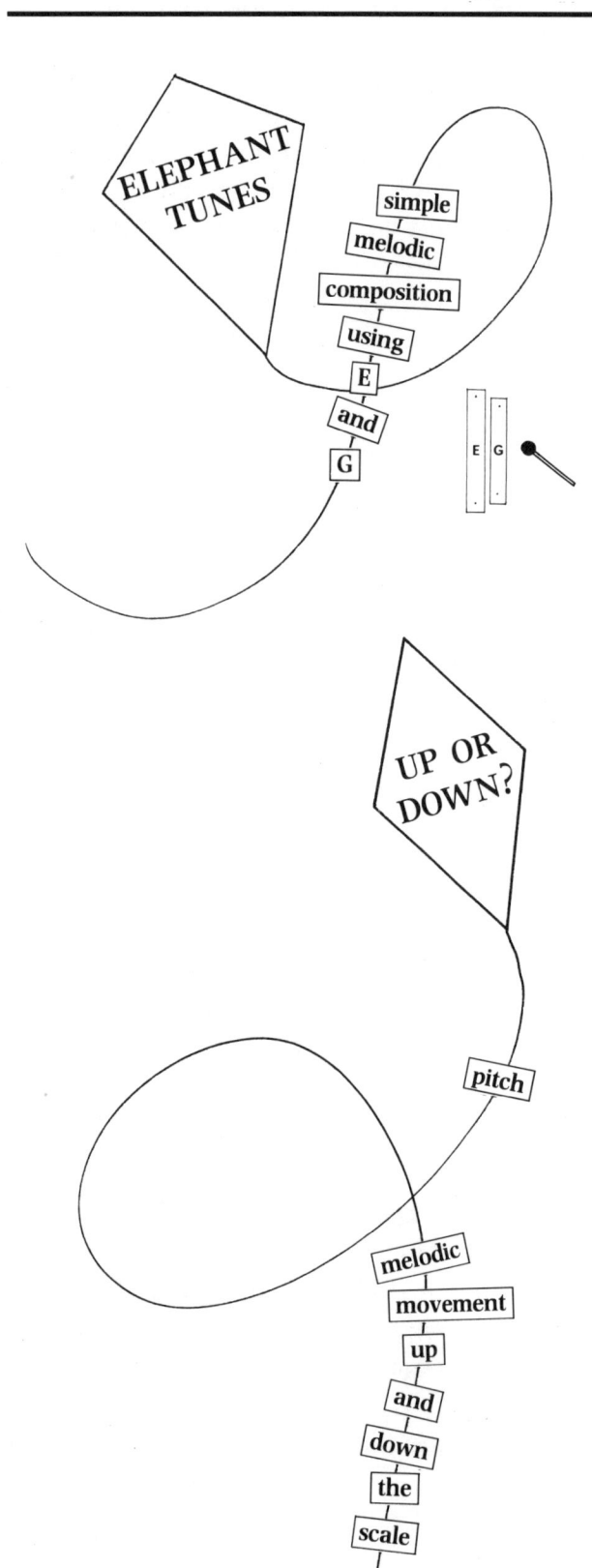

ELEPHANT TUNES — simple melodic composition using E and G

- Set out the chime bars E and G and invite someone to make up a simple tune for the elephant rhythm. Sing. Play the elephant tune on other tuned percussion instruments – but first remove all the bars except low E and G.

- Put E and G in the music corner and invite children whose names have the same rhythm as *elephant* to make up a tune for their own names. Play and sing. Can they think of a way to write their tune down so that they can remember it, and so that other children can play it?

UP OR DOWN? — pitch, melodic movement up and down the scale

- Set out an octave, C to C, on a xylophone: C D E F G A B C'. Remove the other bars. (Any tuned percussion instrument will do.) Beginning on low C, play the rising octave. Talk about it. Play it again and ask the children to draw the tune in the air. Starting on high C', play the descending octave and 'draw' it. Ask the children to listen to the elephant walking uphill. Then downhill. (Slow beat.) Ask them to listen and say whether the elephant is going up or down the hill.

- Play the same game but *behind a screen*. Invite children to go behind the screen to make the elephant music.

- Add variations of speed. The children have to say if the elephant is going up or down hill, slowly or quickly.

- Extend the listening exercise. Play music which describes, for example, an elephant climbing a hill slowly, pausing for a few moments at the top then running halfway down.

- Play the lower note C several times, or the higher note C several times, and ask the children to say if the elephant is at the top or the bottom of the hill.

games and exercises

DRUMS AND BEATERS — *aural discrimination*

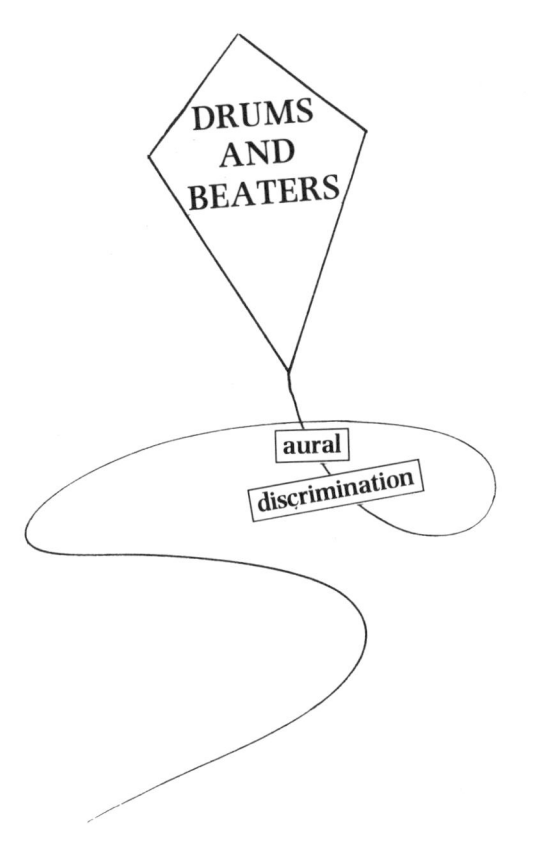

- Set out three or four drums (include tambours if you haven't got many drums) with contrasting timbres or sounds, e.g. snare drums, timp-tomp, cardboard box drum, small tambour. Play them in turn and talk about them – structure, sound, appearance, name. Use the same beater for each.

- Place the drums behind a screen. Play in turn. Can the children identify them by sound? Let the first child who guesses correctly go behind the screen and play another of the drums. And so on.

- Set up as for the drum identification game above, but this time use *one drum* and *a selection of beaters* – wire, soft felt, hard felt, wood, hands. Ask the children to say what type of beater is being used. Use the screen. *What should never be used to tap drums?* (Pencils, rulers, etc.)

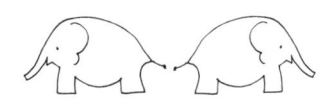

DRUM ROLLS — *instrumental skills*

- Put out your largest free-standing drum or timp-tomp and a pair of felt beaters. (Cut off the ends of the handles if they are too long for small children.) Invite the children to experiment with the beaters and drum. Can they play a drum roll? Using two beaters, play with loose wrists and in the centre of the drum skin. What does it sound like at the edge of the skin?

- Make the sound of thunder, an ogre striding across the mountain tops, a monster, a lion roaring, a hippopotamus yawning. Encourage more suggestions.

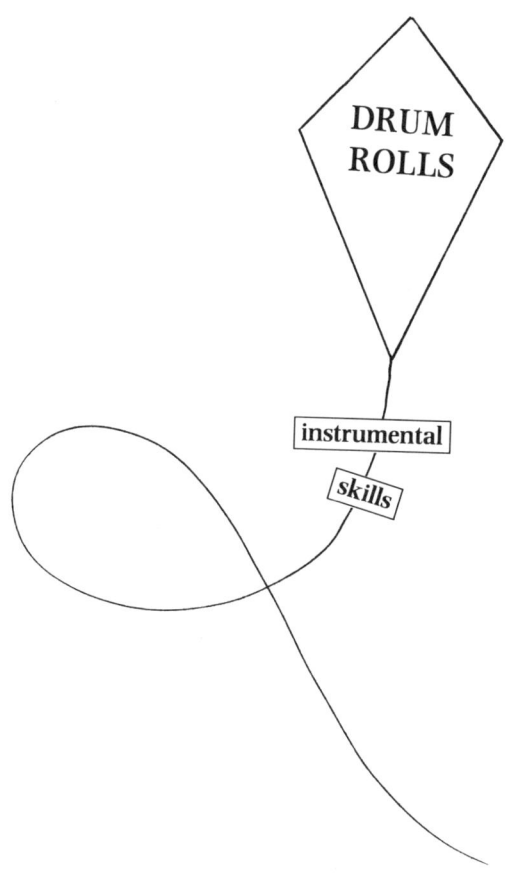

games and exercises

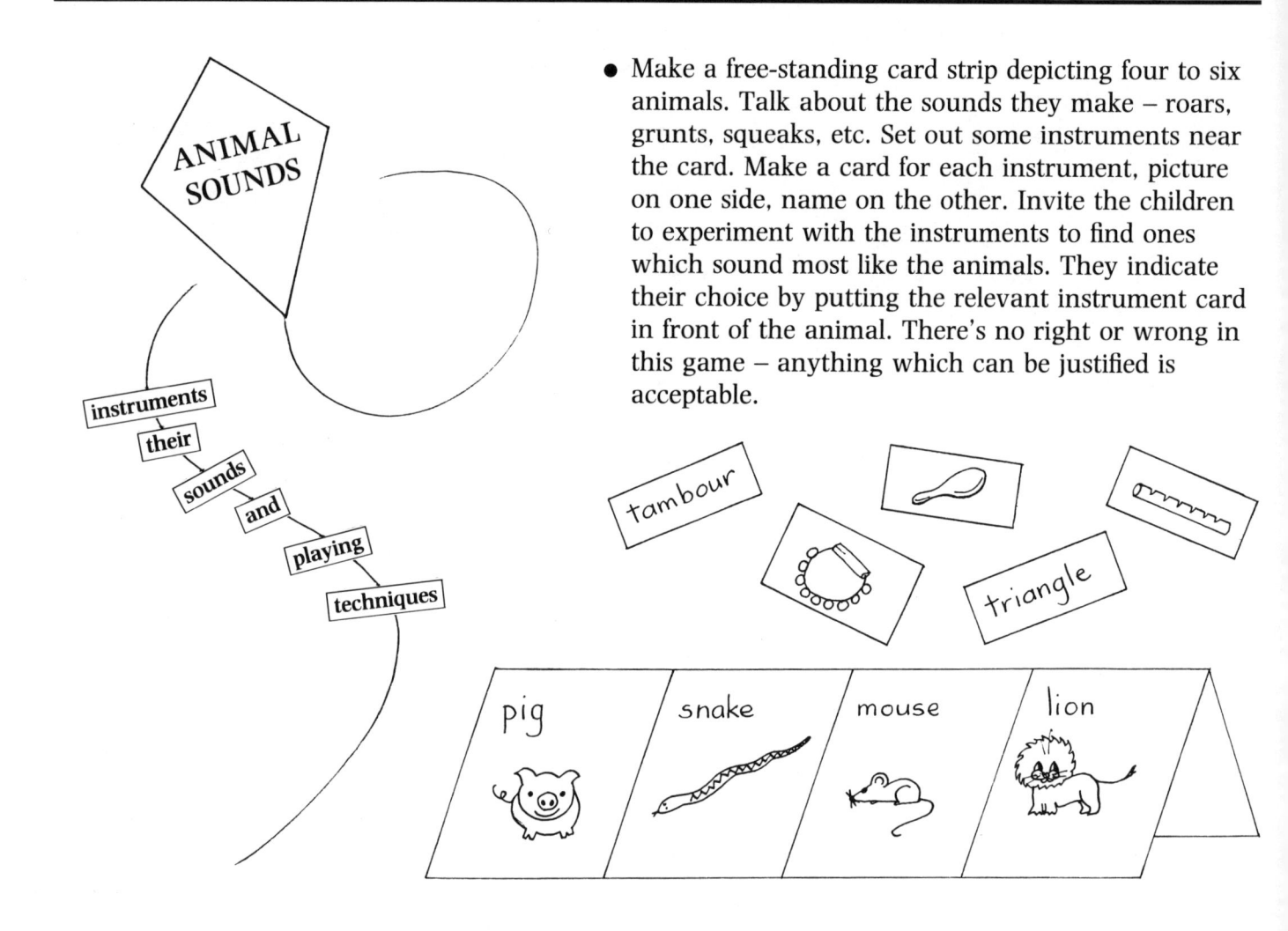

- Make a free-standing card strip depicting four to six animals. Talk about the sounds they make – roars, grunts, squeaks, etc. Set out some instruments near the card. Make a card for each instrument, picture on one side, name on the other. Invite the children to experiment with the instruments to find ones which sound most like the animals. They indicate their choice by putting the relevant instrument card in front of the animal. There's no right or wrong in this game – anything which can be justified is acceptable.

ANIMAL SOUNDS

instruments their sounds and playing techniques

instruments to make and play

It is difficult to make an effective drum or tambour which has a stretched skin, but there are other ways to produce instruments which make a fairly resonant drum-like sound when tapped.

TAMBOURS

Make a collection of shallow tins or boxes of various sizes and in different materials, e.g. wood, metal, plastic, card. Held loosely by the rim and tapped lightly with fingertips or beaters, these improvised tambours can produce a range of interesting sounds. Play a 'proper' good-quality tambour for the children to hear and ask for their comments. Help the children to appreciate that the 'proper' tambour has a more resonant (boomy/bouncy) timbre or sound. Can the children work out why the instrument with the skin is more rich in tone than their

instruments to make and play

homemade tambours? If you possess a tunable tambour, demonstrate what happens when you loosen/tighten the skin. Play the game *Drums and beaters* (see page 35) using a few homemade tambours.

DRUMS

A tambour only has one skin (the other end of the cylinder is open), but a drum has two skins. The simplest form of improvised drum is a biscuit or sweet tin with its lid on. Plastic ice-cream tubs can also be effective. Hold the 'drum' loosely under one arm or in the gap made between crossed legs. A large cardboard box produces a surprisingly resonant sound. Try empty washing powder tubs. The cardboard cylinders can be decorated by the children. Aim for one drum per child.

With adult help, reasonable-quality drums or tambours can be made from strong tins covered either at one end or at both ends with rubber or plastic sheeting. Your school kitchen will probably be able to provide the tins.

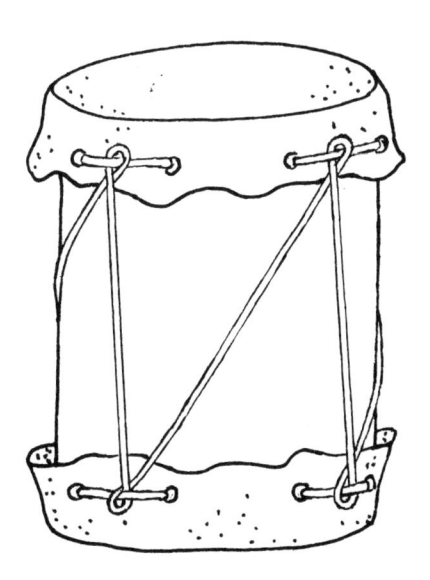

You will need
- Large tin open at one end or at both ends (tins made from thin metal should only be opened at one end).
- Heavy-duty polythene or rubber sheeting – preferably the latter.
- Strong string or cord.
- Leather hole punch.

Instructions
1 Cut out two circles, each 8 cm larger in diameter than the diameter of the tin.
2 Punch an even number of holes (18 to 22 depending on the size of the tin) round the edge of each circle, 2 cm in from the edge.
3 Take a length of string twice the length of the circumference of the tin and thread it in and out of the holes.
4 Place the 'skin' circle on top of the tin and draw it tight. Tie firmly in place. Repeat at the other end if required.
5 With another length of string, lash the two skins together through the threaded string (see diagram). At this stage keep the tension loose. Work round the drum several times, tightening the lashing string until the two skins are stretched tight enough to produce a good tone when tapped. Secure the ends of the lashing string. If you are making a tambour, i.e. only one skin, tie the lashing to a large curtain ring placed centrally under the other base.

BEATERS
1 Make wooden stick beaters from 22 cm long dowelling.
2 Sand any rough edges.
3 For a soft beater, wrap strips of foam rubber or wool around one end.

37

curricular links

> RELATED THEMES: zoos • monsters • giants • endangered species • dinosaurs • jungles • safari parks

Language

Talk about *slow movements*. Make a set of things which move slowly. Why do they move slowly? Can any of them change speed? If so, how and why?

Talk about *loud sounds*. Make a set of things which produce loud sounds. Divide into noisy but nice, noisy and nasty – allow for divergences of opinion. Some things, e.g. sirens, are noisy for a purpose – discuss. Aeroplanes always make a lot of noise when they are flying but we can't always hear them – why? Are all large things loud?

Talk about the letter *e*. Draw an elephant outline and fill it with *e*'s.

Say several words, some of which contain the sound *e* as in 'elephant'. On identifying the letter *e*, the children should stand up, wave a trunk and sit down.

How many words can be made out of *elephant*?

Talk about the sound *ph*.

Give each child an elephant outline and give oral instructions for colouring it, e.g. pink trunk, one green leg, one blue leg, etc.

Read the poem 'Slowly' by James Reeves (*A Puffin Quartet of Poets*). Make up a group poem with each line beginning '*Slowly . . .*', for example, 'Slowly the hands move round the clock' or 'Slowly Juan gets changed for PE'. When it's finished, read it aloud *slowly*. Ask the children to copy it out *slowly* in their best writing.

Make up another poem beginning with *Quickly*. Read it quickly, copy it quickly.

Read the poem 'I like noise' by Barbara Ireson (*Over and Over Again*). Make up individual or class or group poems in the same style, e.g. 'I like noise, The shrieks in the playground, The roar of a rocket'. Older infants can write in block capitals to make their poems *look* loud.

Number work

Make sets of large and small things. Make comparisons using 'larger than' and 'smaller than'.

How many tusks, ears, eyes, legs, tails has one elephant? How many tusks, ears, etc. have two elephants or three elephants? Record findings.

Draw an elephant using geometric templates.

Draw a row of three or four elephants starting with a big one and getting smaller (or vice versa).

Present the children with a row of elephants and give oral instructions, e.g. *Colour the third one orange*, etc.

Using bean bags balanced on backs, see who can transport most bags from A to B in three minutes.

Rules: Only one bag at a time to be carried. Any dropped bags have to be returned to the elephant's back. All 'elephants' must travel on knees and hands. Only bean bags left inside the hoop/bucket will be counted.

Several children at a time can play this.

Put 12 bean bags in a hoop and see who can carry the bags, one at a time, to a given point in the shortest time. Same rules as above apply. Use a stopwatch to time the race. Try again but this time have teams of three elephants working together to do the transporting. Time the race. Compare the results.

curricular links

Introduce the kilogram weight. Find things lighter than, heavier than and the same weight as a kilogram.

Environmental studies

How can you lift heavy objects? Give a few children the task of moving a heavy box (brick box) along the length of the corridor. Provide them with a rope, a large plastic bag and some rollers.

Find a box too heavy to lift and ask a few children (under adult supervision) to try and raise it from the ground a few centimetres. Provide a lever and a few bricks.

Make a study of levers, pulleys and cranes. Watch out for them in your own environment. Make cranes out of construction toys.

Look at the habitats of elephants in Asia and Africa and in Europe (safari parks, etc.)

Study the giants of the past. What animals are in danger of extinction today and why? What can be done to prevent it happening?

Using a tuned drum or tambour, demonstrate how pitch can be changed by skin tension.

Pluck a guitar string (a low one) hard to produce a loud sound. Pluck the same string gently to produce a quiet sound. What do the children notice about the vibrating string?

Art and craft

Make a collage picture of an Asian jungle. Use large stitching with wools and string for fronds and creepers. Cut up green plastic bags for leaves.

Make a full-sized picture of a baby elephant (about a metre wide and a metre tall). Fold strips of paper or card concertina fashion to make a moving trunk.

Construct a 3-dimensional elephant using a large cardboard box and other bits of junk. Make a model of a mouse out of clay and display it near the elephant.

Listen to 'The kind elephant' from the *Play School* cassette tape (see List of resources). This lovely version of the elephant-helps-mouse story, complete with sound effects, is an excellent starting point for any work involving large and small. On the same tape is the song about two hippopotami, 'Mud glorious mud'. Mix some soil and water and make mud pictures – handprints, fingerprints, paintings, etc.

If you can get hold of the book *Elmer*, by David McKee, read it and talk about it. The moral 'be yourself' is nicely put across. Make a patchwork elephant like Elmer, using a variety of fabrics.

Drama and movement

Practise performing several tasks in a *quiet* manner, e.g. taking off shoes, crossing the room. Do it again, but *noisily*.

Repeat but with the contrast of *slow* and *fast*.

Listen to and move to 'The elephant' (*The Carnival of Animals*) by Saint-Saëns and 'Morning' from the *Peer Gynt* suite by Grieg.

Enact some situations where it is good to be noisy/quiet or quick/slow.

list of resources

STORIES

'The elephants' picnic' by E. Colwell in *Tell me another story* (Puffin)
Sam who never forgets by Eve Rice (Bodley Head/Puffin)
Five minutes' peace by Jill Murphy (Walker Books)
The elephant and the bad baby by Elfrida Vipont (Hamish Hamilton)
Barbar stories by Jean de Brunhoff (Methuen)
The elephant's child by Rudyard Kipling (Macmillan Children's Books)
But no elephants by Jerry Smath (Hippo Books)
The trunk by Brian Wildsmith (OUP)
Alistair's elephant by Marilyn Sadler (Hamish Hamilton)
The elephant (pop-up book) by Colin and Jacqui Hawkins (Viking Kestrel)
Elmer by David McKee (Dennis Dobson)
Dinosaurs and all that rubbish by Michael Foreman (Picture Puffin)
I'm coming to get you by Tony Ross (Picture Puffin)
The very worst monster by Pat Hutchins (Picture Puffin)
A lion in the meadow by Margaret Mahy (Picture Puffin)
There's a hippopotamus on our roof eating cake by Hazel Edwards (Picture Puffin)

POEMS

This little Puffin (Puffin)
    The elephant is big and strong
    Slowly, slowly, very slowly
    Slowly, slowly, walks my grandad
    The steamroller
Over and over again (Beaver Books)
    Catch a whale
    If you should meet a giant
    I like noise
When we were very young (Methuen)
    The four friends
Poems for 7-year-olds (Puffin)
    Eletelephony
A Puffin quartet of poets (Puffin)
    Slowly

SONGS

Sing a song one (Nelson)
    Zoo time
    The elephant present
    Going to the zoo
Sing a song two (Nelson)
    Nellie the elephant
Okki-tokki-unga (Black)
    The animal fair
    The prehistoric animal brigade
Apusskidu (Black)
    The animals went in two by two
    The hippopotamus song

INFORMATION

Elephants in the wild by Cliff Moon (Wayland)
Wildlife – the elephant by Jill Coleman and Michael Atkinson (Pan Books)
Animals in the wild – elephant by Mary Hoffman (Windward/Belitha Press)
Hello elephant by Patricia Grey (Longman)
Elephants (Macdonald Starters)
Elephant (Working Animals) by John Stewart (Black)
'Zoos' in *Child Education Special* No. 45

MUSIC

André Previn's Guide to Music vols 1 and 2 (deep woodwind and brass, cello and double bass) (EMI)
'The elephant' and 'The lion' from *The Carnival of Animals* by Saint-Saëns
'The grandfather theme' from *Peter and the Wolf* by Prokofiev
'The broom theme' in *The Sorcerer's Apprentice* by Dukas
'Circus polka for a young elephant' by Stravinsky
'The golliwog's cakewalk' by Debussy/Lewis (*Atarah's Band* · The Blue One)
'The whale' by Paddy Kingsland (*The Soundhouse* · BBC Radiophonic Workshop)
The 'Take Hart' and 'Mr Men' themes (*BBC Children's TV Themes* · BBC Cassettes)
'Nellie the elephant' and 'Mud glorious mud' (*All Aboard* · BBC Cassettes)
'The kind elephant' (story) (*Play School* · BBC Cassettes)

at home

speech rhymes
Bubble, said the kettle   42
A long-haired Griggle from the land of Grunch   42
Dip-dap, dripping tap   43

action rhymes
This is my house   44
High walls   44

poem
The sounds in the evening   45

songs
Somebody's walking up my path   46
When I go to bed   47
My house   48
What happiness   50
Crash! Bang! Ouch! And whoops-a-daisy!   51
Ibble-obble black bobble   53

sound story
No peace for Hammy   54

games and exercises   57

instruments to make and play
Suspended cups, glasses and bottles   61

curricular links   62

list of resources   64

speech rhymes

Bubble, said the kettle

Bubble, said the kettle,
Bubble, said the pot,
Bubble, bubble, bubble,
We are very, very hot.

TRADITIONAL

It's worth spending some time listening to your children's voices and noting their 'type' (high or low or in-between).

Once the children know their voice category they will quickly learn to group themselves in preparation for chanting. Note that children with very low voices may have difficulty with their pitch in singing.

This speech rhyme is for two groups of children or two solo speakers.

1 Get to know the rhyme. Listen to your children and divide them into two groups – high and low voices. The kettles (higher voices) chant line 1, and the pots (lower voices) chant line 2. The third and fourth lines are spoken together, care being taken to sustain the difference in pitch. Later the teacher or a solo child can speak the words *said the kettle* and *said the pot* in between the *bubbles*.

2 Tap or shake or scrape the rhythm of the repeated *bubbles* on any instrument which the children consider to be suitable – drums with soggy skins would come into their own here. Chant as you play. Keep the tempo slow.

3 Using the notes E and G, make up a tune for the last two lines. Sing and play. Find a way to record the tune on paper. Put instruments and 'music' in the music corner.

4 Talk about the rhythm of the words *Bubble, bubble*. Clap, shake, scrape the rhythm as you chant. (Keep the beat going with your foot.) Are they quick or slow claps? (Relate the claps to your tapping foot – in other words, to the beat.) See the game *Quavers* on page 58 for further notes on the quaver pair.

A long-haired Griggle from the land of Grunch

A long-haired Griggle from the land of Grunch
Always giggled when he ate his lunch.
He'd wriggle and giggle and munch and crunch
While nibbling the pebbles that he liked for lunch.

ALICE GILBERT

speech rhymes

Recite *A long-haired Griggle* against a background of eating sounds – crunching, slurping, chewing, swallowing, lip-smacking – and giggling. Make pebble shakers and roll them around as background music. Draw a Griggle eating his lunch. Make up a Griggle menu.

Dip-dap, dripping tap

Dip-dap,
Dripping tap.

Lubble-ubble,
Saucepan bubble.

Hissing-whizzing,
Steam a-fizzing.

Slishing-sloshing,
Dirty washing.

Irgle-wirgle,
Pipes a-gurgle.

Titter-tatter,
Raindrops patter.

Grimbly-grumbles,
Night-time rumbles.

V.C.

This speech rhyme describes various *water sounds* to be heard around the house. (With younger children, reduce the number of stanzas.)

1 Get to know the rhyme. Talk about all the water sounds. Which are liked/not liked? Practise all the *first line water sounds*. Pitch voices to match sound, e.g. low for saucepan and night-time rumbles, high for steam, etc. Exaggerate the dominant letter sounds, e.g. the *s*'s and *z*'s in stanza 3. Talk about the *rhythms* of the first lines. Which is the odd man out? Compare with the rhythm *bubble, bubble* (see opposite).

2 Divide the class into seven groups (or one for each stanza used). Allocate a couplet to each group. Allow time for practice and discussion. Arrange the groups so that they are in the correct order and recite the rhyme from beginning to end. Conduct clearly. Make a tape-recording of the chanting, play back and discuss.

3 Try to find an instrumental (or other) sound to match each couplet. Play with the chanting. Another time, using the instrumental sounds only, bring them in one at a time until the room is full of swishing, gurgling water sounds. Tape, listen and discuss.

4 Play *Water lotto* (see page 57). Sounds depicted on the cards could include water bubbling in a pan, a toilet flushing, a bath filling, a shower, washing up, a washing machine.

action rhymes

This is my house

This is my house,
This is the door.
The windows are shiny
And so is the floor

Outside there's a chimney
Which points to the sky.
On top there's a roof
Which keeps everything dry.

TRADITIONAL

line 1   Draw a large rectangle in the air.
line 2   Draw a smaller rectangle in the air.
line 3   Polish pretend windows.
line 4   Polish a pretend floor.

line 5   Draw a small rectangle high up in the air.
line 6   Point to the sky.
line 7   Use both arms to make a roof over head.
line 8   Hold position.

High walls

High walls,
Windows four,
Climb the steps
To reach the door.

Knock, knock,
Open wide,
Wipe your feet
And walk inside.

V.C.

line 1   Stretch hands and arms above head (stand up).
line 2   Show four fingers.
lines 3 and 4   With flat hands, palms down, mime the climbing of steps by moving hands up and over each other.

line 5   Two knocks.
line 6   Make an opening gesture with both arms.
line 7   Wipe feet on imaginary mat.
line 8   Either move body forwards or stand up and take a step forwards.

Talk about visiting. Whom do your children enjoy/not enjoy visiting? Talk about front doors, paths leading to doors, steps, letterboxes, bells and knockers.

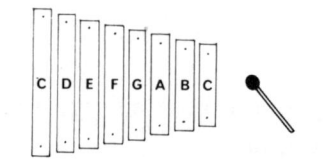

1 Set out an octave of chimes C to the C above. Tap an ascending scale slowly. Ask the children to make their hand(s) climb the steps with the music. Can anyone make 'coming down' music? Play and move hands accordingly.

action rhymes

2 Sing and play the rhyme (see below) tapping the chime bars on the beat to indicate climbing the stairs. Try with other tuned percussion instruments.

C	D	E F	G A	B C
High	walls,	Win-dows four,	Climb the steps To	reach the door.

poem

The sounds in the evening

The sounds in the evening
Go all through the house,
The click of the clock
And the pick of the mouse,
The footsteps of people
Upon the top floor,
The skirts of my mother
That brush by the door.
The crick in the boards,
And the creak of the chairs,
The fluttering murmurs
Outside on the stairs . . .

The queer little noises
That no-one explains . . .
Till the moon through the slats
Of my window-blind rains.
And the world of my eyes
And my ears melts like steam
As I find in my pillow
The world of my dream

ELEANOR FARJEON

1 Insist on stillness before you read this poem to the children. Let them get into a sleeping position on the floor so that they can imagine themselves in the role of a child falling asleep. Talk about bedtime sounds. Which noises do the children like to hear when they are in bed? Which noises frighten them?

2 Try imitating the various sounds described in the first stanza. Bring the sounds in one at a time, sometimes solo, sometimes in conjunction with another. Make a tape-recording of the bedtime sounds and recite the poem against a background of quiet sound effects.

3 Ask the children to describe what it's like just before falling asleep. Read the last four lines and talk about them. Talk about dreams, good and bad. Sing *When I go to bed* (see page 47).

4 Most children enjoy talking about going to bed, their bedrooms, their bedclothes, bedtime rituals, their favourite bedtime toys. Older children will enjoy writing about them.

5 Sing some lullabies in quiet voices. Have a Quiet Day (or hour!) with large signs around the room. Wear plimsolls and whisper.

45

songs

Somebody's walking up my path

TRADITIONAL
ADAPTED BY V.C.

Some-bo-dy's walk-ing up my path, (crunch, crunch) v.4=hel-lo! (Sound effects)

Some-bo-dy's walk-ing up my path, (crunch, crunch) v.4=hel-lo! (Sound effects)

Some-bo-dy's walk-ing, Some-bo-dy's walk-ing,

Some-bo-dy's walk-ing up my path. (crunch, crunch) v.4=come in! (Sound effects)

Somebody's knocking at my door, (knock, knock)
Somebody's knocking at my door, (knock, knock)
Somebody's knocking, somebody's knocking,
Somebody's knocking at my door. (knock, knock)

Somebody's ringing at my bell, (brr, brr)
Somebody's ringing at my bell, (brr, brr)
Somebody's ringing, somebody's ringing,
Somebody's ringing at my bell. (brr, brr)

songs

Somebody's opening the door, (*hello*)
Somebody's opening the door, (*hello*)
Somebody's opening, somebody's opening,
Somebody's opening the door. (*come in*)

1 Add actions at the ends of the first, second and fourth lines. Mime the *crunch, crunch* with either feet on floor or hands on knees. Knock on a convenient nearby surface. Press the tip of the nose for the *brr, brr* and shake hands with self or neighbour on the *hellos* and the final *come in*.

2 Experiment to find suitable sound effects. Buttons or gravel in a tin or plastic container make a good crunching sound. Woodblocks make a realistic knocking sound, although a classroom cupboard door is better still. Make the greetings sound welcoming.

3 Try the tuned percussion accompaniment shown with the song. It can be played by one player or split between two, three or four players, one player per line.

4 Make a game out of verse 1. Line the children up facing you. They may take two steps forward on the *crunch, crunch* sounds at the end of the first, second and fourth lines. Anyone who steps forward at the wrong time has to sit down on the spot. Substitute other types of movement for walking, e.g. jumping, hopping, marching.

When I go to bed

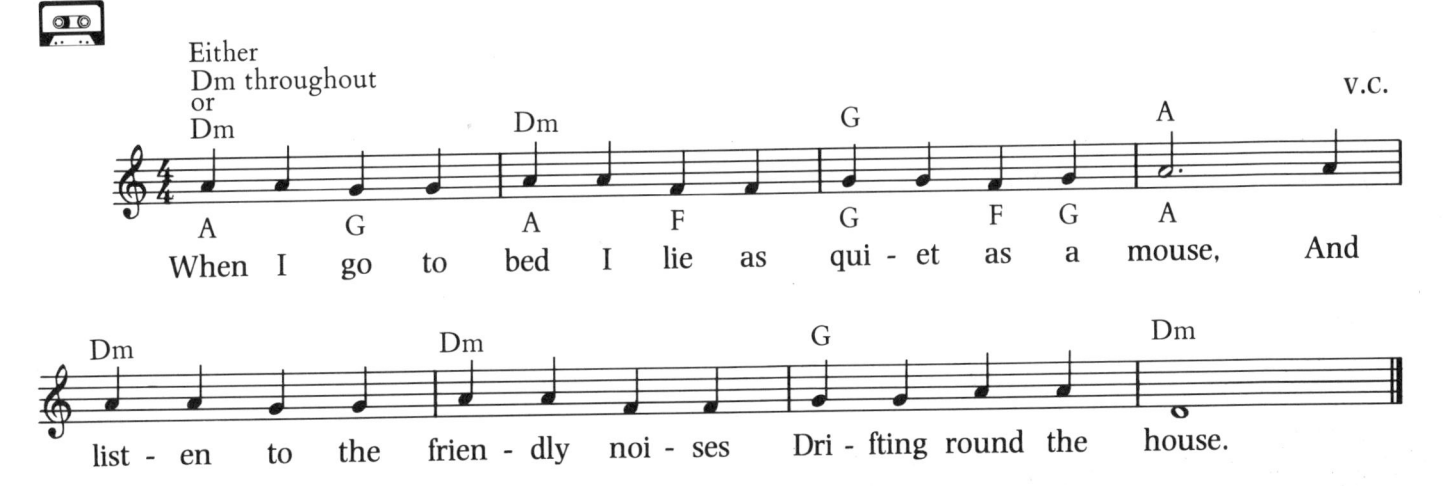

When I go to bed I lie as qui-et as a mouse, And list-en to the frien-dly noi-ses Dri-fting round the house.

The far-off sound of talking and the creaking of the floor,
Music from the radio,
The banging of the door.

songs

1 Sing slowly and quietly. When the children know the song well, invite solo performances, or duets. The children will enjoy putting their hands over their ears as they sing the second verse – their voices will sound far off. Try again, but this time move the hands off and on the ears, in time with the beat if possible. (Press the hands quite firmly over the ears. *Don't hit* the ears.) Talk about the effect.

2 Have a go at sound effects in verse 2.

3 The song can be sung to a repeated chord of D minor. Set out the notes D F and A and invite a few children to tap them gently as and when they want to while the song is being sung. Experiment with different instruments and different beaters. Aim to produce a sleepy sound. (These bars can be displayed in the music corner for further experimentation.)

My house

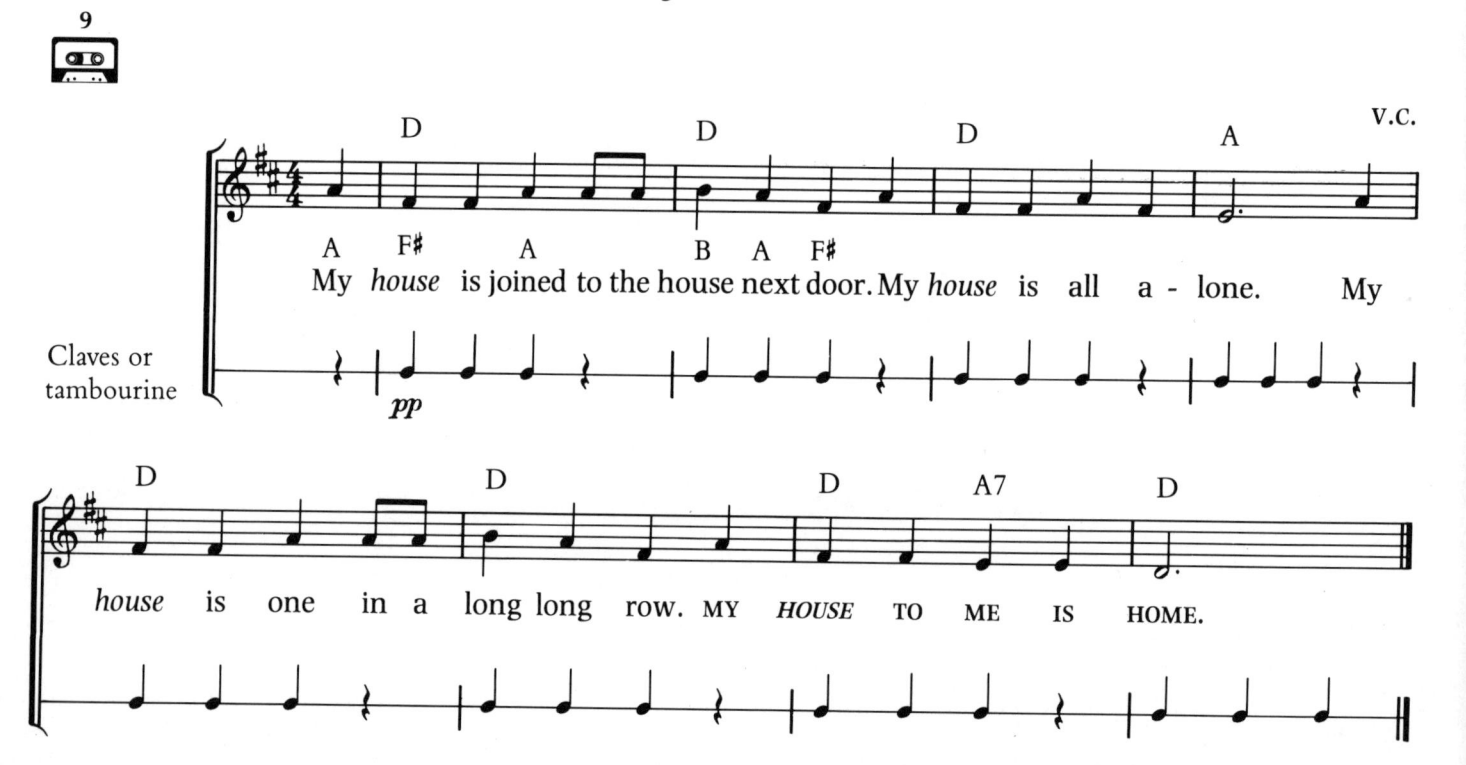

My *house* is joined to the house next door. My *house* is all a-lone. My *house* is one in a long long row. MY HOUSE TO ME IS HOME.

Claves or tambourine — *pp*

My house is high in a block of flats.
My house is a bungalow.
My house is a cottage thatched with straw.
MY HOUSE IS HOME YOU KNOW.

My house is really rather grand.
My house is very small.
My house is something in-between.
MY HOUSE IS THE BEST OF ALL.

songs

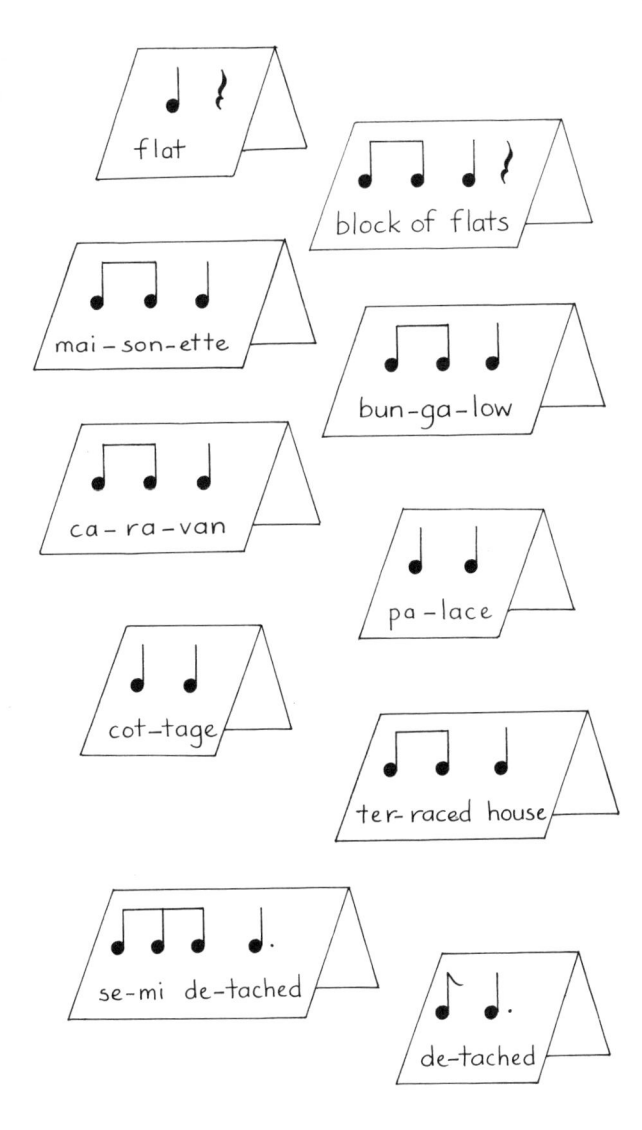

1 Sing the song and talk about the various types of houses mentioned in the song. Help the children to identify their own house type. Concentrating on *verse 1*, divide the children into three groups: those who live in semi-detached houses, those in detached houses and those in terraced houses. Let the children sing the line that applies to them and then *all* join in MY HOUSE TO ME IS HOME. Keep a slow tempo. Older children will be able to treat the other two verses in a similar way, though you might be a bit short of children living in thatched cottages.

2 Play a drone D and A together throughout the song on the slow beat, or just on the repeated word *house*. Or play an ostinato D then A throughout, four notes per line. Try the two accompaniments together.

3 Add untuned percussion. Keep all the accompaniment quiet and light.

4 Older children can clap the *rhythm* of the first verse. Take it quite slowly as there are a lot of notes to fit in. Sustain a quiet beat with either foot or tambour.

5 Clap, tap, shake, scrape all the house rhythms shown on the left, and add any more the children can think of. Display rhythm cards and percussion instruments in the music corner. Leave out chimes E and G and ask children to set the rhythms to music. Encourage the children to record their tunes on paper.

Rhythm cards:
- flat
- block of flats
- mai-son-ette
- bun-ga-low
- ca-ra-van
- pa-lace
- cot-tage
- ter-raced house
- se-mi de-tached
- de-tached

49

songs

What happiness

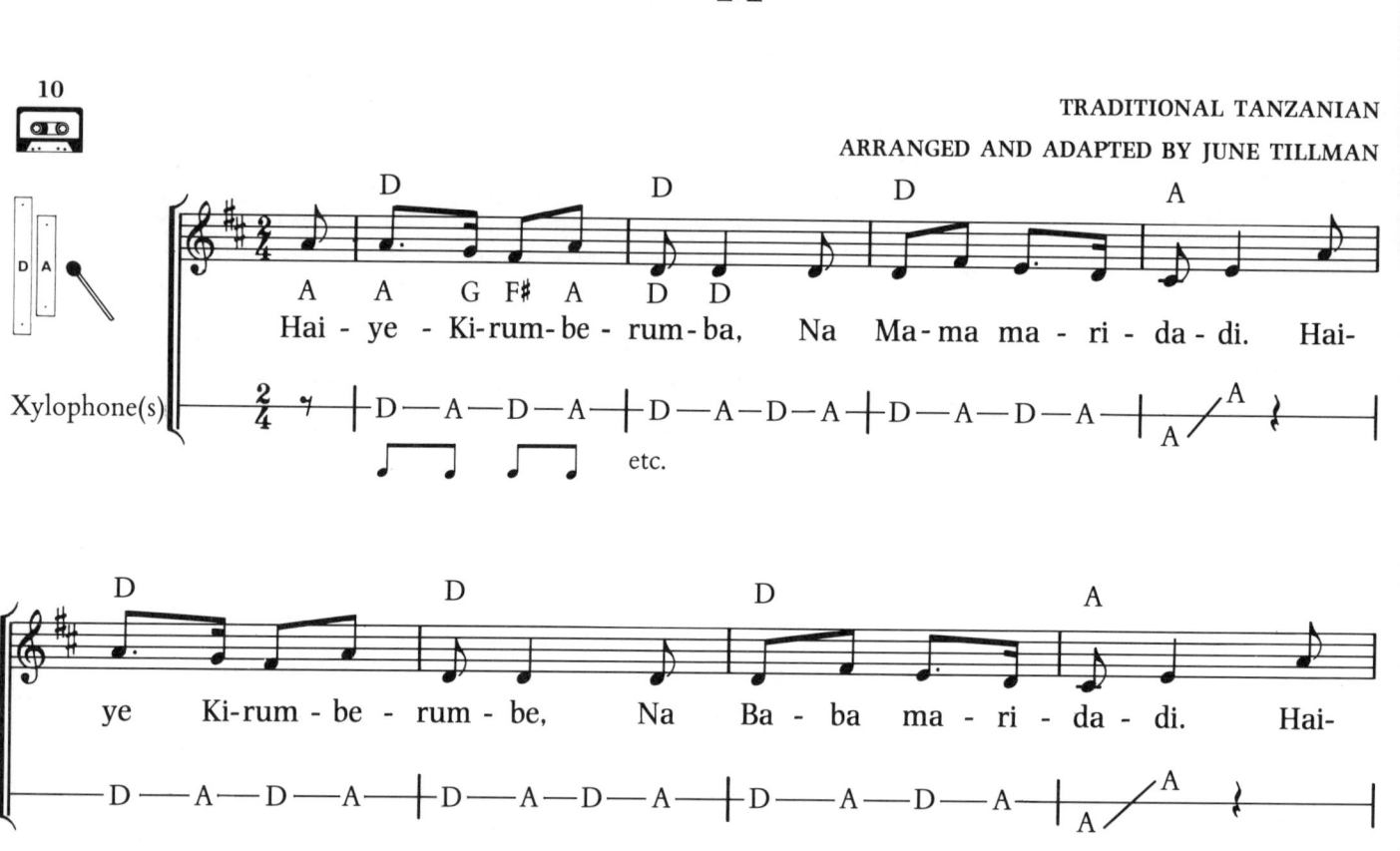

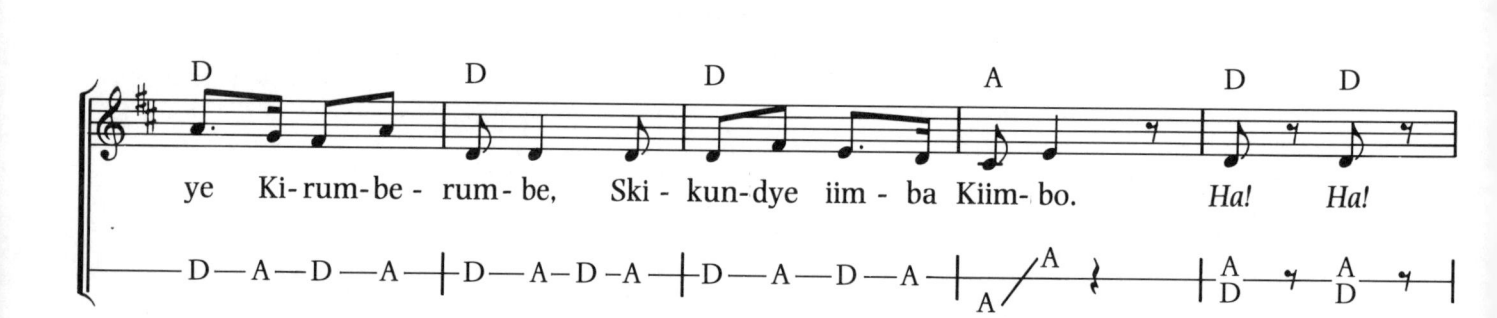

TRADITIONAL TANZANIAN
ARRANGED AND ADAPTED BY JUNE TILLMAN

Hai - ye - Ki - rum - be - rum - ba, Na Ma - ma ma - ri - da - di. Hai-
ye Ki - rum - be - rum - be, Na Ba - ba ma - ri - da - di. Hai-
ye Ki - rum - be - rum - be, Ski - kun - dye iim - ba Kiim - bo. Ha! Ha!
Ha! Ha! Hi - yooo! Ha! Ha! Ha! Ha! Hi - yooo!

Last time, shout HIYOOO!

songs

I'm such a happy person
I have a lovely Mummy.
I'm such a happy person,
(My Daddy is so great-o).
I'm such a happy person,
I sing a happy song-o.
Ha! Ha! Ha! Ha! Hiyooo!
Ha! Ha! Ha! Ha! Hiyooo!

I'm such a happy person,
I have so many friends.
I'm such a happy person,
I have a comfy house.
I'm such a happy person,
I sing a happy song-o!
Ha! Ha! Ha! Ha! Hiyooo!
Ha! Ha! Ha! Ha! Hiyooo! HIYOOO!

It will take some time before the children manage to learn the Tanzanian chorus, but they can make a start with the *Ha! Ha! Ha! Ha! Hiyooo!* lines. When the children do eventually master the foreign words they will feel a great sense of achievement. Have a go at the xylophone accompaniment, and let everyone tap or shake something in the *Ha! Ha!* lines.

Help children with only one parent or with no parents to adapt the words so that they aren't excluded from the singing. This is a happy song which children enjoy (especially if they are allowed to leap into the air on the *Hiyooos*).

Crash! Bang! Ouch! And whoops-a-daisy!

TUNE TRADITIONAL
WORDS V.C.

Verse: Dad's dropped the fish and chips* up-on the kit-chen floor. (*CRASH!*)

Mum's locked her-self out-side, she's thum-ping on the door. (*BANG!*)

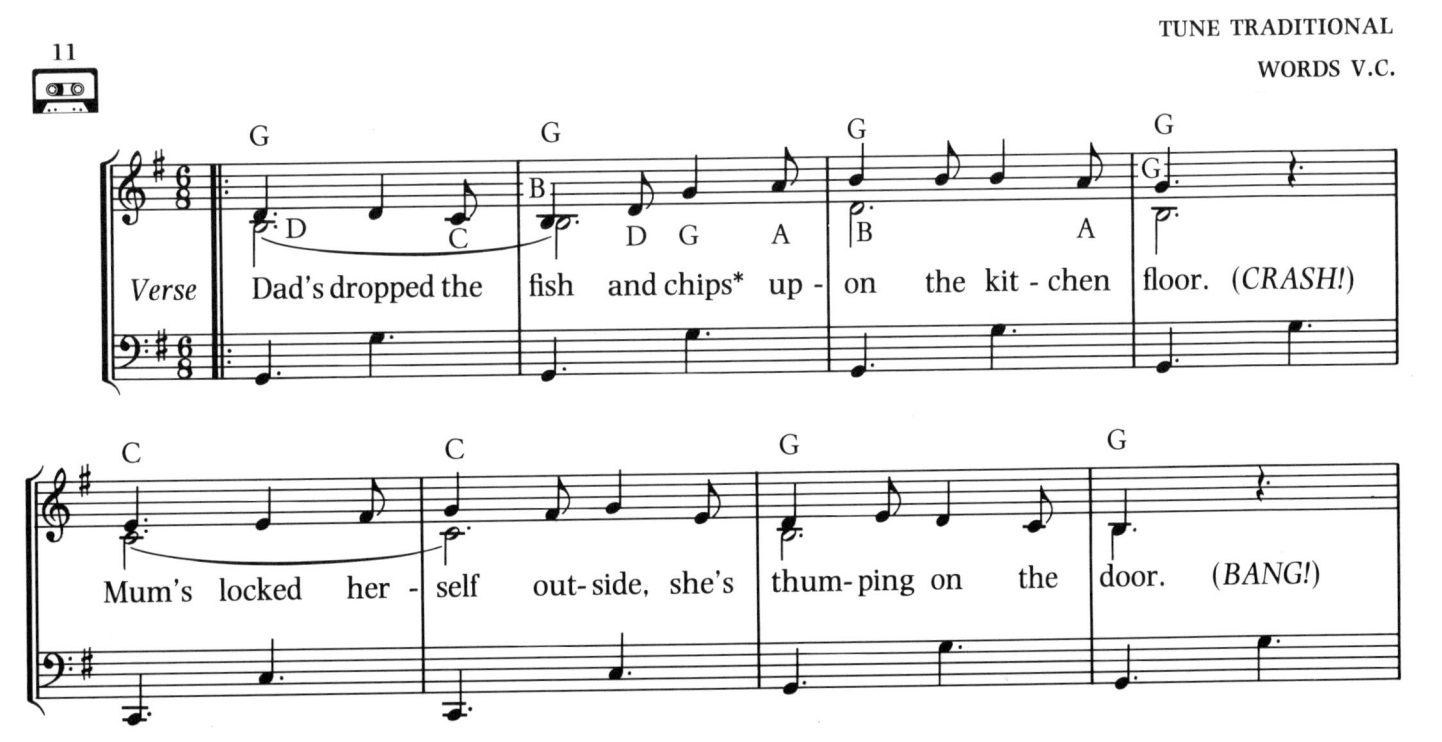

*Change the menu, and for the *fish and chips* substitute *bolognaise, vindaloo, mango spice, apple pie* or anything that fits.

songs

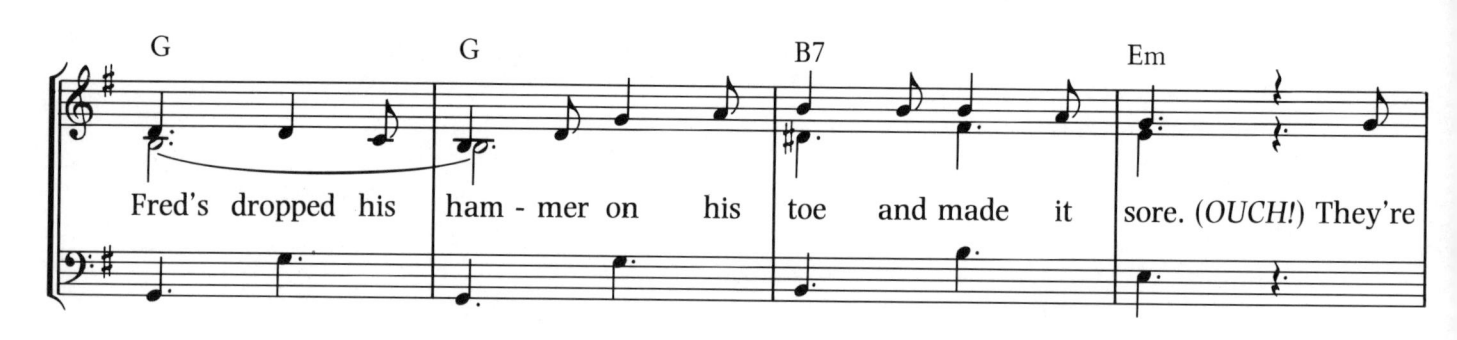

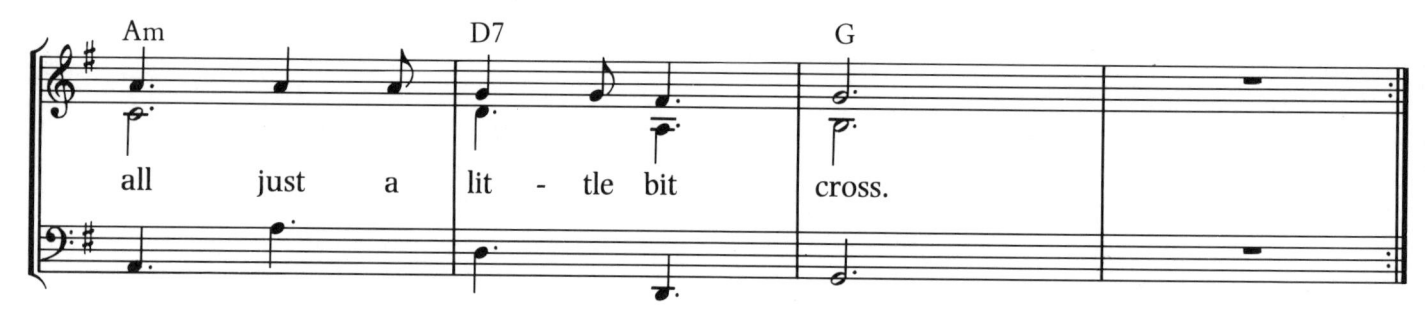

Lyrics with music:

Fred's dropped his ham-mer on his toe and made it sore. (*OUCH!*) They're all just a lit-tle bit cross.

Chorus
Crash! Bang! Ouch! And whoops-a-daisy!
Everyone is going crazy.
Let's have a bit of peace and quiet in the house.
You're making too much NOISE. SH SH SH SH SH . . .

The verse and chorus have the same tune (*John Brown's Body*). Repeat the chorus after the SH SH SH SH SH. Start it quietly and gradually increase the volume and shout the final word, *NOISE*.

1 Choose two percussion instruments, one for the *CRASH!* and the other for the *BANG!* The *OUCH!* can be yelled. Put the sound effects at the end of the appropriate lines in the verse and use them again in the *first line of the chorus*.

2 Add actions to the *chorus*. Clap on *CRASH!*, slap knees on *BANG!*, tread on own foot and shout *OUCH!*, and throw both hands into the air on the word *daisy* in *whoops-a-daisy*. In line 2, shake hands and head in a frenzied manner. Wag forefinger in a warning gesture on the beat in line 3 and clap hands to ears in the last line.

3 When the children are good at combining singing, sound effects and actions, try the following game. Miss out the words of the chorus one line at a time, beginning with the first, *but continue with the actions*. By the time the chorus has been performed four times, observers should *hear* nothing. They will, however, see a funny set of actions. Let the children mouth the words silently. This will help them to keep the tempo.

Ibble-obble black bobble

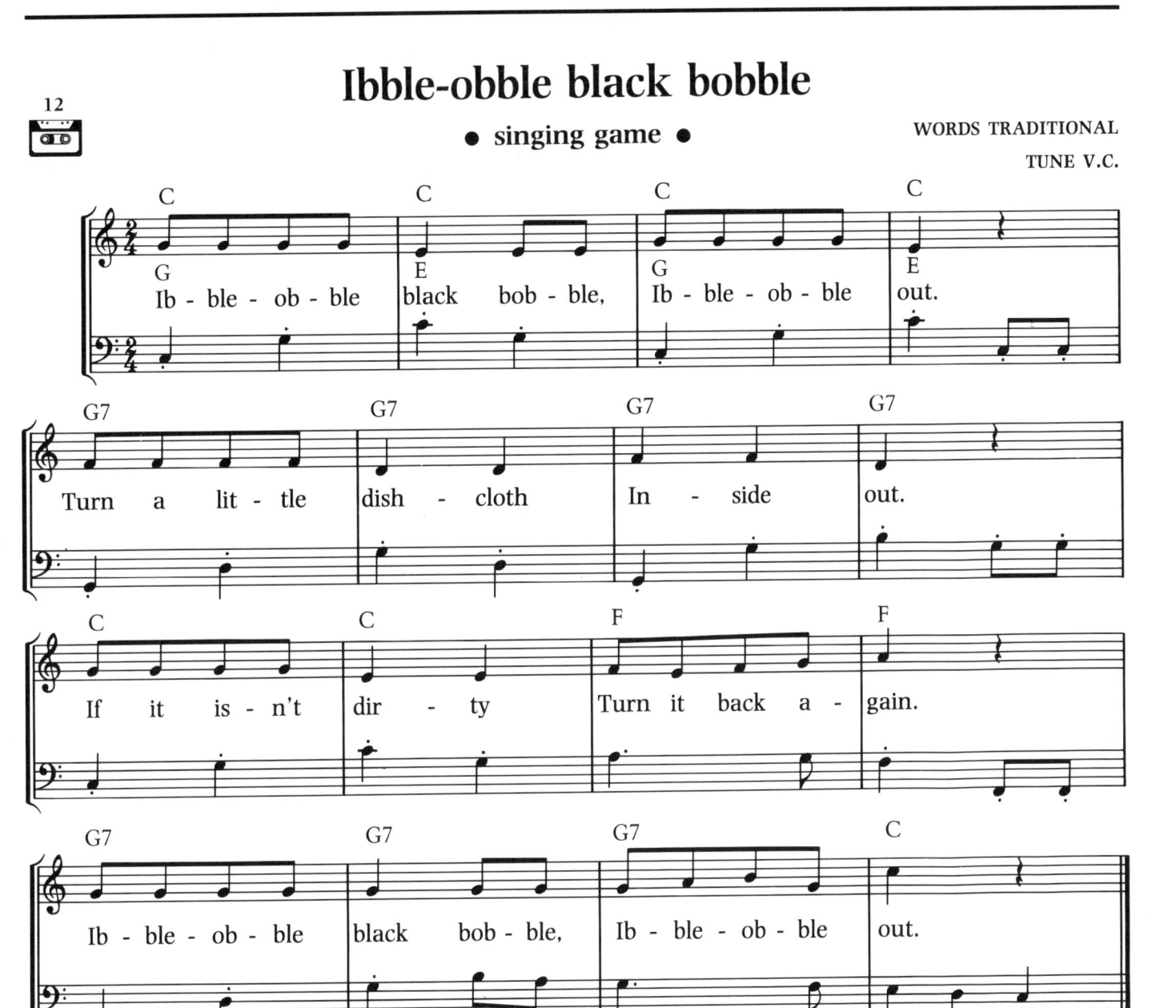

• singing game •

WORDS TRADITIONAL
TUNE V.C.

Ib-ble-ob-ble black bob-ble, Ib-ble-ob-ble out.
Turn a lit-tle dish-cloth In-side out.
If it is-n't dir-ty Turn it back a-gain.
Ib-ble-ob-ble black bob-ble, Ib-ble-ob-ble out.

Try these two games:

1 Stand in pairs facing one another holding hands. Swing the arms from side to side in time with the fast beat. On the words 'Inside out', swing the arms up and over, twisting round until facing each other again. The arms should not be crossed. Continue singing, and on the word *again*, turn back to the original position. On the last *out*, fling both arms up into the air.

2 Make a large circle (of about 15 children). Make a break at one point and appoint one of the children at the break to be the leader. He or she turns the dishcloth inside out (symbolically), and the other child at the break pulls it right way out again. The first child walks in a spiral inside the circle, pulling the rest of the line, walking with the beat. On the words *Inside out*, the other child pulls everyone back in the opposite direction.

sound story

No peace for Hammy

by Veronica Clark

'Oh no,' muttered Hammy, opening one beady eye. 'Not the roaring monster again.' Sighing deeply he put his paws over his ears and curled up into a tight ball. The vacuum cleaner moved relentlessly towards his cage [1]. It growled and sucked round the table, gobbling up the sawdust which had fallen on the floor. It continued to snarl around the room for a few more minutes then disappeared up the passage. 'Aaaah,' sighed Hammy, 'peace at last.'

He shifted into a more comfortable position and was just drifting off to sleep when the woman came in jangling the milk bottles [2]. As she put them in the fridge it began to hum gently [3]. 'Oh dear, oh dear,' shivered Hammy as a cold wave of air from the fridge hit him, 'it's going to be one of those mornings.' Hammy didn't know, however, just how bad it was going to be.

The man walked in and plugged a machine into a socket on the wall. He switched it on [4]. As the drill bore into the plaster of the wall, Hammy shot out of his nest and stood stock still in terror, one paw poised in the air. He stayed frozen in that position until the man had finished drilling. Then covered in a dusting of fine pink plaster, Hammy staggered back to his rapidly cooling tissue-paper nest. Chuntering to himself he made his bed again. The man hammered a rawlplug into the wall [5], screwed in a hook [6], gathered up his tools [7] and rattled off. 'No manners these people,' muttered Hammy, 'no manners at all.'

The previous night Hammy had been very busy on his wheel. He had put on rather a lot of weight over Christmas because of all the mincepie crumbs the children had poked through the bars of his cage. His New Year's resolution had been to do 50 turns on his wheel each night when he woke up. Last night he had managed 55 and he was extremely tired as a result. He yawned an enormous yawn, showing his two long, yellow front teeth and the inside of his little pink mouth, then he curled up in his nest.

sound story

He was just nodding off when the telephone rang [8]. Then the dog started to bark [9] which woke the baby [10]. 'Suffering sunflower seeds', exclaimed Hammy, 'I've had enough. I'm leaving home.' He swung up the bars of his cage and started to gnaw frantically at the catch of his door, but after a few bites on the metal he gave up and went back to bed.

Hammy slept until six o'clock that evening. He woke up just as the family was finishing tea. He had a quick sip of water then climbed up into his wheel to do his exercises. Round and round trundled the wheel, faster and faster [11]. Hammy loved the squeaky, grinding noise it made. The bars of the wheel became blurred and Hammy was able to pretend that he was running across the desert, a warm wind in his whiskers. He sang:

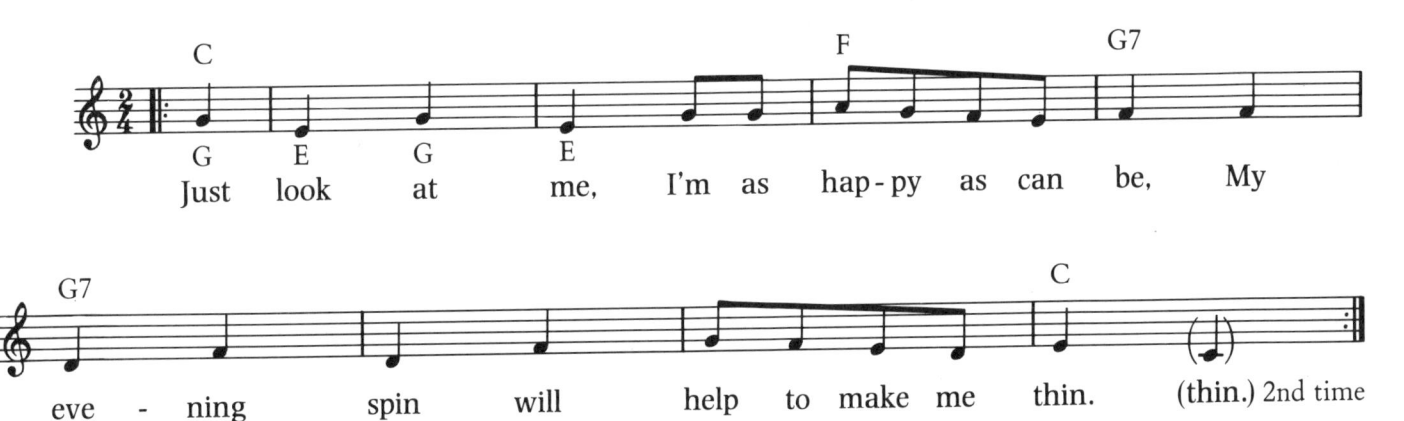

Just look at me, I'm as hap-py as can be, My eve-ning spin will help to make me thin. (thin.) 2nd time

Suddenly his dream was shattered. 'Drat that hamster!' shouted the man. 'If he doesn't stop making that racket I'll wring his scrawny little neck!' Hammy stopped mid-spin and nearly fell out of the wheel. He couldn't believe his ears. How dare that man with the ear-splitting drill, the banging hammer, the rasping screwdriver, the jangly tools, not to mention the ringing telephone, the barking dog and the shrieking baby, *dare* to complain about his lovely, lovely wheel.

'Well, well, well,' said Hammy sadly stepping off his wheel and walking over to a piece of carrot, 'Well, well well. Next thing I know they'll be moaning about my carrot.' And he sank his teeth into the carrot and started to eat [12].

sound story

Read the first paragraph then stop and establish who or what is Hammy. What is the roaring monster? Read the story through without sound effects. Talk about hamsters, their origins, cages, diet, exercise, appearance, etc. Another time, add body sounds (see chart). Try the instrumental sound effects and compare the two. Choose the more realistic effects for a taped performance. Think about the starting and stopping of the sound effects. Some are sudden sounds, others need to be faded in and faded out.

story sounds	body sounds	instrumental or other sounds
1 vacuum cleaner +	vocal roaring	experiment with various fillings inside **tin** or **plastic containers**
2 milk bottles +	*jingle jangle* or *clingle clink* spoken as realistically as possible	the real thing (*very* gently)
3 humming fridge +	quiet, steady hum	no substitute for voices
4 electric drill	invite renderings of drill sounds and select the best	**guiro** or **clappers** played rapidly, or **tape-recording** of the real thing
5 hammering	knocking	**woodblock**
6 ratchet screwdriver	Donald Duck type noises with mouth	**guiro**, or real thing
7 tools +	Say *doi-ing, ding, ting, tang* as realistically as possible	rattle a few **metallic objects** together in a tin
8 telephone	*brr* with voice	no substitute for voice unless you have a **tape-recording** of real thing
9 dog barking	vocal imitation	voice, or **tape-recording** of real thing
10 baby crying	vocal imitation	voice, or **tape-recording** of real thing
11 the wheel +	vocal squeaks	rub a **damp cork** against a **milk bottle**
12 carrot	vocal imitation	crunch a real **carrot**

+ sounds which can be made by several children

Now would be a good time to play *House lotto* (see opposite). Use the sounds in the story as a basis for your game.

games and exercises

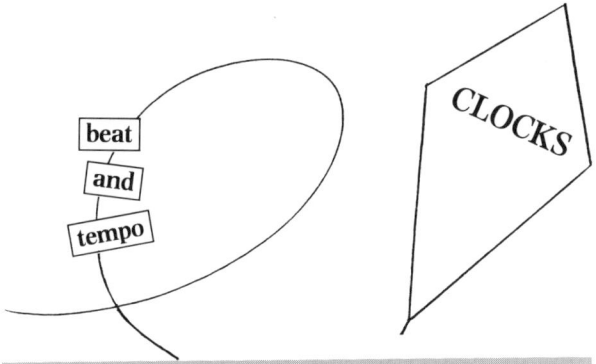

CLOCKS — beat and tempo

The **beat** of music is like the ticking of a clock. It is regular – that is, it stays the same. Some clocks have a slow tick, others have a fast tick. Some music has a slow beat (*Rock-a-bye baby*), some music has a fast beat (*Here we go round the mulberry bush*). Now and then the beat is allowed to speed up or slow down for special effect.

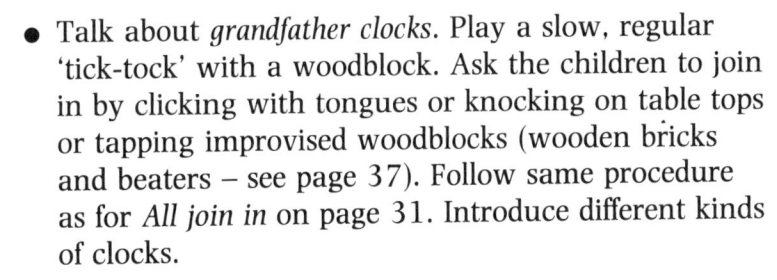

- Talk about *grandfather clocks*. Play a slow, regular 'tick-tock' with a woodblock. Ask the children to join in by clicking with tongues or knocking on table tops or tapping improvised woodblocks (wooden bricks and beaters – see page 37). Follow same procedure as for *All join in* on page 31. Introduce different kinds of clocks.

- Use the woodblocks to play *Traffic lights* (see page 31). When the red light shows the children should keep the ticking going in their heads ready to join in again when the green light shows.

- Still using the clock theme, play *Pass it on* (page 32). Pass the ticks along a line of children equipped with woodblocks.

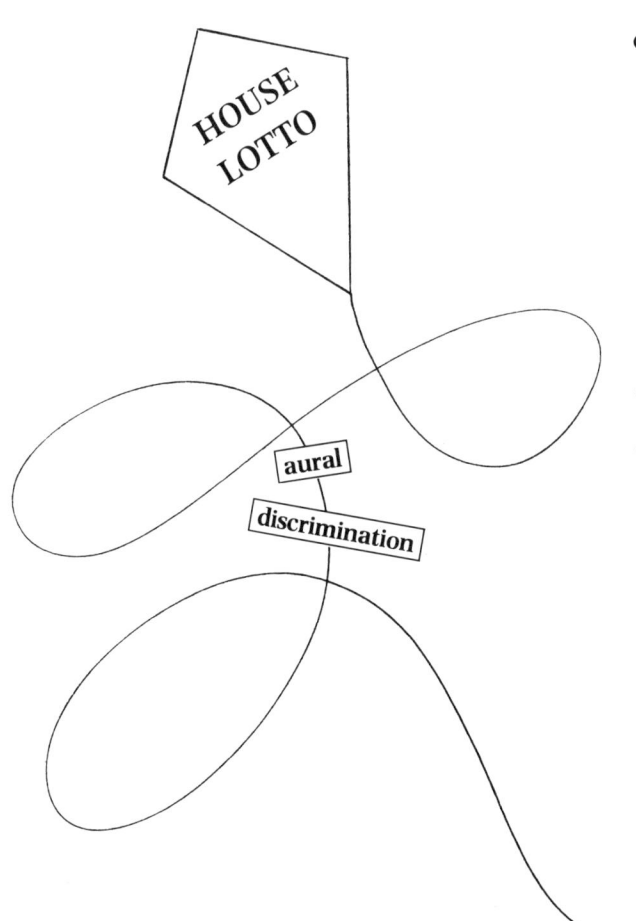

HOUSE LOTTO — aural discrimination

- Prepare a lotto 'card' for *House lotto*. On A4 paper draw six to eight boxes for all or some of the following: *vacuum cleaner, water running into bath, washing machine spinning, frying egg, slamming door, telephone bell, someone running up stairs, television*. Draw pictures in the boxes and make photocopies. The children will enjoy colouring in the pictures. For extra strength, mount the paper on card and cover with transparent plastic.

- Collect the sounds on tape.

- The sound lotto games described in this book *are not competitive*. The children all have the same 'card' and simply place a counter on each picture as they hear its corresponding sound.

- More specialised house lotto games can be prepared – water lotto, electric lotto, TV programme lotto, bathroom lotto. The cards and tapes can be placed in the music corner.

57

games and exercises

- Ask the children to join in chanting *bubble bubble bubble bubble* over and over again, *slowly* (refer to the speech rhyme on page 42, *Bubble, said the kettle*). When the rhythm is established, quietly chant the speech rhyme against a background of a few bubbling 'kettles' and 'pots'. This must be a very controlled exercise. At first the children will find it strange and will want to abandon their bubbling and chant the words with you. Try the exercise several times on consecutive days until the two parts can be sustained without difficulty. Half the class can bubble, the other half can chant the words. Remember, the repeated *bubble* must be rhythmically regular.

- On another occasion gently slap the *beat* on the thighs as you chant. There are four beats per line. The beat falls on the words *búbble*, *sáid* and *kéttle* ′𝄽. The fourth beat in lines 1, 2 and 4 falls *after* the last word. *It is important to acknowledge this beat.* Clap, tap or shake the beat as you chant.

- Another time, tap the beat as you chant a repeated *búbble búbble* – one tap for each word on the first syllable – *not too fast*. Then invite someone to clap the rhythm to the *bubbles*. Keep the rest of the children tapping the beat. What do they notice? (The *bubble* claps are quicker.) They aren't the same as the beat, so they can't be crotchets.

> *Quick notes are called quavers (N.B. QUavers and QUick begin with same sound), and are joined together in pairs or 3s or 4s with a little bridge* ♫, ♫♪, ♫♫ *One on its own looks like this* ♪

- Draw a long line of quaver pairs on the board and write *bubble* under each pair. Clap and chant the words and follow the notes as you speak.

Don't agonise over explaining quavers – talk about them 'in passing' and draw the attention of the children to them as they occur in such rhythmic patterns as ♫ ♩ *and in the children's names. The children need to know that they are quick notes.*

bub-ble bub-ble bub-ble bub-ble

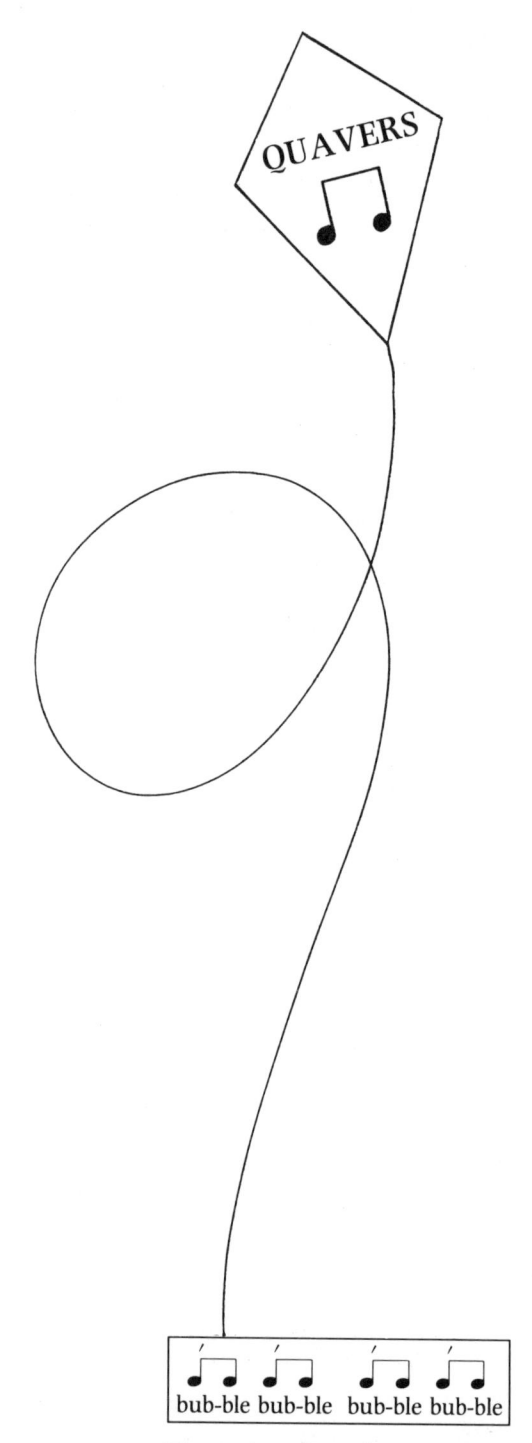

The strokes above the notes show the beat.

games and exercises

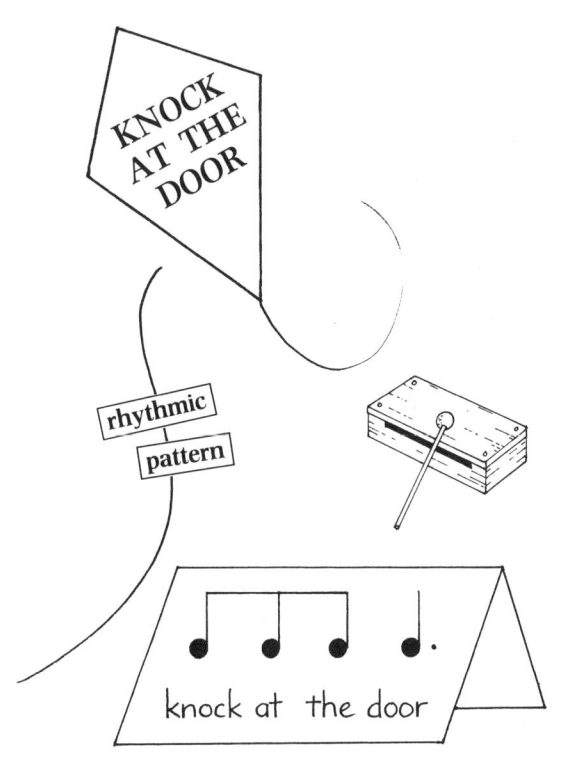

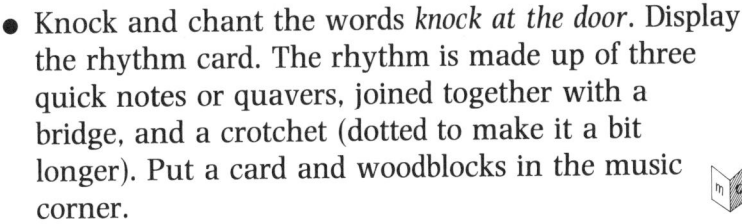

- Knock and chant the words *knock at the door*. Display the rhythm card. The rhythm is made up of three quick notes or quavers, joined together with a bridge, and a crotchet (dotted to make it a bit longer). Put a card and woodblocks in the music corner.

- Find other words or phrases that fit in with this rhythm, e.g.
    How do you do?
    Take off your coat.
    Sit on the floor.
  Chant and play their rhythms.

- Make up tunes for the phrases using E and G. Sing and play. Try to write the tunes down so that others can play them.

- Get into the habit of singing instructions to the children using E and G, e.g. *put up your chairs, get in a line, close your books, stand up straight.*

- Display pairs of things found in the house (either real things or pictures), e.g. *knife and fork, cup and saucer, brush and comb*, etc. Chant and play the rhythms on instruments. Use the objects on display as instruments if possible – tap the knife and fork together, tap the cup against the saucer. How many taps for each pair? How many notes? Draw the noteheads (no sticks or bridges) above the words.

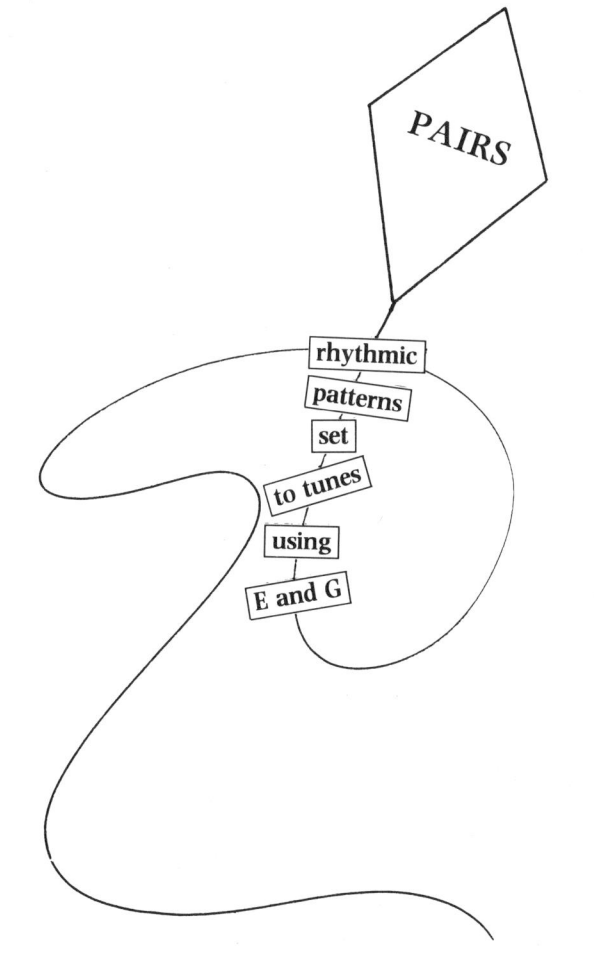

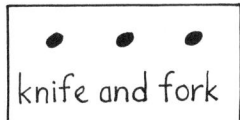

- Make up tunes for the pairs using E and G. Record.

games and exercises

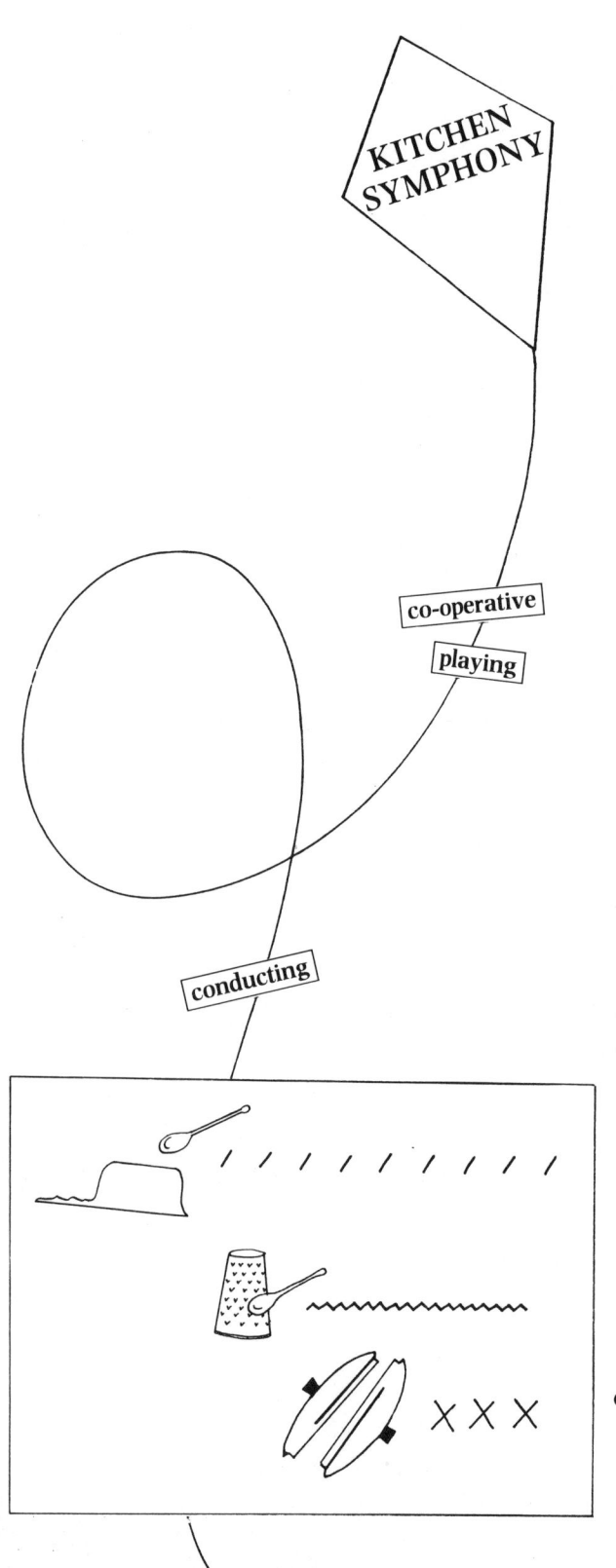

KITCHEN SYMPHONY

co-operative playing

conducting

- Collect all sorts of kitchen implements which make sounds – pots, pans, whisks, graters, palette knives, wooden and metal spoons, etc. Experiment with them and describe their sounds. Group into sound categories – things which scrape, ring, crash, etc.

- Sit the children in a circle and give an implement to each child. Play a steady beat and ask the children to join in *quietly*. They should stop and start with you. Change the tempo. Change the volume. Change the leader.

- Tell the children you are going to conduct them *like an orchestra*. Use the gestures described below. Make them generous and positive.

everyone play	– open wide both arms and conduct from this position
everyone stop	– start with both hands just crossing, palms down, then sweep them apart
one player play	– point a finger directly at the player
one player stop	– show the player in question a flattened palm
play quietly	– bring two palms closer together
play loudly	– move two palms away from each other

The 'symphony' can be played with a controlling beat throughout, or with more random sounds suitable to each implement, e.g. the grater can grate pretend cheese, the whisk can be used to beat an imaginary egg, etc. Variations of speed can be introduced. Ask the children to think up hand signs for *play more quickly* or *play more quietly*.

- Let the children, in pairs or threes, each with a different 'instrument', make up their own kitchen music. They can play together or solo or in sequence. Can they record their music on paper?

instruments to make and play

Many kitchen utensils make pleasant sounds when tapped, shaken, blown or scraped. Make a collection of such items and let the children experiment with them. Don't forget to include a range of spoons to use as beaters. Bottle brushes rubbed gently against metal trays make a lovely sound.

Note: Some of the utensils will be breakable and the children should be aware of the dangers of tapping or shaking too hard.

SUSPENDED CUPS

Collect mugs and cups of various shapes, sizes and thicknesses and suspend from a frame (dressing-up clothes rack) with strong string. Hang them a fair distance apart so that they won't swing against each other when tapped. Let the children experiment with rubber, metal, wooden and plastic beaters. *Discuss the safety aspects of this exercise.* Talk about the sounds produced. Do any cups produce identical sounds/notes? Are any of the sounds singable, i.e. do they produce a clear note? If they do, try to match the note with a chime bar. Label with its letter name.

GLASSES

1 Display two fairly large, tall, good-quality, identical glasses. Tap each in turn and compare their sounds. Pour an eggcupful of coloured water into one of the glasses. Tap each glass again and compare the sounds. Continue adding water to the same glass an eggcupful at a time, and tap the glasses after each addition. The change in pitch will at first be difficult to detect, but as the water gets nearer the top of the glass, the lowering of the note becomes more evident. Notice also the difference in the sound quality or **timbre**. As the glass fills up the tone becomes duller.
2 Repeat, but this time pour in the water in a steady stream and tap the glass with the free hand as the glass fills up.
3 Experiment with both glasses and try to produce two distinct notes. Can you, for example, make the opening notes of *Baa baa black sheep?* Match with the notes on a tuned percussion instrument, then label.
4 Using several identical glasses, make a wide range of notes and arrange in order of pitch (and therefore, probably, fullness).
5 Make a collection of empty glasses – tall, short, wide, narrow, thick glass and thin glass. Tap and discuss the sounds produced.

Any experimentation with glass should be closely supervised.

BOTTLES

These can be filled with varying amounts of water and tapped as described above, but lovely sounds can be produced by blowing across the tops of the bottles. Place the bottles on a low table and ask the children to kneel as they blow. Provide paper towels or disinfected cloths for the children to wipe around the tops of the bottles after they have finished blowing. Provide several different types of bottle and you will be able to produce a range of sounds. Another time set out four or five *identical* bottles ands fill with varying amounts of water. What do the children notice when they blow across the necks? Relate their discoveries to the glasses experiment described above.

If you are managing to get a good range of sound, make up a story incorporating the sounds in the text.

Pitch in relation to length

By filling glasses or milk bottles with varying amounts of water, the children can be introduced to the principle that pitch is affected by the length of the vibrating column of air.

curricular links

> RELATED THEMES: houses • families • machines in the home • people who help us at home • water in the home • sources of energy for the home • bedtime and night-time • babies • holiday houses • houses in the past • house building • animals' houses

Language

Ideas to put to the children:

Talk about your house. Describe each room.

Talk about houses you like to visit/don't like to visit.

If your reading books feature people who live in 'special' houses, talk about them.

What makes *your home* so special to you?

Draw a house shape and fill with lots of letter *h*'s.

Talk about the sound *ou*.

Draw a house with windows and a door. Cut the windows and doors so that they open (like the real thing) and mount on card. Label the various parts of the house. The words *window* and *door* can be written beneath the hinged flaps.

Write about *My favourite room, Smells I like, Sounds I like, Things I like to feel*.

Describe *My dream house*.

Read *A dark dark tale* by Ruth Brown and write personal versions of what's in the cupboard.

Number work

Make a class survey of houses – detached, semi-detached, flat, etc. Record pictorially or as a block graph.

Prepare a worksheet to be taken home to discover how many rooms/clocks/mirrors/beds, etc. in the children's houses. Count using a tally system: ͟H͟H͟T͟ ͟I͟I͟ . Discuss the results using *more than, less than, the same as*, etc. How many altogether?

Measure round your bed in feet – your own. Make a plan of each bed using squared paper, one square representing one foot length.

Use stairs to teach ordinal numbers – make up a story about an untidy child who leaves his or her toys lying around on stairs: *He's left his teddy on the fifth step*, etc. The children can record the story in picture form on a prepared sheet featuring a staircase.

Draw houses/castles/churches/tents, etc. using geometric templates.

Using junk, construct houses with chimneys, garages, etc. Analyse the solid shapes used – cuboid, cone, etc.

Ask the children to imagine that the front has been taken off their house – draw the rooms which would be visible from the street. Relate this to a dolls' house.

Ask each child to make a rough plan of one room in her or his house.

Environmental studies

Visit a well-known local house – castle, stately home, church.

Walk around the streets near the school and pay attention to the different types of houses you pass – note the various styles of architecture, the names of roads, odd and even house numbers, length of roads, names of houses, number of storeys, etc.

curricular links

Visit a building site and watch a house in the process of being built – notice lifting mechanisms, machines for carrying, foundations and diggers, frameworks, brick laying, cement mixing, etc.

What makes things *work* in the house? How is your house heated? Make a collection of household gadgets (catalogue pictures) and group into sets, e.g. electrical, gas, run by batteries, etc.

Look at *water* in the home – its source, its movement, its uses.

What effect does boiling water have on vegetables/rice/eggs,etc? What would happen to a pan of water if it was left to boil for a long time? What happens when steam meets a cold surface?

Art and craft

Make a large dolls' house out of cardboard cartons, one carton per room. Make furniture out of odds and ends. (*Tilly's House* by F. Jacques will provide ideas for the furnishings.) Eventually, stick all the rooms together and let the house become a permanent feature of your classroom.

Paint or make a collage gingerbread house.

Design a house for a mouse, rabbit, owl – see *House by Mouse* by George Mendoza.

Make a frieze of the three little pigs and their houses, using straw, sticks and pretend bricks.

Make clay houses. Try igloos.

Make individual mini-rooms using cereal boxes with one large side cut off. Line the walls with wallpaper and stick pictures from catalogues on the back wall. Add furniture made from corks and matchboxes.

Drama and movement

Pretend to be in the dark and feel your way round a strange house. Climb stairs, open doors and cupboards, bump into things, reach high and low, recoil on encountering cobwebs, etc.

Mime routine activities – teeth brushing, eating an egg, tying shoe laces, etc. Make a guessing game out of it.

Play *Who am I?* – children mime the actions of someone who helps us in the house, e.g. plumber, electrician, window cleaner, doctor, etc.

Pretend to be blind and feel a piano, a dog, an ironing board, etc.

Everyone except two children sits in a space and pretends to be a piece of furniture. One of the two remaining children is blind (eyes closed), the other is the guide. The guide has to direct the blind person across the room without bumping into the 'furniture', using spoken instructions only. (The children will have to know their lefts and rights to play this game.)

What household jobs are best done in pairs? In twos, mime folding a sheet, cleaning a car, putting up Christmas decorations, wallpapering.

list of resources

POEMS

Nursery rhymes
    The house that Jack built
    Old Mother Hubbard
    Little Polly Flinders
    Diddle diddle dumpling

The young Puffin book of verse (Puffin)
    Little girl
    House coming down
    Wanted
    The cold old house
    The deserted house
    The old woman

The book of a thousand poems (Bell and Hyman)
    The washing-up song
    Noises in the night

Poems for 9 year olds and under (Puffin)
    Lightships

Sense and nonsense – Tasting (Macdonald)

Rhymes around the day illustrated by Jan Ormerod (Picture Puffins)

All in a day poems selected by Kaye Webb (Ladybird)

SONGS

Knock at the door (Ward Lock) (songs and poems)
    I wish how I wish that I had a little house
    Yellow submarine
    The clock is on the dresser (rhyme)
    Mix a pancake (rhyme)
    There was a little house (rhyme)

Sing hey diddle diddle (Black)
    There was an old woman who lived in a shoe
    Polly put the kettle on
    Goosey goosey gander

Tinderbox assembly book (Black)
    How many people live in your house?
    A home is a house for me
    All alone in the house

Okki-tokki-unga (Black)
    Ten fat sausages
    Someone's in the kitchen with Dinah
    In a cottage in a wood
    The wise man and the foolish man
    I'm a little teapot
    Cousin Peter
    I jump out of bed in the morning

STORIES

The mice who lived in a shoe by R. Peppe (Puffin)
Peace at last by Jill Murphy (Macmillan)
The patchwork cat by W. Mayne & N. Bayley (Cape/Puffin)
14 rats and a rat catcher by J. Cressey and T. Cole (Black/Puffin)
House by Mouse by George Mendoza (Deutsch)
A dark dark tale by Ruth Brown (Andersen Press)
Tilly's house by F. Jacques (Heinemann)
Moonlight and sunshine by Jan Ormerod (Kestrel) (picture book)
Mrs Pig's bulk buy by Mary Rayner (Piccolo Picture Books)
The tiger who came to tea by Judith Kerr (Picture Lions)
Not now, Bernard by David McKee (Andersen Press)

FAIRY TALES

Goldilocks   Hansel and Gretel
The three little pigs

MUSIC

Hansel and Gretel by Humperdinck
'Morning' from the *Peer Gynt Suite* by Grieg
Eine kleine Nachtmusik by Mozart
'Lullaby' by Brahms
'Building up my house' (*Bang on a Drum* · BBC Cassettes)

INFORMATION

How we live by Anita Harper and Christine Roche (Picture Puffin)
My kitchen by Harlow Rockwell (Julia MacRae Books)
Henry's house by Helen East (First Starters Macdonald Educational)
Building a house by Althea (Dinosaur)
Homes around the world by Anne Sproule (Macdonald)
How do people live? by Philip Steele (Macdonald)

hens and chicks

speech rhymes
Hickety pickety my black hen *66*
The big brown hen and Mrs Duck *66*
Eggs are laid by turkeys *67*

action rhyme
Tipper tipper tap *68*

poems
Egg thoughts *69*
Miracle *69*

songs
Five warm eggs in an incubator *70*
Humpty Dumpty *71*
Kokoleoko *72*
Harriet Brown *74*
Chicks grow into chickens *76*
One little cockerel bright and gay *77*
Five warm eggs rolling round about *78*

sound story
The beautiful egg *79*

games and exercises *83*

instruments to make and play
Hand jingles, jingle poles, jingle whips and tambourines *86*

curricular links *88*

list of resources *90*

speech rhymes

Hickety pickety my black hen

Hickety pickety
My black hen,
She lays eggs
For gentlemen.
Sometimes nine
And sometimes ten,
Hickety pickety
My black hen.

TRADITIONAL

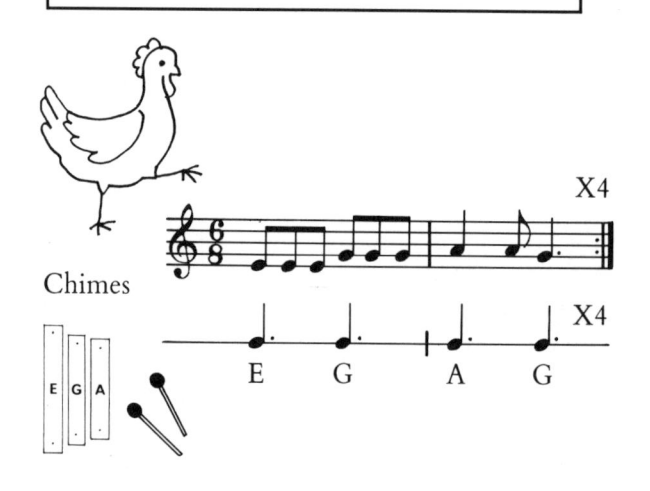

1 Chant the rhyme a few times and encourage the children to join in the first and last two lines. Bring out the consonants – *ck, p, t*. Clap the *beat* quietly as you chant. Tap the *beat* on claves.

2 Choose a child to speak lines 5 and 6 on his or her own.

3 Clap, tap, shake, etc. the *rhythm* of the first two lines.

4 Try combining beat and rhythm with the chanting.

5 Put out the chimes E G and A. Either sing the rhyme to the tune given here or make up your own.

6 Add a bit of variety by pausing after the word *nine* and either clapping nine times or dropping nine clay or plastic eggs into a top hat. Do the same but with one more clap (or egg) after the word *ten*.

Chimes
E G A G

The big brown hen and Mrs Duck

The big brown hen and Mrs Duck
Went walking out together;
They talked about all sorts of things –
The farmyard and the weather.
But all I heard was 'Cluck, cluck, cluck'
And 'Quack, quack, quack' from Mrs Duck.

ANON

speech rhymes

1 Talk about the poem. Can animals really talk about things like the weather? What sort of messages *can* animals communicate with their purrs and growls and hisses – danger, hunger, fear, pleasure, etc.?

2 Practise the three *clucks* and the three *quacks*. Find an instrument to accompany each.

3 Help the children to make up variations of the poem, e.g. *The small white lamb and Mr Dog went walking out together*, or *The fat black cat and Mrs Mouse went walking out together*. Add the appropriate animal noises.

4 Talk about animal sounds, e.g. *baa, grunt, moo, miaow, gobble, hiss, woof,* etc. Hunt for instruments which best match each sound. Play and speak together. Make a card for each sound and display in the music corner.

Eggs are laid by turkeys

Eggs are laid by turkeys,
Eggs are laid by hens,
Eggs are laid by robins,
Eggs are laid by wrens.
Eggs are laid by eagles,
Eggs are laid by quail,
Pigeon, parrots, peregrines:
And that's how every bird begins.

MARY ANN HOBERMAN

1 Read the poem and talk about it. Try to find pictures of all the birds mentioned in the poem.

2 Clap or play an instrument every time the word *eggs* is spoken. Then ask one child to clap on the first *eggs*, to be joined by a second child in the second *eggs*, a third on the third *eggs*, and so on until six children are clapping or playing.

action rhymes

Tipper tipper tap

Tipper tipper tap, ♪♪ ♪♪ ♪
First a hole, then a crack,
Then a glimpse of feathers in a squirming back.

Chirpy chirpy cheep ♪♪ ♪♪ ♪
Pipes the busy little beak,
Then a chick pops out and collapses in a heap.

Flipper flipper flop, ♪♪ ♪♪ ♪
Like a small, damp mop,
Our chicken goes exploring with a wriggle and a hop.

Fluffy and dry,
And not a little bit shy,
Our new-born chick blinks a beady eye.

V.C.

Make the actions *in the first line of each stanza only*. The following ideas for percussion accompaniment are suggestions only. Experiment to find other appropriate sounds.

Stanza 1
- Mime the action of the pecking chicken inside its shell.
- Tap the rhythm of the words in the *first line* on a woodblock.

Stanza 2
- With the fingers and thumb of one hand, make a beak and mime the opening and shutting beak.
- Shake the rhythm of the *first line* with jingle bells.

Stanza 3
- Move the elbows of both arms in imitation of small wings.
- Flap a pair of clappers to the rhythm of the *first line* words.

Stanza 4
- With both hands make a round shape suggestive of a fluffy chicken. Wiggle fingertips slightly to give the impression of fluffiness.
- Give one gentle tap of the cymbal (large) with a wire brush on the word *fluffy*.

Movement ideas

Mime the quick tapping movements of the beak with various parts of the body. Curl up small, begin to wriggle and squirm, then – at a given signal – suddenly hatch out and collapse in an extended shape. Stretch one limb at a time, explore the space around. Practise walking, as though for the first time, on stiff legs. Walk in straight lines. Use an instrument to indicate when the chickens should run and when they should stop. Practise blinking and moving the head from side to side in a jerky way. Listen to 'Hatching chicks' from *Pictures at an Exhibition* by Mussorgsky.

poems

Egg thoughts

I do not like the way you slide,
I do not like your soft inside,
I do not like your many ways,
And I could go for many days
Without a soft-boiled egg.

Poached eggs on toast, why do you shiver
With such a funny little quiver?

RUSSELL HOBAN

1 Make some slither boxes – rice or sand inside long, flat containers (shoe, date or chocolate boxes). Tip the boxes from side to side in time with the slow beat of the words. Experiment with instruments and beaters to produce shivering sounds to accompany the final couplet.

2 How do the children like their eggs cooked? Make a block graph to show preferences.

3 Use eggs in cookery sessions to make meringues, omelettes, pancakes, soufflés, cakes and buns.

Miracle

It's funny
How a thing as runny as an egg,
With a shell so smooth,
No groove,
But round and hard and cold,
Could house this chick –
Just one day old:
This little ball of fluff,
Pale golden stuff,
All light and airy
As a fairy.
A trick . . . ?
No trick,
This chick –
A miracle.
A flipping, flapping miracle.

V.C.

1 This poem describes the contrast between the smooth, cold eggshell and its runny contents, and the fluffy warmth of the newly-hatched chick. Ask the children to say *slimy, slithery, sloppy* and *runny* in a voice suggestive of liquid. Then try *smooth* in a smooth voice. *Round, hard* and *cold* should sound clipped. Finally, say *fluffy, light, airy* and *fairy* in breathy, high voices. Write the words in an appropriate way, e.g.

2 Using tuned and untuned metallic instruments, make up some 'miracle music'. Gently rub the beaters up and down the bars or tap them at random. Gently hit the edge of a large cymbal with a selection of beaters, including, if possible, a wire brush. Indian bells, jingles and triangles can sound magical if played sympathetically.

songs

Five warm eggs in an incubator

• singing game •

v.c.

Five warm eggs in an in-cu-ba-tor, Tip-per tip-per tap and a lit-tle bit la-ter Bro-ken shell in the in-cu-ba-tor, One damp chi-cken on the floor.

Four warm eggs in an incubator,
Tipper tipper tap, and a little bit later –
Broken shell in the incubator,
Two damp chickens on the floor.

Two warm eggs in an incubator,
Tipper tipper tap, and a little bit later –
Broken shell in the incubator,
Four damp chickens on the floor.

Three warm eggs in an incubator,
Tipper tipper tap, and a little bit later –
Broken shell in the incubator,
Three damp chickens on the floor

One warm egg in an incubator,
Tipper tipper tap, and a little bit later –
Broken shell in the incubator,
Five damp chickens on the floor.

songs

The combination of reducing numbers at the beginning of each verse and increasing numbers at the end, is tricky for young children. You can help by preparing a set of flashcards, eggs on one side, damp chicks on the other. You can use the clenched fingers of one hand as an aid to counting. As the eggs hatch, show the fingers one by one. The straight fingers represent the chicks, the fingers still curled up are the eggs. Better still, act out the song. Choose five (or ten) children to be eggs. They should curl up in a tight ball. The eggs can roll a little on the spot – eggs do move shortly before hatching as the emerging chick struggles to get out. On *Tipper tipper tap* the teacher or a child touches one of the 'eggs' lightly on the back. This is the signal for that egg to crack open and hatch. In the last line of each verse the newly-hatched chick flops over to join the other chicks and lies still.

This is a delicate song requiring clear diction. Embellish the *Tipper tipper tap* with claves and accompany *Broken shell* with a lightly tapped tambourine. The number of chicks (first word in the last line of each verse) can be highlighted with a single chime on the Indian bells or a triangle. The hardest letter to enunciate (as those who have heard the cassette will acknowledge) is the letter *p* on the end of *damp*. Omit the *p* and you'll end up with '*damn*' chickens all over the place!

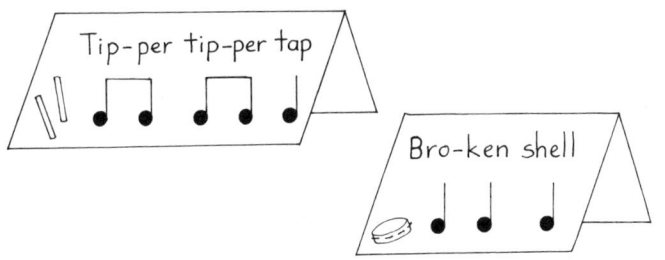

Extra texture can be added by playing the skeleton melody on a xylophone. The simple accompaniment of thirds played on a chiming tuned percussion instrument adds a magical touch.

Humpty Dumpty

Don't forget this most famous of all egg songs. It's quite a tricky song for young voices because of its wide range. Sing it in G major (see below) and you should have no trouble. Clap the beat as you sing. Play a descending slide on a xylophone for the fall followed by a smash (tambourine or dropped cymbals). In the last two lines the king's horses can gallop in time with the words (coconut shells or woodblocks). Sigh a drawn-out, regretful *Ahhhh!* at the end.

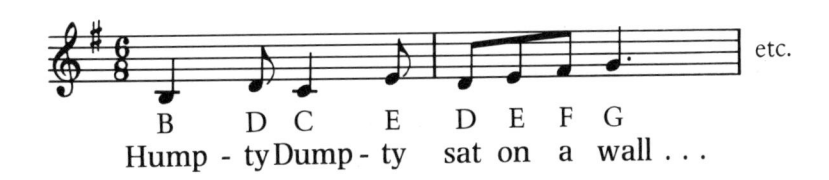

```
    B   D C   E   D E F G
  Hump-ty Dump-ty  sat on a wall ...
```

71

songs

Kokoleoko

TRADITIONAL AFRICAN SONG

Ko - ko - le - o - ko chic - ken, ko - ko - le - o - ko,

Ko - ko - le - o - ko chic - ken, crow - ing for day.

MORE ACCOMPANIMENT SUGGESTIONS

Descant melody

72

songs

Sun is rising in Bethlehem,
Kokoleoko chicken, crowing for day.

Mary and Joseph are searching for a room,
Kokoleoko chicken, crowing for day.

Someone has found them a bare and rocky cave,
Kokoleoko chicken, crowing for day.

Baby Jesus is born today,
Kokoleoko chicken, crowing for day.

Baby sleeps on a bed of hay,
Kokoleoko chicken, crowing for day.

Shepherds come and they bring Him a lamb,
Kokoleoko chicken, crowing for day.

Wise men come with some precious gifts,
Kokoleoko chicken, crowing for day.

Everybody sing for joy,
Kokoleoko chicken, crowing for day.

Everybody clap for joy,
Kokoleoko chicken, crowing for day.

Kokoleoko chicken, kokoleoko,
Kokoleoko chicken, crowing for day.

This simple and catchy African song lends itself to several easy instrumental accompaniments (see music). The children will be able to improvise freely on drums, tambours and shakers when they know the song well. It's a lovely song to clap to. The teacher or a soloist can sing the 'story line' with everyone joining in the repeated *Kokoleoko chicken, crowing for day.* Older children can tackle the descant tune on recorders or glockenspiel, and the 'bass' line accompaniment on either xylophone or piano. Adapt the volume to match the words. The cassette tape will help the children to match the words to the melody.

This song lends itself to adaptation. Use it for any celebration, for example, *Sharon Robinson is six today, Kokoleoko chicken, crowing for day*, or *Spring is here and the leaves are green, Kokoleoko chicken, crowing for day.*

songs

Harriet Brown

v.c.

Chorus How many eggs have you got in your nest, Harriet Brown (best hen in town)?

Glockenspiel, chimes — E — F♯ — G — A — | — E — F♯ — G — A

How many eggs have you got in your nest Under a blanket of down?

Harriet I'm moody and broody So please go away, There's no need to stay. Echo (No need to stay.) To

Glock., chimes F♯ — A — F♯ — D

be a good mother These eggs I must cover All night and all day. Echo (Night and all day.)

Glock., chimes F♯ — A — F♯ — D

songs

Chorus How many eggs have you got in your nest,
Harriet Brown (best hen in town)?
How many eggs have you got in your nest
Under a blanket of down?

Harriet I'm blinking and thinking,
There's no time to talk,
Or go for a walk.
Echo   (Go for a walk.)
Nine, ten or twenty,
I know I have plenty,
Now go or I'll SQUAWK!
Echo   (Go or I'll SQUAWK!)

Repeat chorus

Fairly recently a parent of one of the children in my class offered to lend me a broody hen called Penelope Brown. We obtained a dozen fertilised eggs and Penelope dutifully sat on them in a pen in a disused outside toilet. Unfortunately Penny (re-named Harriet in the song to help the scansion), proved to be a reluctant sitter. One by one the eggs were broken or got cold, and the question *How many eggs have you got in your nest?* became a daily and increasingly anxious enquiry. Eventually, Penny, no longer broody, and with nothing to show for her long sit, was returned to her fellow fowls. In an attempt to restore the children's faith in the wonderful process of procreation (and in me), I contacted our rural studies centre to book an incubator. The latter proved to be a great success and the 18 multicoloured chicks which hatched inspired most of the songs and poems in this section.

The song can be effectively split up between soloists and a group of singers, as is demonstrated on the cassette. Harriet should sound extremely ratty. Keep the tempo slow as there are a lot of words to fit in. Squawk the final *SQUAWK!* Set out the chimes E F# G and A and ask the children to try to pick out the tune which accompanies *Harriet Brown (best hen in town)*. Incorporate it into the song to accompany the singing. Can anyone hear this particular bit of tune anywhere else in the song?

Try also the *no need to stay* fragment using the notes D F# and A. Always encourage the children to draw the tune fragments they sing and play, either in the air, or on paper. *Harriet Brown (best hen in town)* would look something like this:

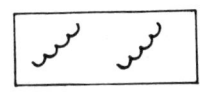

75

Chicks grow into chickens

16 Sung on the cassette in the higher key of D
(see chords in brackets)

DAVID MOSES

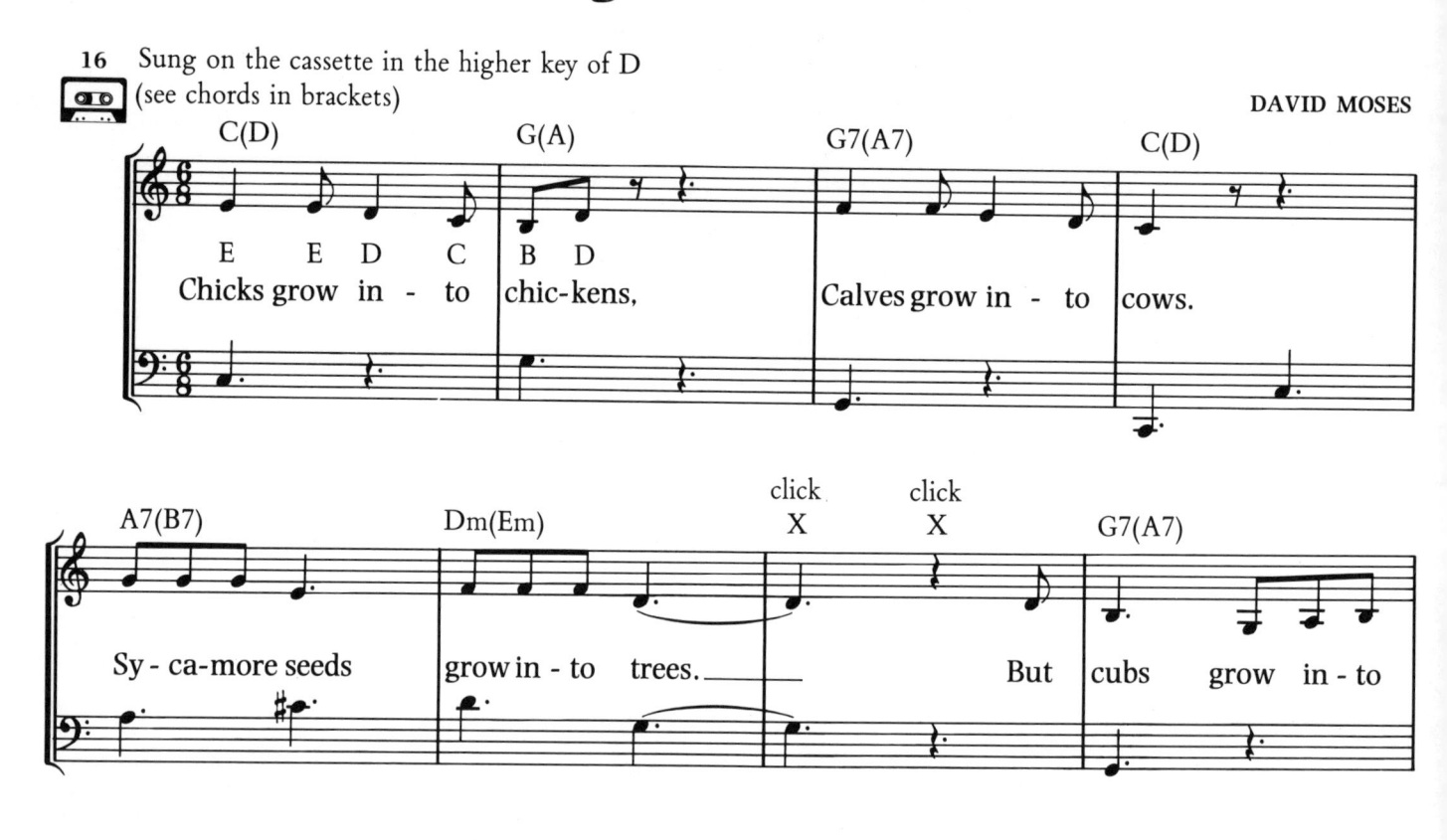

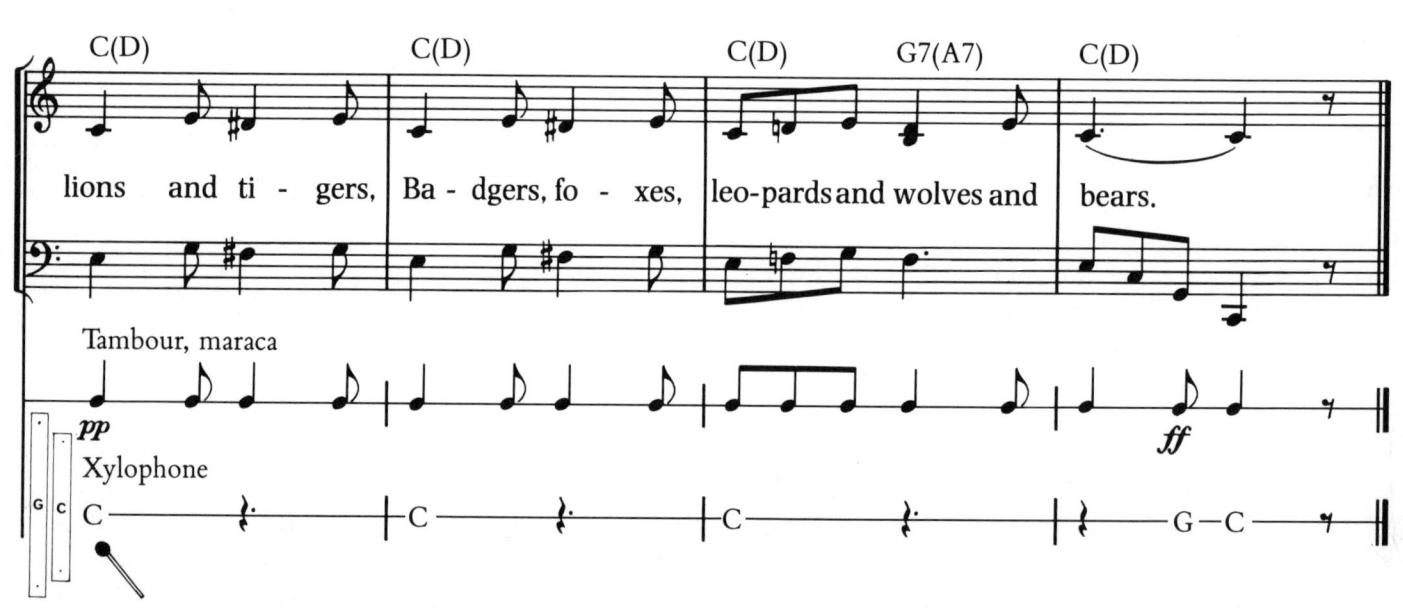

Chicks grow in-to chic-kens, Calves grow in-to cows.
Sy-ca-more seeds grow in-to trees. But cubs grow in-to
lions and ti-gers, Ba-dgers, fo-xes, leo-pards and wolves and bears.

Foals grow into horses,
Kittens grow into cats.
Fresh green shoots sprout out of roots,
   But cubs grow into lions and tigers,
   Badgers, foxes, leopards and wolves and bears.

Pups grow into seals, or dogs,
Lambs grow into sheep.
Bulbs grow into daffodils,
   But cubs grow into lions and tigers
   Badgers, foxes, leopards and wolves and bears.

songs

To start with, ask the children to join in the last two lines only. Talk about the baby animals mentioned in the song. How many more can the children think of? If you are nippy you'll be able to fit in a quick animal noise at the ends of the first two lines of each verse. Help the children to feel the two rest beats in the middle of the song by clicking (listen to the cassette). Copy the rhythm of the words in the last lines on tambour or maraca or claves. A skeleton chorus can be played on a xylophone – see music.

Put out the chimes D E F G and ask the children to try to pick out the tune which accompanies the words *Sycamore seeds grow into trees*. Start on G. Draw the shape of the tune fragment.

One little cockerel bright and gay

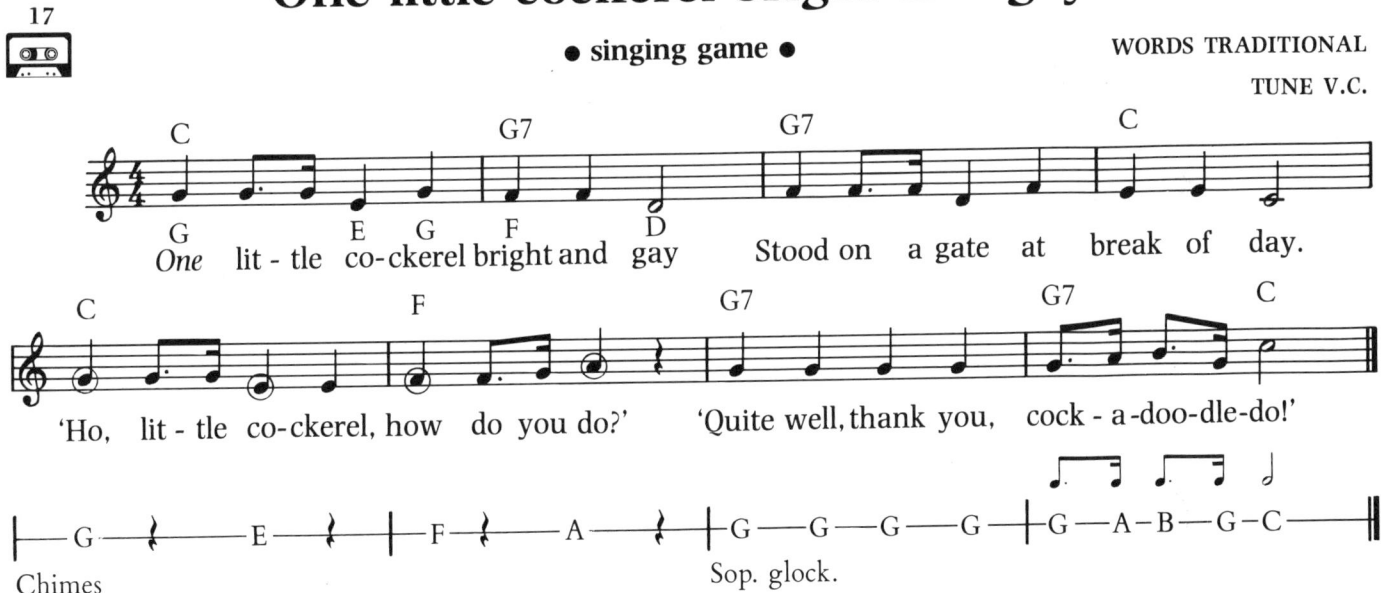

• singing game •

WORDS TRADITIONAL
TUNE V.C.

Two little cockerels bright and gay
Stood on a gate at break of day.
'Ho, little cockerel, how do you do?'
'Quite well, thank you, cock-a-doodle-doo!'

Three little cockerels . . .
Four little cockerels . . .
Five little cockerels . . .

All the children except one form a circle. The remaining child is the cockerel and stands in the centre of the circle. The children walk, skip or slip-step round in time with the fast beat of the music (eight beats per line) as they sing lines 1 and 2. In line 3 everyone stops as they sing *'Ho, little cockerel, how do you do?'* and the cockerel replies *'Quite well, thank you, cock-a-doodle-doo!'* The cockerel chooses a companion and so the song continues. The last cockerel to be chosen is the one who chooses the new cockerel.

Put out the chimes E F G A B and C', and encourage the children to play and sing the final bar or the final two bars.

77

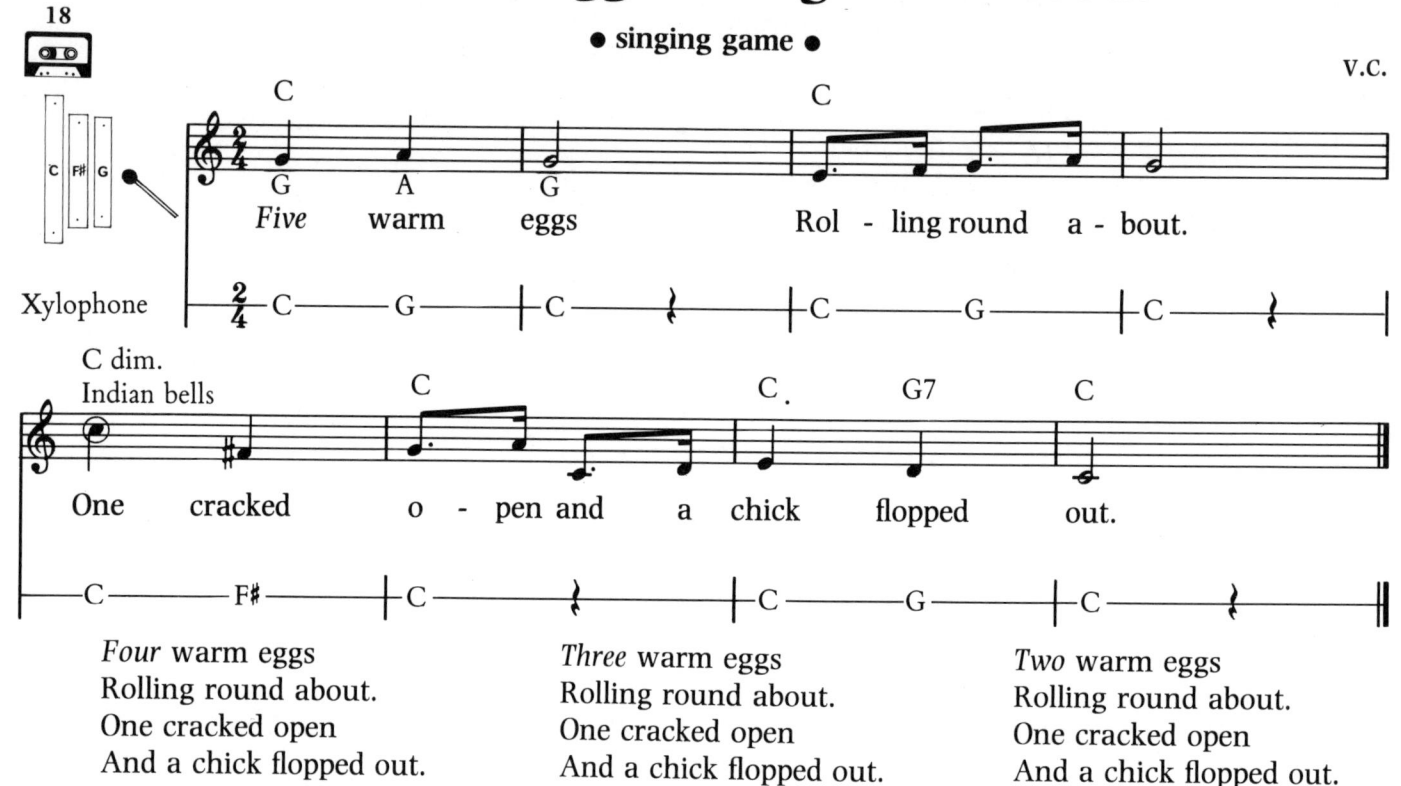

songs

Five warm eggs rolling round about

• singing game •

v.c.

Five warm eggs / Rol - ling round a - bout.

One cracked o - pen and a chick flopped out.

Xylophone

C dim.
Indian bells

Four warm eggs
Rolling round about.
One cracked open
And a chick flopped out.

Three warm eggs
Rolling round about.
One cracked open
And a chick flopped out.

Two warm eggs
Rolling round about.
One cracked open
And a chick flopped out.

One warm egg
Rolling round about.
It cracked open
And a chick flopped out.

No warm eggs,
Just a golden heap.
Five small chickens
Singing 'Cheep, cheep, cheep!'

Prior to hatching, the struggling of the chickens inside their shells causes their eggs to roll around, sometimes quite vigorously. In this song a number of children are chosen to be eggs (ten or five), and one by one, as they are touched on the back by the teacher or by another child, they hatch and flop over to the side. It's helpful to use a PE mat as the 'base' where the newly-hatched chicks can gather. One child can be a lamp. Young chickens need warmth and it is not unusual to see a clutch of chicks dozing together under a lamp.

Lightly tap a triangle or Indian bells on the numbers (5,4,3,2,1). You could use the same number of triangles as there are eggs, and reduce the number of players to match the number of eggs.

Try clapping the rhythm of the song. Draw the children's attention to the dotted or 'snappy' notes.

Can anyone pick out the melody of the first two lines? Set out the chimes E F G and A.

Find an instrument to make a floppy sound to describe the *movement* of the newly-hatched chicks. Clappers and castanets are rather harsh. Can they be muted in any way? Experiment with rubber gloves, the flapping pages of a book, a few large, moist leaves, etc.

sound story

The beautiful egg
by Veronica Clark

The warm egg lay on the sand at the edge of the beach. The midday sun shone down on its smooth, hard shell, and every now and then the egg gave a little roll. The most unusual thing about the egg, apart from its size (it was very big), was its colour. It was neither white nor blue, turquoise nor green, but a heavenly mixture of them all. The colour whirled and swirled round the curves of the egg like the rollers of the ocean. It was a truly beautiful egg.

Down at the water's edge the waves sparkled as they lapped the sand [1]. A light breeze rustled the leaves of the giant palm trees [2], and in the dark jungle behind, brightly coloured parrots whooped and screeched [3].

The first creature to discover the egg was Mrs Ostrich. She stepped elegantly along the beach, her feathers curling in the breeze. On seeing the egg she stopped, poked her long neck forward and gasped, 'Oh! But you are lovely!' Folding her legs underneath her, she sat down beside the egg and sang:

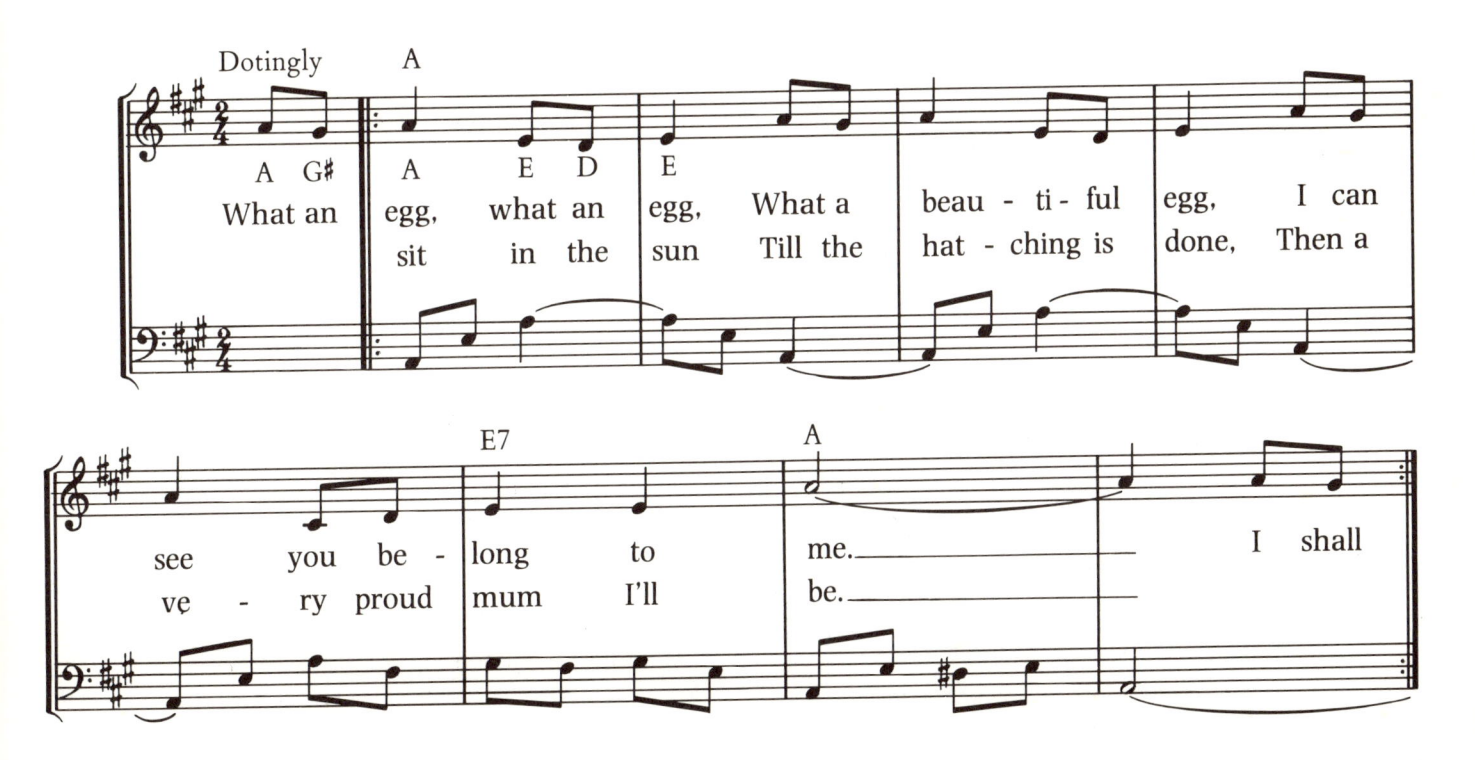

Dotingly

What an egg, what an egg, What a beau-ti-ful egg, I can see you be-long to me. I shall
sit in the sun Till the hat-ching is done, Then a ve-ry proud mum I'll be.

79

sound story

She had barely finished crooning, when who should come crawling out of the swamp but Mrs Crocodile. Her powerful tail swished from side to side making pretty patterns in the sand ⟨4⟩. When she saw the egg she opened her toothy mouth wide and croaked, 'Cor! What a smasher!' Settling down next to Mrs Ostrich she sang in a creaky voice: *What an egg, what an egg*, etc.

Mrs Turtle hadn't meant to come as far up the beach, but hearing the singing she decided to investigate. She was somewhat surprised to see Mrs Ostrich and Mrs Crocodile sitting down together, but she forgot about them altogether when she caught sight of the egg. 'Oh my goodness gracious me,' she fluttered, 'What a dear, dear egg'. And blinking her beady little eyes she sang in a breathless voice: *What an egg, what an egg*, etc.

'You really are being ridiculous,' snorted Mrs Ostrich. 'This is my egg. It's far too big to belong to either of you.'

'Don't talk so daft,' interrupted Mrs Crocodile rudely, 'Any eggs found lying around the swamp are mine.'

'Pardon me', said Mrs Turtle, 'but this egg is the colour of the sea so I think it must be a turtle's egg.'

Now all the time the three creatures had been arguing, the egg had been rolling to and fro, and faint tapping sounds could be heard from inside ⟨5⟩. Suddenly, CRACK ⟨6⟩, a small hole appeared in the side of the shell and the tip of a beak could be seen. 'There, what did I tell you?' gloated Mrs Ostrich. 'It's a bird.'

There was another CRACK ⟨6⟩, and a long scaly tail poked out of the hole. 'Ha ha,' smirked Mrs Crocodile. 'That's *my* baby'.

There was one more CRACK ⟨6⟩ and the rounded hump of a turtle's shell could be seen. 'Oh my precious,' crooned Mrs Turtle, waddling over to the newly-hatched creature.

Then she stopped. The baby that stood blinking in the sunlight was a most peculiar-looking little thing. It had the beak of a bird, the tail of a crocodile, the back of a turtle *and* the ears of a monkey, the neck of a giraffe and the legs of a camel. 'Oh no,' breathed Mrs Ostrich.

sound story

'Cor!' croaked Mrs Crocodile. Mrs Turtle just blinked her beady eyes. Then, without another word they all three turned their backs on the bewildered baby and walked away.

The baby began to cry. Huge tears welled up out of its eyes and dripped off the end of its beak. It made a strange whimpering sound which turned into hiccups 7. Its thin legs began to wobble and its neck drooped.

Mrs Baboon, who had been swinging through the palm trees at the edge of the beach, heard the funny noise and loped over to see what was going on. When she saw the baby she went over and walked all round it. Then she smiled. 'Hmmm,' she said, patting it gently on its back. 'You are a funny little thing – but I like you.' Bending down she scooped the baby up in her strong arms. The baby immediately stopped crying and began to make a soft purring noise 8. Mrs Baboon loped back towards the jungle singing:

> What a fright, what a sight,
> I can see you're not quite
> What a baby baboon should be.
> But you're not all that bad,
> And I can't have you sad,
> So I'll take you along with me.

Out at sea the waves sparkled and sighed 1. A light breeze rustled the leaves of the giant palm trees 2, and in the dark jungle behind, brightly coloured parrots whooped and screeched 3.

And high up in the branches of a tall, tall tree, a kind baboon rocked her new baby to sleep, and as she rocked she hummed.

(Hum tune of song getting quieter and quieter.)

Read the story without sound effects and talk about the four main characters. Encourage the children to make their singing voices match the animal. The environmental sounds should all be muted to create a dreamlike atmosphere.

sound story

story sounds	body sounds	instrumental or other sounds
1 *sparkling waves* +	an undulating *shsh* sound or a swishing sound made by rubbing palm of hands over clothing	random **Indian bells** for the sparkles
2 *rustling leaves* +	a light blowing combined with rapid champing noises made by rapid tongue movements against the top and bottom of the mouth	for the breeze, rub the palm of one hand gently and slowly over a **sheet of paper** for the leaves gently shake **milk bottle tops inside a small plastic bag**
3 *parrots* +	experiment to find the most realistic bird calls	experiment with **recorder tops**, blow through **trapped paper**, or use **party blowers**
4 *swishing tail*	rub palms of hands rhythmically together	experiment with various **beaters** on **drum skin**
5 *tapping noises*	back of nails on table top	**claves** or **woodblock**
6 CRACK	Donald Duck type vocal sounds	**Velcro shoe fastenings**, or pop the air bubbles in **plastic packaging**
7 *crying*	vocal whimpers, sobs and hiccups	try out quick jerky taps on a **high-pitched instrument**
8 *purring*	vocal	**guiro**

+ sounds which can be made by several children

Use the story as a talking point for appearances and attitudes. Why did the three animals each want the egg so much? Why did they change their minds? Just because people look different, does it mean that they think or feel differently? Who was the kindest animal and why? Older children will appreciate the story of *The Good Samaritan*.

games and exercises

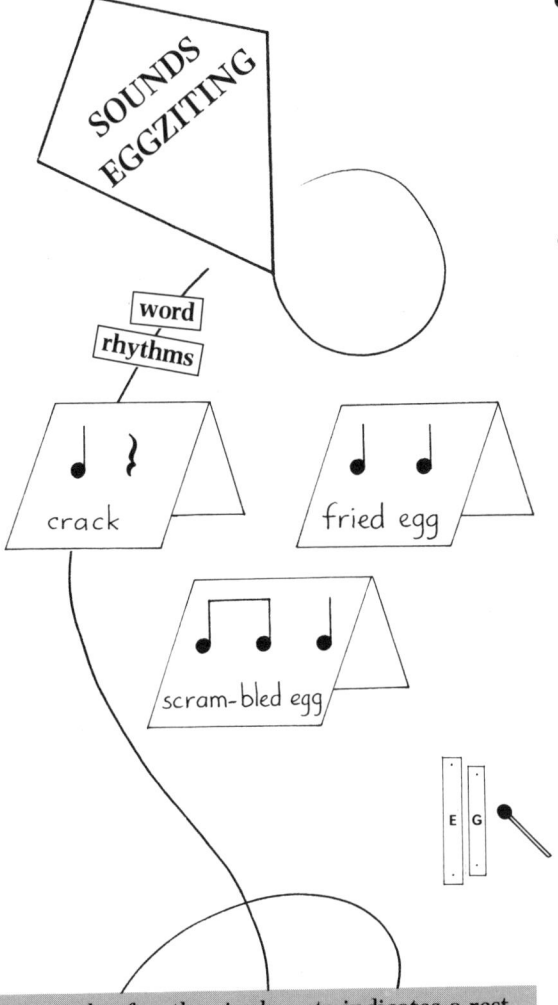

- Make a collection of 'eggy' words, e.g. *yolk, slither, scrambled egg, meringue, splatter*. Clap and chant them. Make voices match the word. Play the rhythms on suitable instruments, e.g. play *fried egg* with maracas (sizzling fat), play *boiled egg* with claves (tapping the shell).

- Another day, repeat the above but with a more analytical approach. How many claps has each rhythm? Make a rhythm card for each word or phrase. Group similar rhythms together. Ask one group of children to play the 'one-clap' words, another the 'two-clap' rhythms, and so on. The following lists may be helpful:

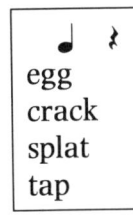

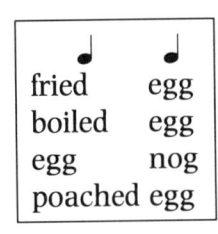

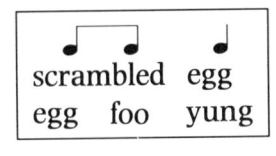

egg	fried egg	scrambled egg
crack	boiled egg	egg foo yung
splat	egg nog	
tap	poached egg	

- Set out chimes E and G. Invite the children to make up simple tunes for each rhythm. It won't always be possible to 'use up' both notes. *You don't have to change notes at all if you don't want to.* Write down the tunes. Put the tunes in the music corner so that others can play them.

- Older children can be introduced to a more standard way of writing down tunes. Draw two parallel lines: the higher one is for the higher note G, the lower one is for the lower note E. When reading the music, the eye must travel from note to note, left to right. Some children will read along the top line first, then move down to the bottom line. This isn't likely to

- happen with short melodic phrases. Thus the following tune would be written down as:

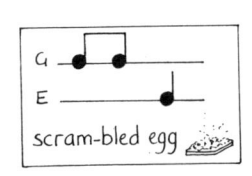

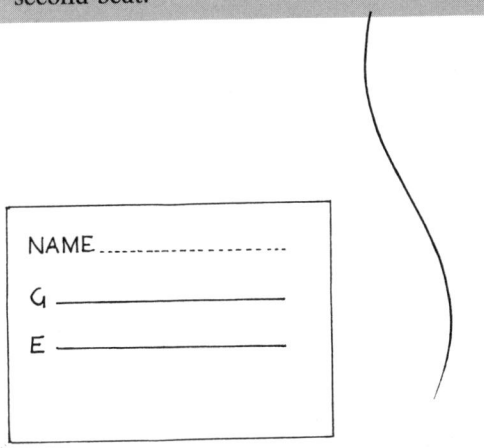

You can prepare simple worksheets like the one shown on the left.

SOUNDS EGGZITING

word rhythms

crack / fried egg / scram-bled egg

The squiggle after the single note indicates a rest or a beat of silence. It completes the pattern of two beats into which all these 'eggy' words fit. To 'play' the rest, keep the hands together after the clap on 'crack', and incline them forward on the second beat.

NAME..........
G _____
E _____

83

games and exercises

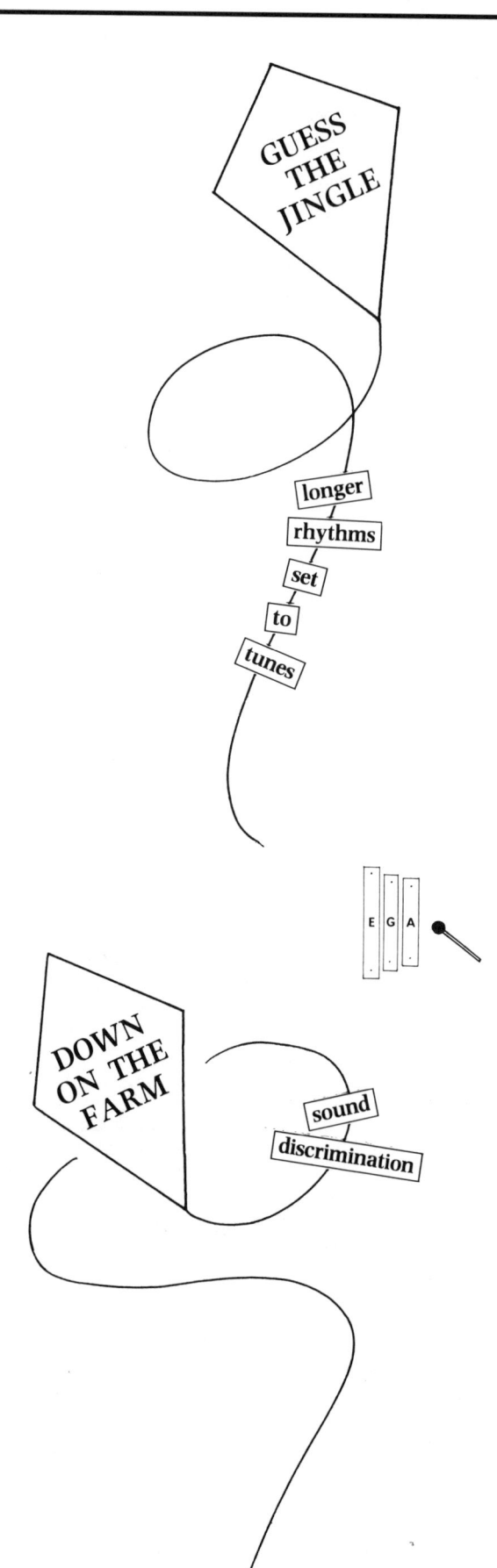

GUESS THE JINGLE

longer rhythms set to tunes

- Learn, chant and clap the following three jingles:

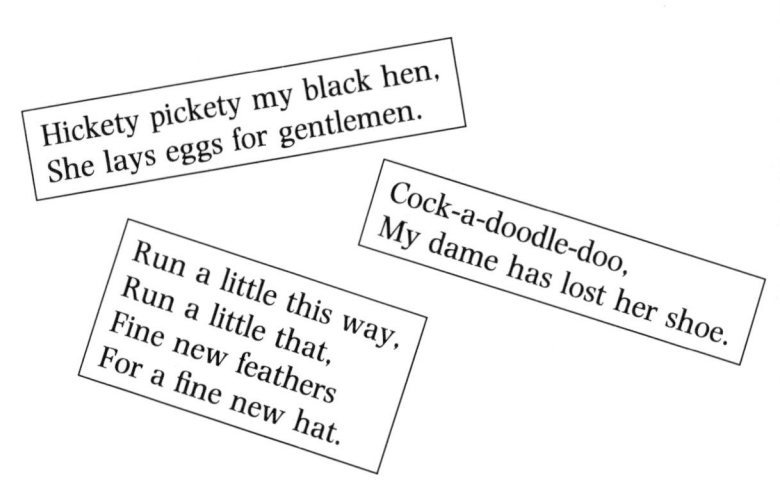

> Hickety pickety my black hen,
> She lays eggs for gentlemen.

> Cock-a-doodle-doo,
> My dame has lost her shoe.

> Run a little this way,
> Run a little that,
> Fine new feathers
> For a fine new hat.

Each jingle represents a different *rhythmic type*. The first has a strong 'walking' beat, the second 'skips', and the third gives the impression of running around.

- When the children know the jingles well, ask them to play the *rhythm* of each. Keep the tempo fairly slow as there are a lot of notes to fit in. Play on instruments.

- Play the *rhythm* of one of the jingles and ask the children to guess which one is being played.

- Set out chimes E G and A. Make up and sing simple tunes for the jingles.

DOWN ON THE FARM

sound discrimination

- This is a well-known party game. Each child is told (whispered) the name of one farmyard animal. At a given signal the children make a noise of their animal as loudly as they can. On finding someone making the same sound, they join up until their group is complete. Don't have more than six in each group. For a class of 30 the following combination works well: 6 cows, 6 cockerels, 6 dogs, 6 cats and 6 ducks.

- Other suitable farmyard sounds for the game are *whistling farmers*, *noisy tractors*, *hissing geese* and *grunting pigs*.

games and exercises

COCKEREL RONDO

bird cries – imitation and ordering

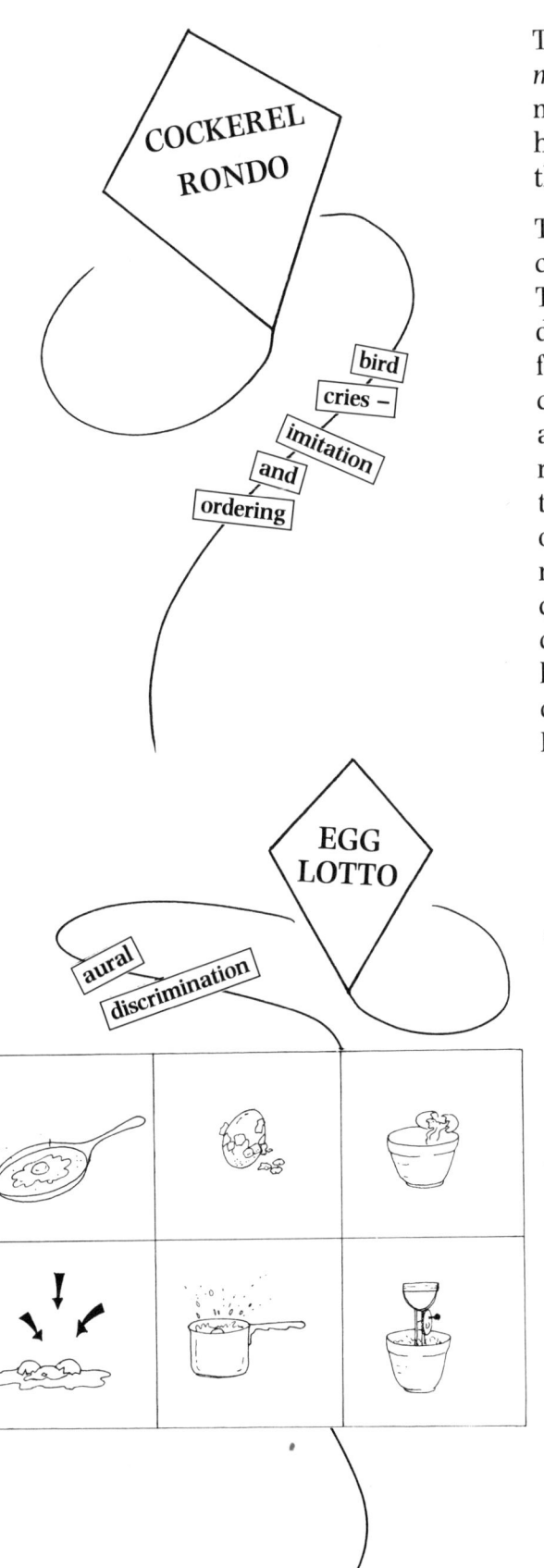

The distinctive feature of a *rondo* is that there is *one main theme which keeps returning*. It's a bit like a multilayered sandwich with a lot of pieces of bread holding in different fillings. The bread is the returning theme.

The *Cockerel rondo* is made up of bird cries. Each bird cry is followed by the *cock-a-doodle-doo* of a cockerel. Talk about farmyard birds and imitate their sounds – ducks, geese, hens, chickens, turkeys. Choose the four favourite sounds and give one each to four groups of children. Practise in turn. Now choose a cockerel. Find a child who can crow *cock-a-doodle-doo* loudly and rhythmically. Stand her or him on a chair. Start with the cockerel (two crows), and follow it with one of the other sounds. The other bird calls don't have to be rhythmic or conform to a beat – just let the children quack or hiss for about ten seconds, then return to the cockerel. Continue until each of the four bird groups has performed. Finish with the cockerel. Conduct the children either by pointing or by holding up pictures. How could you write down what you have played?

EGG LOTTO

aural discrimination

- Make lotto cards with a box for each of the following: an egg frying, an egg being beaten, an egg falling on the floor, a hard-boiled egg being peeled, an egg being broken on the edge of a bowl then dropped in, and an egg boiling vigorously. Prepare a tape of the six egg sounds.

- First play the tape and talk about the sounds. Then put the tape and tape-recorder and lotto cards in the music corner and invite small groups of children to play *Egg lotto*. For counters, stick small yellow tiddlywinks on slightly larger circles of white card (fried eggs). Some of the sounds are similar so the children may need to talk amongst themselves to make the best choice.

instruments to make and play

HAND JINGLES

These are suitable for young children because they are easy to play. Also, they can be played en masse without undue strain on the nerves. Some of the commercially manufactured jingles are harsh and loud and teachers may prefer to make and use the simple form of jingle stick described here.

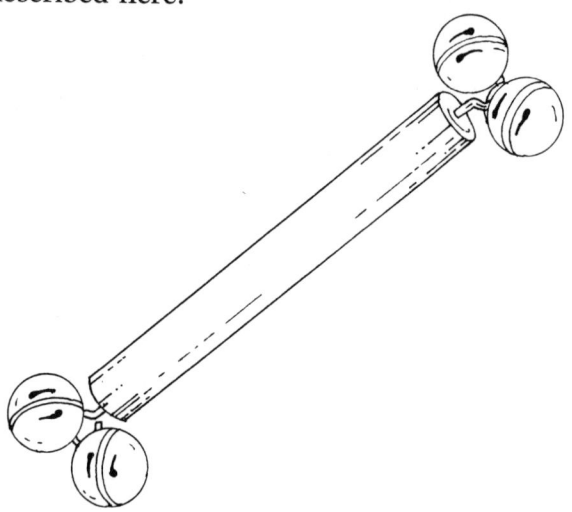

For one jingle stick you need:
- 10 cm length of dowelling (15 mm diameter)
- 2 screw hooks
- 2 or 4 small bells (with small metal loops for attaching to the hooks)
- button or brushing polish

Instructions
1. Sandpaper any rough ends on the dowelling.
2. Either polish, varnish or paint the stick. To polish, give the wood three coatings of either button or brushing polish, smoothing each coat with glass paper when it has had time to dry.
3. Screw a hook into each end of the dowelling handle.
4. Thread one or two bells onto each hook and close the open ends of the hooks with pliers.

JINGLE POLES

Short jingle poles are popular. They are either shaken or tapped lightly on the floor. If a rubber door-stop is screwed into one end, the pole can be bounced up and down on the stopper. Shorter poles are played from a kneeling position.

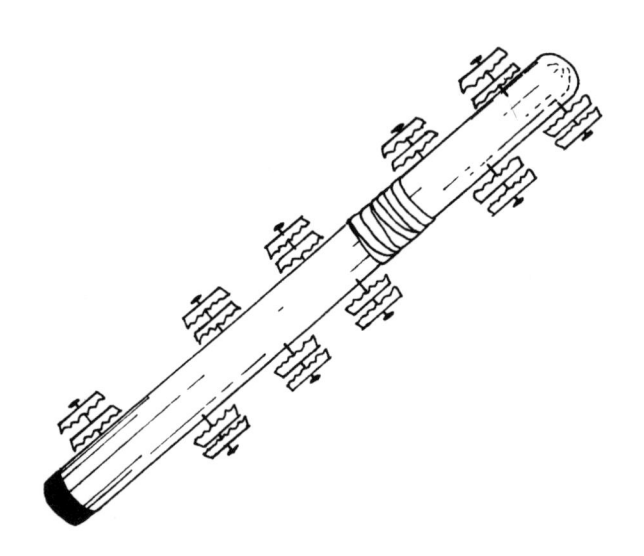

For one jingle pole you need:
- half a broom handle
- a good supply of metal bottle caps
- 20 mm wire nails
- enamel paints

Instructions
1. Sand the sawn-off edge of the broom handle. Polish, varnish or paint.
2. Remove the cork or plastic disc in the centre of the bottle caps and clean the caps. Dry them thoroughly. Paint the inside of the caps with brightly coloured enamel paints.
3. Nail the caps loosely to the broom handle in pairs (back to back) in any pattern. Leave room between caps for holding near the top.

instruments to make and play

JINGLE WHIPS

These are useful for gentle sound effects – rustlings and clatterings. Let the strings hang down and shake gently with a loose wrist.

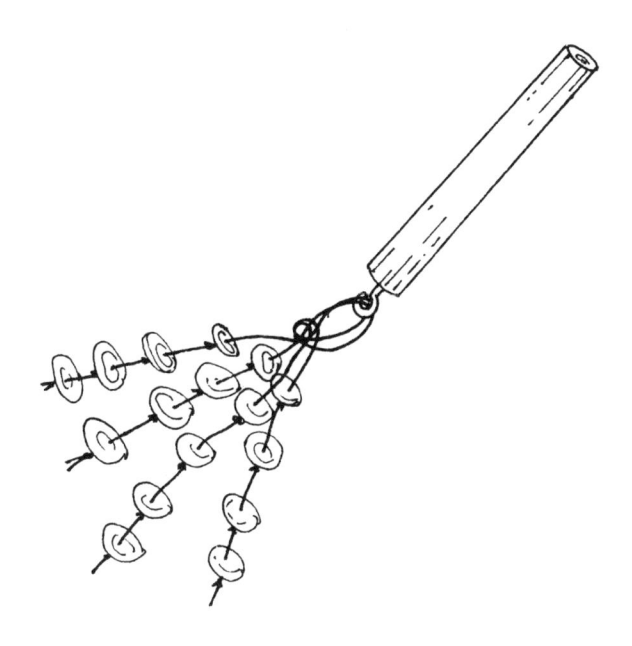

For one jingle whip you need:

- 15 to 20 cm length of dowelling (15 mm diameter)
- one screw eye
- string
- bottle tops or caps

Instructions

1 Sand any rough edges on the dowelling.
2 Polish, varnish or paint the stick.
3 Screw the eye into the end. Thread two 40 cm lengths of string through the eye and tie together near the eye so that four equal lengths of string are hanging down.
4 Prepare metal bottle tops as described above (see *Jingle poles*). Make a hole through the centre of each one with a nail. Thread the caps on to the string, using knots to separate them. You can use milk bottle tops instead of metal bottle caps – they are surprisingly durable.

TAMBOURINES

The lovely sound of a good-quality tambourine cannot be reproduced with a homemade instrument such as the one described below. However, plate tambourines are fun to make, attractive, and make a reasonable sound.

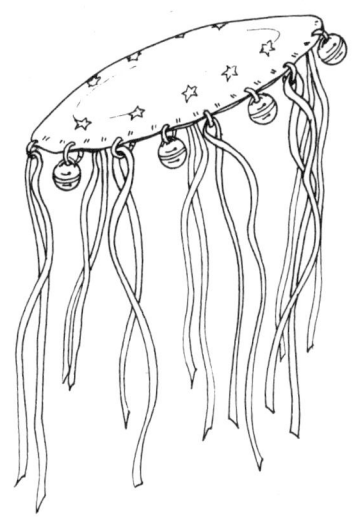

For one tambourine you need:

- 4 cardboard plates
- key rings or open-ended curtain rings
- bells or bottle caps
- ribbon or tape

Instructions

1 Glue the plates together. The plates can be coloured with felt-tip pens or poster paints, or decorated with self-adhesive plastic shapes. One or two coats of varnish on top of the felt-tips/paint will help to preserve the patterns.
2 Using a leather punch, punch an *even* number of holes round the edge of the plates, about 1 cm in from the rim. Thread a key ring or curtain ring through *every other* hole.
3 Thread either a bell or two bottle caps on to each ring. Close the rings.
4 Thread brightly coloured ribbon or tape or paper or plastic strips through the remaining holes and tie firmly in place.

87

curricular links

> RELATED THEMES: birds • farms • baby animals • creatures which hatch from eggs • feathers • cooking with eggs • Easter • Spring

Language

Draw the outline of an egg and fill it in with letter *e*'s.

Talk about the sound *ch* – *ch*icken, *ch*irp, *ch*eep. With a large brush, paint the two letters *c* and *h* on a card, using a strong glue. Sprinkle chicken meal over the glue and shake off the excess meal, leaving the sound *ch* filled in with the chicken food. Let the children stroke over the letters saying *ch* for *chicken* (*food*). Alternatively you could stick on chicken bones.

Chant or sing *Humpty Dumpty*. Make a collection of all the words containing *all*. Add others to the list. Make up variations of *Humpty Dumpty*, e.g. *Humpty Dumpty sat on a ball*. Extend the game to include other rhyming pairs, e.g. *Humpty Dumpty sat on a seat, Humpty Dumpty fell on his feet*.

Look at *Rosie's walk* by Pat Hutchinson. Make up a similar story about a zebra hunted by a lion, or a mouse stalked by a cat – oral, written or in pictures.

Pass round a raw hen's egg – carefully! Collect describing words and phrases and write them up on large, suspended egg shapes.

Make a collection of fragile objects and talk about them. Display with a *PLEASE DO NOT TOUCH* notice nearby.

Make up stories about eggs: *The huge egg, The golden egg, The glass egg, The teeny weeny egg.* Where was it found, what hatched out, what happened next?

Easter is a time of happiness and of sadness. What makes the children happy or sad?

Read the poem *Miracle* on page 69. What is a miracle? What do the children consider to be miraculous?

Number work

What shape is an egg? Make a collection of things that are ovoid – acorns, some sweets, seeds.

Collect various types of eggbox and talk about rows and columns, e.g. a carton of *six* eggs has two rows of 3, *or* three columns of 2 (depending on which way you look at the carton).

How many ways can children arrange four eggs (clay or plastic or real) in a carton with six spaces? Record results on squared paper.

Ask the children to each make three clay eggs, one small, one middle-sized and the third bigger than the other two. Play games with the eggs using appropriate vocabulary, e.g. largest, smallest, etc.

Balance real (hardboiled) eggs with a variety of units, e.g. plastic cubes, beads.

Take three eggs the same size. Boil one, blow one and leave the other raw. Let the children see you doing this. Which egg is the lightest/heaviest? First guess, then verify using a balance.

How long do the children like their eggs cooked? Boil one for a minute, crack open and examine contents. Boil another for two minutes and do same. Continue for 3/4/5 minutes.

What can the children do in the time it takes to boil an egg? (How many times round the playground, how many times can they bounce

curricular links

and catch a ball, write their name, etc.?) Use sand timers or stopwatches. Record the results.

Environmental studies

Talk about *heat* in relation to hatching and babies in general. What happens if the mother bird abandons her eggs? How do we keep newborn babies warm?

Talk about *heat* in relation to cooking eggs – hot water, hot fat, hot air.

Watch an egg boiling. Why do small bubbles rise from the egg?

Take the egg out of the hot water and watch the shell carefully – why does it dry so quickly?

Measure out 500 ml or five eggcupsful of water. Boil for 15 minutes. Let the water cool and measure the water left in the pan.

Place a mirror near a kettle of boiling water. Watch what happens to the steam as it meets the surface of the mirror. Talk about evaporation and condensation.

Place a raw, a boiled and a blown egg in a bowl of water. Do they float? Why?/Why not?

Read the poem 'Pace-egging' and sing the 'Easter song' from *Seeing and doing*. Try rolling hardboiled eggs down a wide plank of wood or a table top. Change the gradient. Try with balls and beads. How far does each object roll? What's the best shape for rolling? Cover the gradient surface with material/foam rubber/a towel, and roll again. What happens?

Look at and talk about all sorts of eggs – fish, snail, insect, frog eggs.

Talk about the protection of wild birds and their eggs.

Collect and look at feathers – their shape, function, position on bird, weight. Write with them (quill pens), make prints, arrange in order of size.

Art and craft

Make cress people out of half eggshells half-filled with soil.

Make collage chicks using sawdust, feathers, cottonwool, yellow and black fabrics, yellow and black wool. Tie onto a frame and suspend to make chicken mobile.

Decorate hardboiled or blown eggs.

Make Easter bonnets or hats.

Prepare some white and brown paint. Ask the children to experiment with mixing to produce as many different coloured eggs as they can (using only the white and brown). Try with two different colours, e.g. yellow and blue.

Make a huge Humpty Dumpty stuffed toy. The body can be made from a pillow case (machine-stitch the oval shape) stuffed with soft rags. Stitch or sew on eyes, mouth, belt, etc. Add arms and legs. Let the children play with him. They can make up falling-down music for him, or gallop with him to the accompaniment of coconut shells.

Drama and movement

Talk about opening things. Mime unzipping a banana, opening a tin of beans, unscrewing a sauce bottle, opening an envelope, etc.

Pretend to break out of a large paper bag, break down a locked door, dig your way out of a snow drift.

Watch a feather floating to the ground. To the accompaniment of light, airy percussion sounds, float and drift around the room and finally sink to the ground as the music stops. Make the sound of a gentle breeze. Move as dictated by the breeze, sometimes slowly, sometimes swirling wildly, sometimes barely at all. Listen to 'Morning' from *Peer Gynt* by Grieg and move as the music suggests.

list of resources

POEMS

Seeing and doing (Methuen)
  The guppy
  Hen's song
  Easter song
  The farmyard
  Pace-egging

The book of a thousand poems (Bell and Hyman)
  I had a little hen
  Peter and Michael
  Cock-a-doodle-doo
  The mouse the frog and the little red hen
  Eggs for breakfast
  The clucking hen

The young Puffin book of verse (Puffin)
  The chickens
  Ten little chickens

Now we are six (Methuen)
  The little black hen

All in a day (Ladybird)
  Yellow poem
  Egg thoughts

SONGS

Harlequin (Black)
  My Easter bonnet
  It happens each Spring

Someone's singing Lord (Black)
  The golden cockerel

Nursery rhymes for today (Kestrel)
  Mother Goose comes to Cable Street

MUSIC

'Hatching chicks' from *Pictures at an Exhibition* by Mussorgsky
'Morning' from *Peer Gynt* by Grieg
'The hen' from *The Birds* by Respighi
The Firebird by Stravinsky
'Spring' from *The Four Seasons* by Vivaldi
The Golden Cockerel by Rimsky Korsakov
The Ugly Duckling by Prokofiev
'Down on the farm' (*Bang on a Drum* · BBC Cassettes)

STORIES

The crows of Pearblossom by Aldous Huxley (OUP)
Hare and the Easter eggs by Alison Uttley (Collins)
The goose that laid the golden egg by Geoffrey Patterson (Andre Deutsch)
Early morning in the barn by Nancy Tafuri (Julia MacRae Books)
Across the stream by Mirra Ginsburg (Puffin)
Here a chick, there a chick by Bruce McMillan (Scholastic)
Little chicken story by Mary deBall Kwitz (World's Work)
'The little rooster and the diamond button' in *Stories for 5-year olds* (Puffin)
'Mother hen' in *Tell me a story* (Puffin)
'Chanticleer and Pertelotte' in *Stories for 6-year olds* (Puffin)
The little red hen illustrated by Paul Galdone (World's Work)
Rosie's walk by Pat Hutchins (Picture Puffin)
The tale of Jemima Puddleduck by Beatrix Potter (Warne)
Meg's eggs by Helen Nicoll and Jan Pienkowski (Picture Puffin)
The very hungry caterpillar by Eric Carle (Picture Puffin)
The egg by Dick Bruna (Methuen)
Ahhh! said stork by Gerald Rose (Picture Puffin)
Humpty Dumpty by Rodney Peppé (Picture Puffin)
The Joss Bird by Sarah Garland (Faber)
Horton hatches the egg by Dr Seuss (Collins)
The hen who wouldn't give up by Jill Tomlinson (Magnet)

INFORMATION

The egg and the chicken by Ilea and Enzo Mari (Black – Books Without Words)
The chicken book by Garth Williams (Patrick Hardy Books)
Egg the chick by Millicent Selsam (World's Work)
Hens by Gunilla Ingves (Black)
Poultry on the farm Down on the Farm series (Wayland)
'Spring' in *Child Education*, Mar. 1984
'Farms' in *Child Education Special* No. 36

trains

speech rhymes
Slam the door and blow   *92*
Piggy on the railway   *92*

action rhyme
All sorts   *93*

poems
With a slam and a bang and a whistle   *94*
High on a hill   *94*

songs
Pat works upon the railway   *95*
I love to travel by railway   *96*
Crossing gates   *98*
One red engine   *100*
The train is carrying coal   *102*

sound story
The Bluebell Railway   *103*

games and exercises   *106*

instruments to make and play
Maracas, slither boxes, sandpaper blocks and rasps   *109*

curricular links   *110*

list of resources   *112*

speech rhymes

Slam the door and blow

Slam the door and
Blow.

Ready steady
Go.

Shudder judder
Jerk.

Carry us to
Work.

V.C.

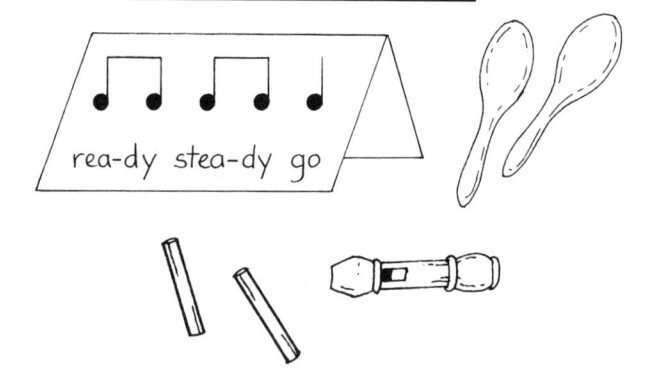

1. Swap train experiences. Does anyone you know go to work by train? Talk about the preliminaries to setting off – doors slamming, whistle blowing, the slow stirring into motion accompanied by creaks and jerks.

2. When the children are familiar with the rhyme, help them to clap the *beat* on the first word of each line. Transfer to untuned percussion.

3. The *rhythm* of each stanza is the same. Clap and chant the rhyme to the first stanza. Play the rhythm on shakers or claves. Blow the rhythm on a recorder mouthpiece or PE whistle. Put the rhythm card and a few instruments in the music corner – you'll have to make some arrangement for cleaning the mouthpiece of any blowing instruments.

4. Add a touch of drama by blowing a PE whistle on the word *blow*. Then gradually increase the tempo as though the train is gathering speed. At the end, repeat *Carry us to work*, getting faster and faster, and fade ———.

Piggy on the railway

Piggy on the railway
Picking up stones,
Along came an engine
And broke poor Piggy's bones.
'OW!' said Piggy,
'That's not fair.'
'Huh,' said the driver,
'I don't care.'

TRADITIONAL

1. Read the rhyme and invite comments. Talk about the dangers of playing near railway lines. Act out the rhyme – one child, Piggy, pretends to pick up stones, and four or five other children form a train and bump into him. Piggy and the engine driver can each speak their own lines, high voice for Piggy, low voice for the engine driver.

2. All practise squeaking Piggy's lines in high voices. Pause after *OW!* while the teacher or a child says *said Piggy*, and continue with *That's not fair*. Stand up and stretch high into the air as Piggy's words are spoken, then crouch down for the engine driver's lines. Let half the class be Piggy and the other half be the engine driver. Swap over.

speech rhymes

3 Continuing the theme of high and low, listen to some *unpitched* percussion instruments and try to arrange them in categories — high/low/can't say. *Allow for some divergence of opinion.* Encourage the children to give *reasons* for their choices.

4 Chant *That's not fair* to the accompaniment of one of the 'high' instruments, and *I don't care* to the accompaniment of a 'low' instrument. Put rhythm cards and a few instruments in the music corner for the children to play with. Encourage them to chant (or sing) as they play.

action rhyme

All sorts

Huffing, chuffing,
Steaming, puffing,
Old steam train.

Rumble, tumble,
Plain and humble,
Slow freight train.

Swaying, rocking,
Often stopping,
Branch-line train.

Gently humming,
Smoothly running,
Diesel train.

Dashing, whizzing,
Flashing, fizzing,
High-speed train.

V.C.

1 Talk about different types of trains – their functions, appearance, speeds.

2 Practise chanting a stanza at a time, matching voice and movements to the type of train:

steam train	breathless, use arms as pistons
freight train	bring out the dark sound of the words, roll hands round and round
branch-line train	sway gently from side to side
diesel train	increase tempo and decrease volume, move gently forwards and backwards
high-speed train	emphasise the sibilant sounds, move head rapidly from right to left (or vice versa) in time with the pulse as though watching things pass by a train window

3 Find a percussion instrument for each stanza and play it on the beat to accompany the chanting.

4 Divide your class into five groups and allocate a train stanza and an instrument to each group.

93

poems

With a slam and a bang and a whistle

With a slam and a bang and a whistle
The train is ready to go:
It jerks into life and begins to move off,
Its carriages pulled in a row.

It rattles and wobbles across all the points
Until it has found the right track,
Then it carries its passengers past the high flats,
Past dirty canals, still and black.

Out of the city and into the suburbs,
Hundreds of houses in rows,
Gardens with washing and swings and old sheds,
Gardens where nothing much grows.

Into the countryside, open and green,
Bridges and trees zipping past.
The train seems to say as it races away,
'I'm free and I'm smooth and I'm fast.'

V.C.

The poem describes the journey of a train which starts off in the city and moves out to the countryside. Start off slowly and gradually increase the tempo. Let the children join in the last line.

High on a hill

I was high on a hill amidst bracken and gorse
Looking down on a patchwork plain,
When out of a tunnel far below
Crawled a long thin worm of a train.
With barely a sound it hurried along
Between miniature hedges and trees,
So slow and so small it was hard to believe
There were people inside just like me.

V.C.

Read the poem and talk about it. Discuss the effect of distance on size and sound. Make a backcloth of sound for the poem. Include humming insects, a gentle breeze, birdsong (damp corks rubbed on glass). At the point in the poem when the train emerges from the tunnel, a child can chant quietly, *diddle-de-dee*. The train sound should continue to the end of the poem and a bit beyond, then fade away.

Pat works upon the railway

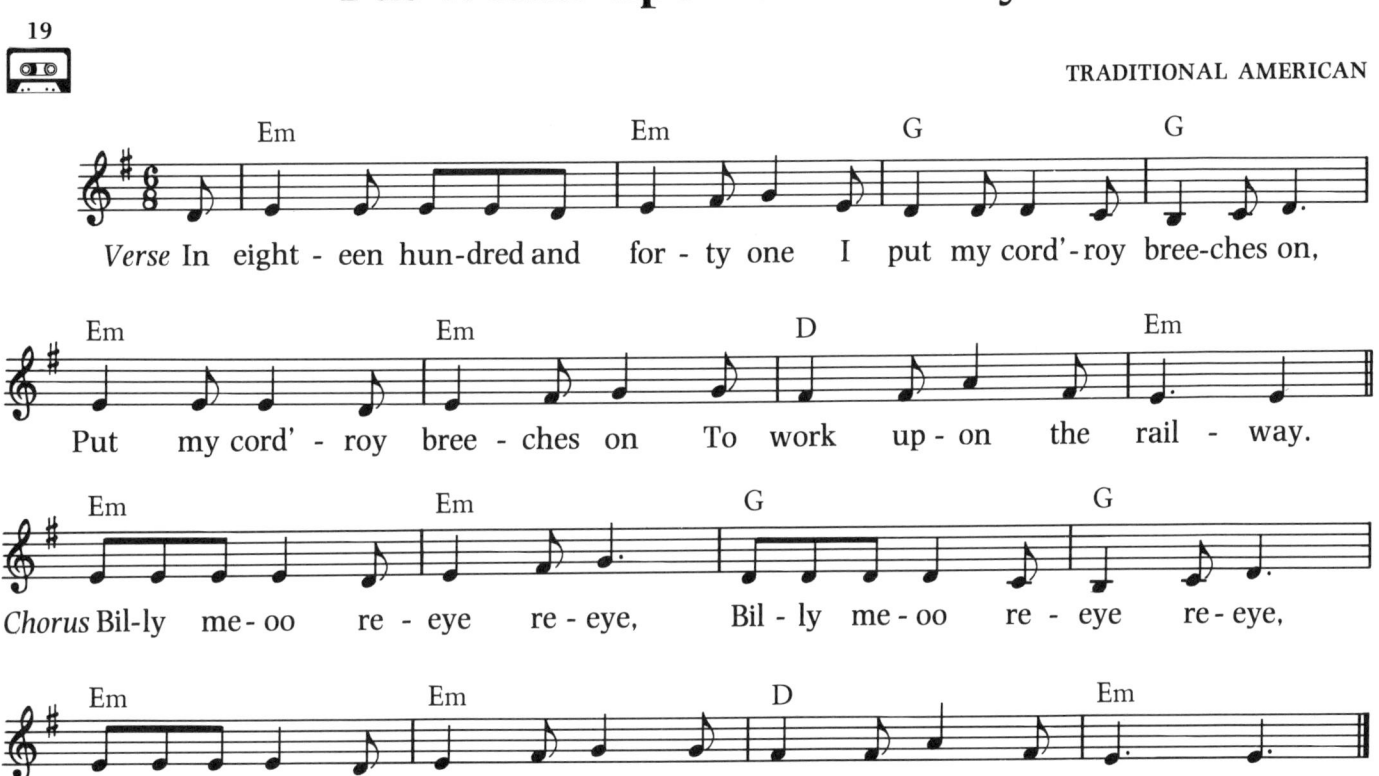

TRADITIONAL AMERICAN

Verse In eight-een hun-dred and for-ty one I put my cord'-roy bree-ches on, Put my cord'-roy bree-ches on To work up-on the rail-way.

Chorus Bil-ly me-oo re-eye re-eye, Bil-ly me-oo re-eye re-eye, Bil-ly me-oo re-eye re-eye, To work up-on the rail-way.

Chorus Billy me-oo re-eye re-eye,
Billy me-oo re-eye re-eye,
Billy me-oo re-eye re-eye,
To work upon the railway.

In eighteen hundred and forty three
'Twas then I met sweet Biddy McGee,
An elegant wife she's been to me
While working on the railway.

It's 'Pat do this', 'Pat do that',
Without a stocking or cravat,
Nothing but an old straw hat
To work upon the railway.

In eighteen hundred and forty two
I left the old world for the new,
'Twas my bad luck that brought me through
To work upon the railway.

In eighteen hundred and forty five
I thought myself more dead than alive,
I thought myself more dead than alive
While working on the railway.

In eighteen hundred and forty seven,
Sweet Biddy McGee went up to heaven,
If she left one kid she left eleven
To work upon the railway.

This song tells the tale of a young man who leaves his home country (Ireland?) for America where he gets a job working on the railway. The one bright spark in his life is the elegant Biddy McGee, who incredibly bears him at least eleven children in the space of four years. Introduce a tambourine or two to help the chorus go with a swing.

95

songs

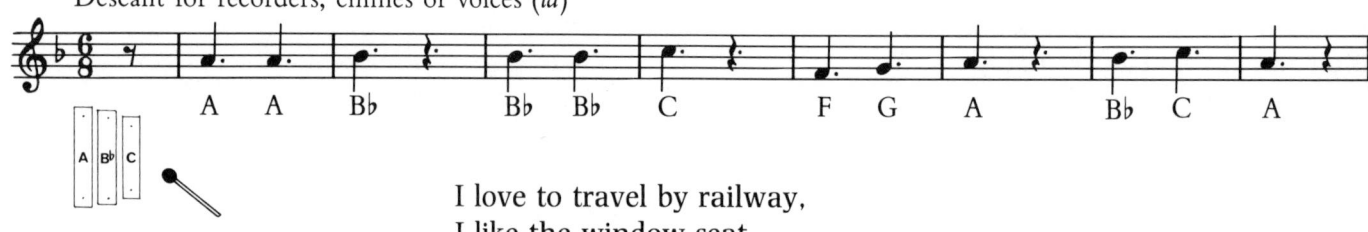

I love to travel by railway

v.c.

Capo 5th fret and play chords in brackets

I love to tra-vel by rail - way. I like the win-dow seat. It's
fun to watch the trees zip by To tra-vel by train is a treat.

Chimes, xylophone

Descant for recorders, chimes or voices (la)

I love to travel by railway,
I like the window seat.
It's fun to overtake the cars,
To travel by train is a treat.

Alternative third lines
It's fun to count the telegraph poles
It's fun to make the traffic stop
It's fun to see the cows and sheep
It's fun to wave at passers-by

songs

For many children nowadays, travelling by train is a rarity and a treat. This song tries to catch the excitement of a train journey. It's an easy song to learn because of the repeated lines (the children can make up their own third lines). Encourage the children to clap on the fast beat (four per line) as soon as they have grasped the tune. Later a more sophisticated clapping pattern can be taught – see the emphasised words with the music. Try shaking a quiet beat with maracas. Someone might be able to sustain a quiet ♩ ♪ ♩. pattern throughout on claves or tambourine. Two ideas for tuned percussion accompaniment are given with the music. The 'descant' can be played on recorders or hummed. Very easy, but effective, is a drone C and F tapped on the first strong beat of each line.

To capture the rising sense of excitement caused by the train ride, encourage the children to increase the volume slightly in line 3. What happens to the tune at this point? Put the chimes C F G and A in the music corner and ask the children to find the tune of the last line. Start on A.

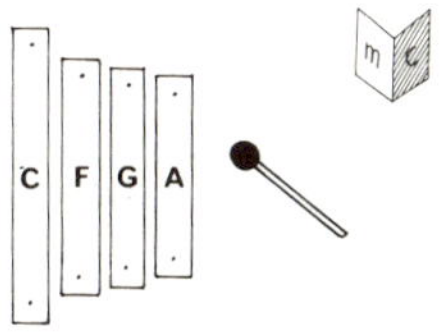

A few older children who know the tune well will be able to clap, tap, shake the *rhythm* of the words. Keep a fairly slow tempo – there are a lot of notes to fit in, especially in the last line.

Play around with the beat. There is a strong feeling of four about this song – there are four beats for each line. Try *clapping* two of these beats, and *slapping the thighs* for the remaining two. Keep the beat going at the end of the second line where there is a long note on the word *seat*. Older infants in pairs will love to 'clap' a *thighs · clap · hands together* (twice) pattern, or a *thighs · clap · one hand · the other hand* pattern. Try splitting the four beats between two instruments, e.g. *tambour* (2) then *tambourine* (2), or *tambour · tambourine · tambour · tambourine* – one tap or beat each. Use four instruments. The children can invent their own patterns. When children know a song well they often play (improvise) complex and extremely effective rhythmic patterns. Keep an eye on what's going on and draw attention to some of these rhythms. Let everyone have a go. Ask them to draw their four-beat patterns (see below).

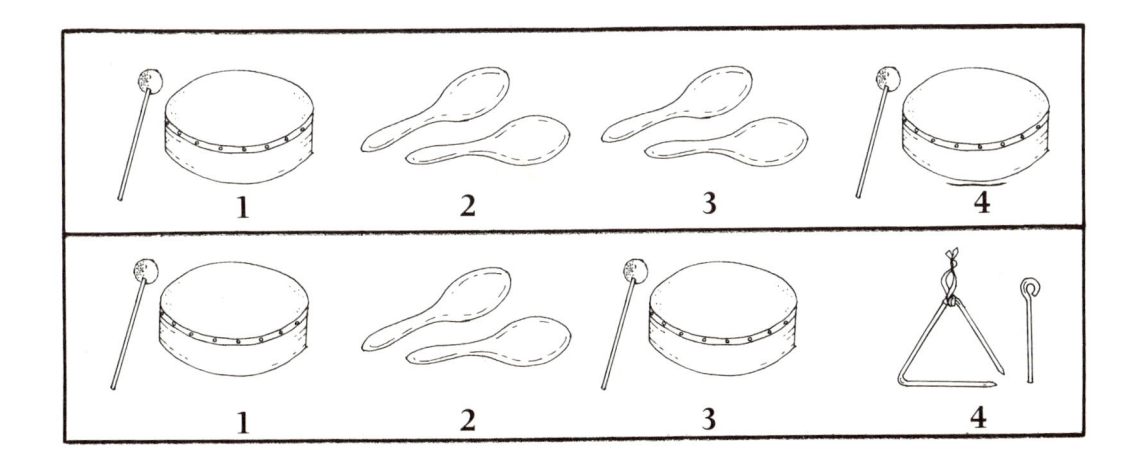

97

songs

Crossing gates

21

C7 (throughout)

v.c.

Chorus Hear me blow, See me fly, Watch me as I hur-ry by.

Tuned percussion, piano

G — C' — | G — C' — | G — C' — | G — E —

C7 (throughout)

Verse Ev'-ry-thing Stops for me, Cars and bikes wait pa-tient-ly.

E — G — | E — G — | E — G — | E — C —

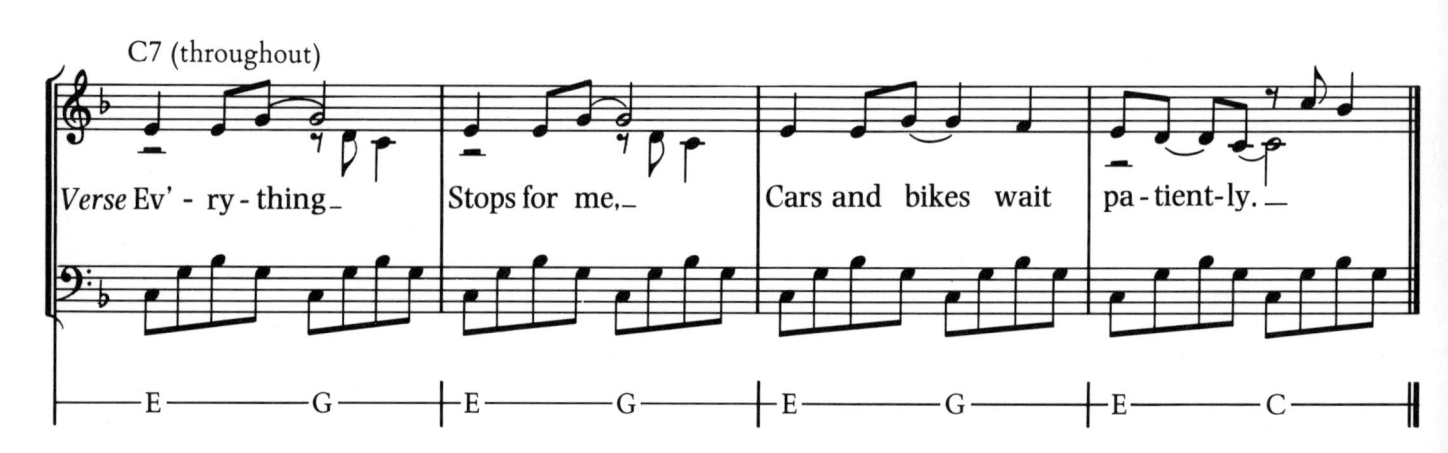

Chimes, metallophone, glockenspiel

or

Xylophone

98

songs

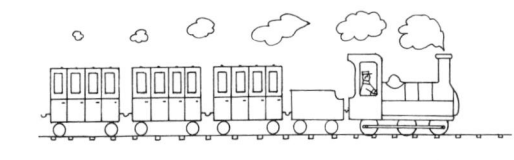

Chorus Hear me blow,
    See me fly,
    Watch me as I hurry by.

Giant trucks
Bearing freight
Line up at the crossing gates.

Chorus Hear me blow,
    See me fly,
    Watch me as I hurry by.

Passers-by
Watch me pass,
Wave at faces seen through glass.

Chorus Hear me blow,
    See me fly,
    Watch me as I hurry by,
    Hurry by, hurry by, hurry by.

I have yet to meet a child who doesn't enjoy waiting at crossing gates for a train to pass through. This song tries to capture the superiority of a train as it brings the road traffic to a halt. Talk about *level crossings*. How do they work, why are they necessary, what are their advantages/disadvantages over bridges, are there alternatives to the gate system? Do the children like waiting for the train to pass through? What do they do while they are waiting for the train to pass? Do they wave?

At first sing the part of the train yourself and let the children join in the chorus, *Hear me blow*, etc. The chorus melody is meant to sound a bit like a breathy train whistle, so don't be too fussy about a clean jump to the top C. A bit of pitch variation adds a touch of realism. Ask the children to keep their ears open for train whistle sounds. You'll probably be inundated with a motley collection of pipes, whistles and recorders. Listen to all of them and talk about the different sounds. We searched for a long time to find a whistle to use for the recording session, but finally, one week before the deadline, we were brought an old wooden whistle found on the way to school!

When the children have heard the song a few times, choose one child or a small group of children with 'low' voices to sing the part of the self-important train (the verses). Talk about the two tunes. Are they similar? How are they different? The chorus and verse sound exciting sung together (as on the cassette). A relatively simple way to approach this two-part harmony is to get the 'train' voice(s) to sing verse 2, but to keep repeating the last two words *crossing gates* while the chorus is sung through. The chorus singers can repeat their last phrase *Hurry by* several times, then the two parts can fade as though the train is disappearing. Finish with a faint train whistle.

The tune is based on one chord, C7, which is made up of the notes C E G B♭. These notes form the basis of any tuned percussion accompaniment to this song. The simplest accompaniment is to play the two notes G and the C above (together as a drone, or singly) with the beat of the music. Alternatively, try the four-note arpeggio accompaniment given with the music, or hand out as many chime bars C, E, G and B♭ as you have and let the children play what they want. Fade the music in and out. Don't tackle any accompaniment until the children know the song well.

songs

One red engine
● singing game ●

WORDS TRADITIONAL
TUNE AND ACCOMPANIMENT V.C.

One red engine Puffing down the track,
Two red engines puffing, puffing back.

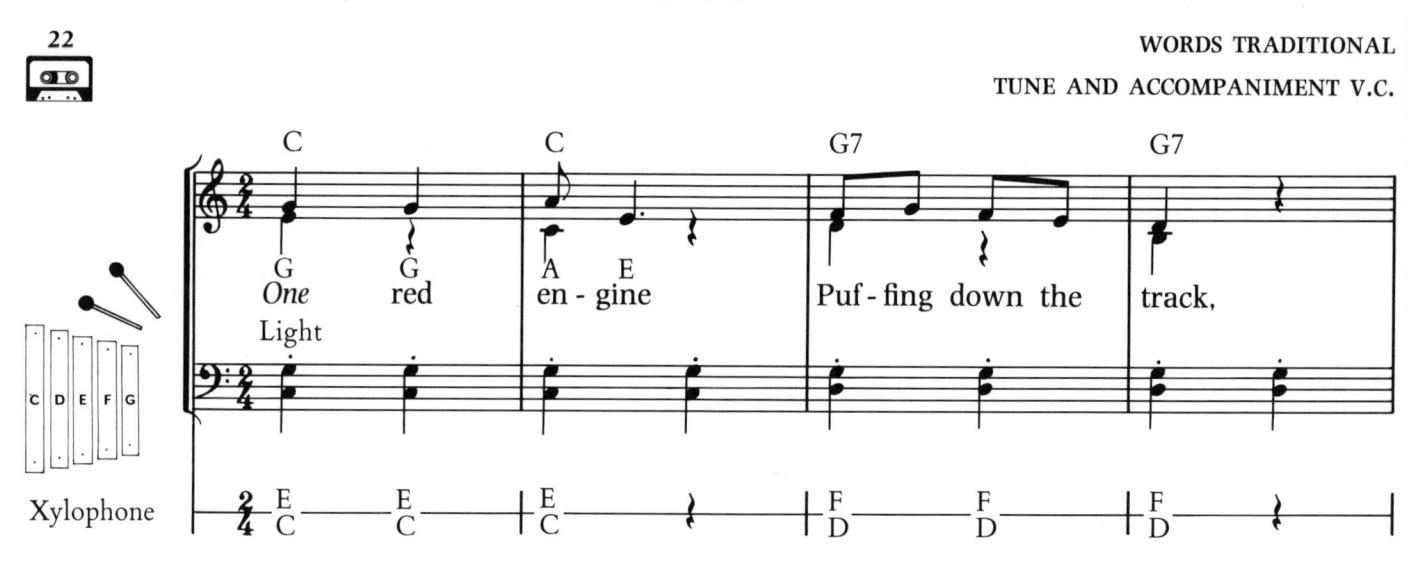

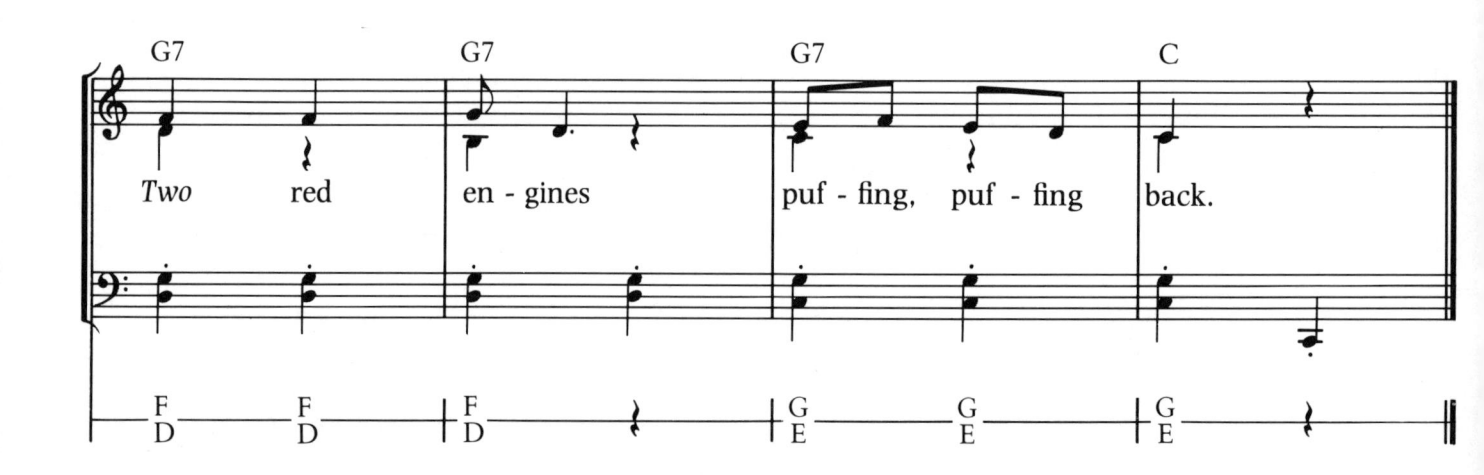

Two red engines puffing down the track,
Three red engines puffing, puffing back.

Three red engines puffing down the track,
Four red engines puffing, puffing back.

Four red engines puffing down the track,
Five red engines puffing, puffing back.

songs

This is a cumulative game where the number of engines increases during the course of the song. Sort the children into groups of five and line them up along the long side of the room. The leader of each group walks forward about two metres and stands with his or her back to the other engines in his or her group. During the first line the first engine chuffs backwards (7 beats/7 steps) and the next in the line joins on, putting hands on waist. In the second line of the couplet the two engines chuff forwards 7 steps. And so on. To start with, just have one set of five engines so that the rest of the children can see as they sing what is happening.

1. Practise shaking a slow beat with two maracas, one in each hand. Use alternate hands. Move as you play, chanting *chuff-chuff chuff-chuff*, etc. Half the class can sing the first couplet while the other half shake and chuff. Swap over.

2. Try the simple xylophone accompaniment included with the music.

songs

The train is carrying coal
• singing game •

TRADITIONAL
ARRANGED BY V.C.

The train is carrying coal, It has five trucks you'll find. At ev'ry station the train will stop... And leave a truck behind.

Xylophone ostinato: E F F# F

The train is carrying coal (rocks, steel, cars, etc.),
It has *four* trucks you'll find.
At ev'ry station the train will stop . . .
And leave a truck behind.

Talk about freight. Talk about the various ways of transporting goods round the country. In this song the number of trucks *decreases* each verse. The easiest way to play the game is for five children (five trucks) to stand facing the class. During the last line of each of the five stanzas, one child sits down. Or let the trucks (plus an engine) move on a circular route round the room. The station can be the teacher's desk or the carpet.

Make a good pause at the end of the third lines to allow for one truck to 'disengage' and sit down. Introduce a metallic rattling sound effect to suggest the uncoupling of the truck. When the children know the song well, try the ostinato E F F# F melodic accompaniment shown with the music. The two high notes (D and E) shown in the second, fourth and last bars, sound effective played by a metallophone or glockenspiel, or an octave lower on recorders.

102

sound story

The Bluebell Railway

by Veronica Clark

'We're there,' said Nick, 'slow down.' By the side of the road was a sign which said *Bluebell Railway Sheffield Park.* Mr Greaves flashed the indicator and slowed down. He turned off the main road and into a car park. At the entrance a boy wearing a cap and coat several sizes too large for him, directed the car to an empty parking space. 'Why is he wearing those funny clothes?' said Jennifer.

'I think he's wearing the uniform of a railway guard who used to work here a long time ago,' said Mrs Greaves.

'They must have had big heads,' said Julia, who was only three and a half.

Everyone, including Nan Rowland, got out of the car and stretched. A fine drizzle was falling so Nan put on her plastic rainhat. Julia and Jennifer shared a broken umbrella. At the ticket office Mr Greaves bought return tickets for the next steam train. They had half an hour to wait and it was a cold day so everyone except Nick and Mrs Greaves went into the waiting room where a real coal fire was blazing. Nan Rowland sat on a leather seat and looked at the posters on the walls. She liked them because, she said, they reminded her of when she was a little girl. Julia and Jennifer played ticky-off-the-ground until they were told off.

Suddenly Nick came running in. 'It's coming,' he yelled, and shot off again. On the platform everyone peered down the line in the direction of a faint chuffing noise [1]. 'Here she comes,' said Mr Greaves, 'Stand back.' Like a huge dragon the steam train approached, getting bigger and bigger and louder and louder. It whistled loudly [2]. Julia disappeared under Mrs Greaves' coat. With a lot of wheezing and hissing the train stopped [3]. Julia came out again.

The doors of the train opened and crowds of chattering passengers climbed down onto the platform [4]. The station suddenly seemed to come alive. Nick and Jennifer got up into

sound story

the nearest carriage and rushed for the window seats. Nan Rowland was heaved and shoved up the step and she collapsed into the nearest seat. Julia complained because the seats were itchy. She took off her coat and sat on it.

The children were very excited and wanted the train to start immediately but it didn't. After what seemed a very long time the doors were all slammed shut [5] and the guard, also wearing an old-fashioned uniform, blew his whistle [6].

Slowly the train steamed out of the station [1]. Gradually it got up speed until it was whizzing through open countryside. Smoke and soot flew past the windows and the children bounced up and down on the seats in time. 'Diddle-dee-dee, diddle-dee-dee,' chanted Jennifer, and the other two joined in: 'Diddle-dee-dee, diddle-dee-dee, diddle-dee-dee, diddle-dee-dee.' Now they were travelling on an embankment high above the fields, and the children were able to see a long way on both sides. The train went over a bridge. Underneath the bridge a small stream snaked away across the meadows. The grazing cows took no notice of the smoky monster which rumbled along above them. Suddenly the ground seemed to rise up and the train was passing between steep banks covered with tall trees. The smoke from the engine swirled up through the dripping branches. Julia spotted a rabbit. It disappeared into a hole with a flick of its powderpuff tail.

Everyone jumped as the train let out two loud whistles [2]. 'I think we're nearly at Horstead Keynes,' said Mrs Greaves.

'What's that?' said Julia.

'That's where we're going. Then we'll stop and the engine will shunt round to the other end of the train ready to take us back to Sheffield Park,' explained her mum.

'Oh,' said Julia, but she didn't really understand. She thought Horstead Keynes was something to do with horses.

The train began to slow down. It pulled into the station and stopped [3]. 'What do we do now, Dad?' asked Nick. 'Can we get out?'

'I'm stopping here,' said Nan Rowland. 'My knees are too stiff for all this climbing up and down.'

sound story

'We'll bring you a cup of tea from the station buffet,' said Mrs Greaves. She lifted Julia down the step onto the platform.

'I like steam trains,' said Julia, 'They smell nice.' She let go of her mother's hand and trotted after Nick who was looking at the key rings in the souvenir shop.

The Bluebell Railway is in East Sussex near Haywards Heath. It operates vintage steam trains between Sheffield Park and Horstead Keynes. Some of your children will have visited similar railways. Talk about early trains and about steam power. Talk about coal fires. What is steam? Boil a kettle and place it near a window so that the steam condenses on the glass. How many of the children have ever travelled by train? It might be worth considering taking the children on a short train journey.

Read the story without sound effects. Ask the children to join in the *diddle-dee-dees*. Another time, add vocal sound effects. Talk about speed and volume. When should the train sound loud, when should it sound far off? Can the children make their train sounds increase in volume as the train approaches the station? As the train travels away from the station and into the countryside, the speed will gradually increase then settle down to a regular tempo.

story sounds	body sounds	instrumental or other sounds
1 chuffing train +	voices – *ch ch ch ch*	**shakers** (small gravel, small buttons, macaroni, etc.), or **wire brush on drum or tambour**
2 train whistle	voices – *whoo-whoo*	**recorder tops**
3 escaping steam +	*pshshshsh*	rapid side-to-side shaking of **maracas** or **slither boxes** (rice, cornflakes, sand, etc.)
4 chattering passengers +	help the children to improvise suitable chatter	
5 doors slamming	aim for a random effect – clap hands	slam **books** or **bricks** down on table top
6 guard's whistle	whistle with mouth	**PE whistle**

+ sound effects which can be made by several children

games and exercises

TRAIN WHISTLE BLOWING — rhythmic patterns

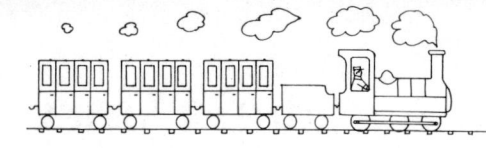

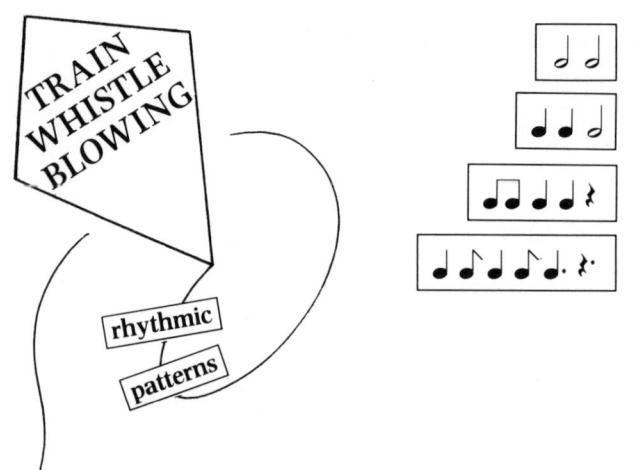

- This is a copying game. Don't analyse the rhythms. Blow one of the rhythms (left) and ask a child to imitate it on his or her recorder. *Repeat the teacher–child pattern until the imitation is accurate.* Do it again and let the rest of the class join in with a vocal imitation, *toot toot*. Try again with a different rhythm. Groups of children can copy if you have enough 'train whistles'. Make up some more whistle rhythms – they don't have to be written down.

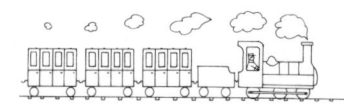

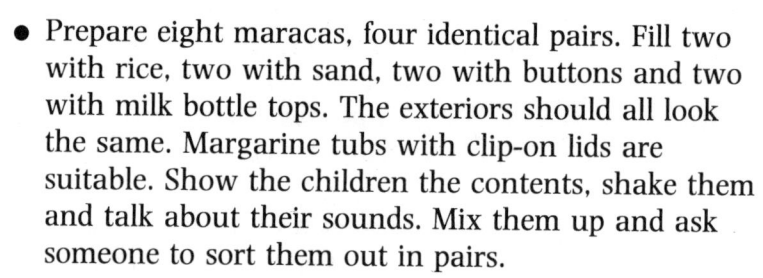

MARACA SNAP — aural discrimination

- Prepare eight maracas, four identical pairs. Fill two with rice, two with sand, two with buttons and two with milk bottle tops. The exteriors should all look the same. Margarine tubs with clip-on lids are suitable. Show the children the contents, shake them and talk about their sounds. Mix them up and ask someone to sort them out in pairs.

- Take four of the shakers behind a screen leaving their four partners on display. Ask a child to go behind the screen and shake one. By a process of trial and error another child tries to find its partner. *Snap!* (The screen isn't really necessary, but it makes the game more exciting.)

- Put the maracas and four labels — *rice, sand, buttons, bottle tops* – in the music corner for matching.

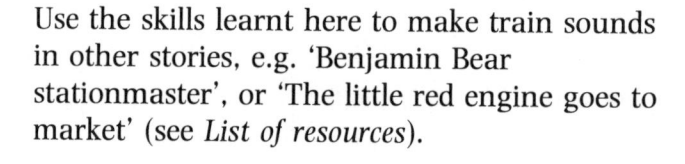

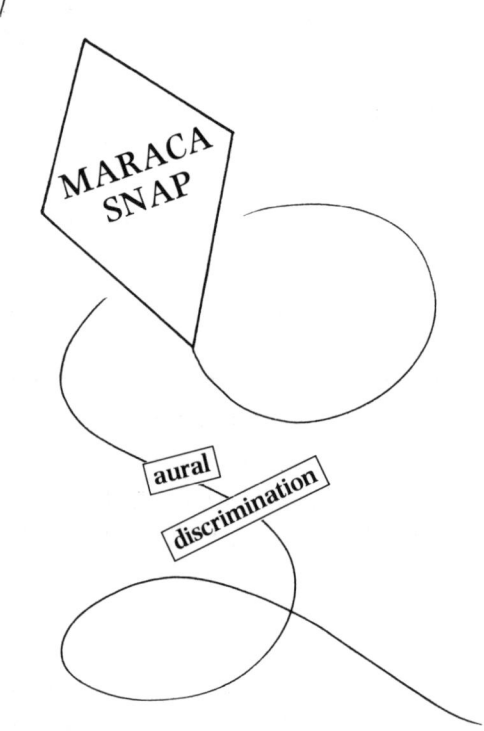

Use the skills learnt here to make train sounds in other stories, e.g. 'Benjamin Bear stationmaster', or 'The little red engine goes to market' (see *List of resources*).

games and exercises

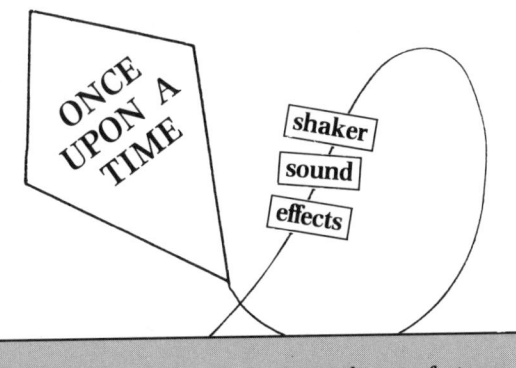

ONCE UPON A TIME — shaker sound effects

gravel in plastic pot	→ machinery, feet on gravel
sand in slither box	→ breeze, lapping waves, breathing
milk bottle tops in plastic pots	→ rustling leaves, rain
buttons in box	→ applause

- Make a collection of shakers with sounds which can be readily associated with environmental sounds (see left). See page 109 fur further suggestions for making shakers.

- Invite the children to make a simple statement beginning *Once upon a time . . .* followed by a description of something relating to one or more of the maraca sounds. For example, *Once upon a time I was walking down the garden path* (sound effect) *when I heard a hedgehog in the leaves* (sound effect).

- Gradually build up the collection of sound effects — not just shakers — and use them for poems and stories. Let the children experiment with them in the music corner.

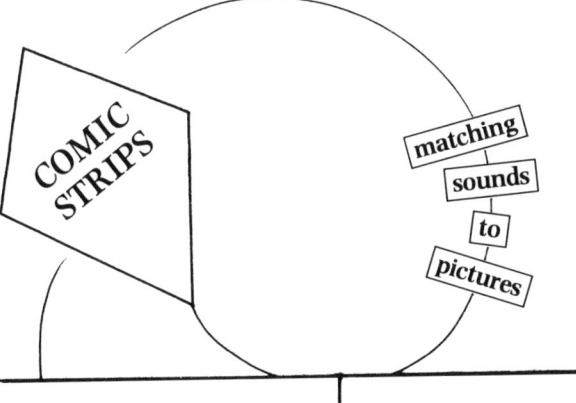

COMIC STRIPS — matching sounds to pictures

- Make a collection of comic strips similar to the two below. The four pictures in each strip should indicate a sequence of changing sound. Provide sound effects for a few of them in a class session before moving pictures and instruments to the music corner. Pay attention to speed, timbre, volume and pitch. The sounds can be accompanied by a simple monologue.

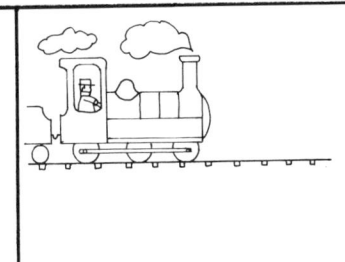

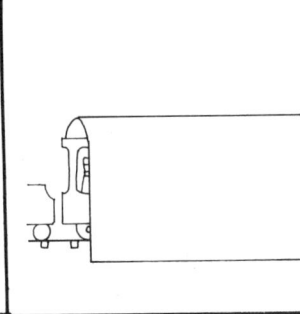

games and exercises

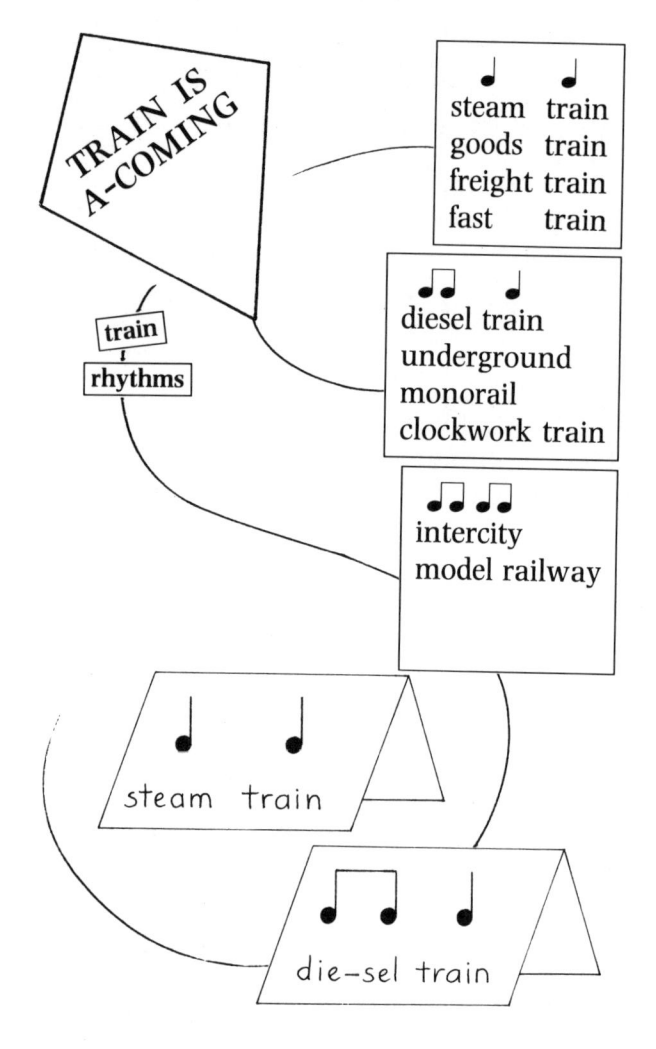

TRAIN IS A-COMING

train rhythms

♩ ♩
- steam train
- goods train
- freight train
- fast train

♪♪ ♩
- diesel train
- underground
- monorail
- clockwork train

♪♪ ♪♪
- intercity
- model railway

[card: steam train ♩ ♩]

[card: die-sel train ♪♪ ♩]

- Talk about different kinds of trains, their appearance, function, speed, etc. As they are mentioned, clap their rhythms and place each in one of the three categories shown on the left.

  Chant and clap at a *speed suitable for the type of train*. Add instruments – shakers, maracas, sandpaper blocks, guiros, rasps, recorder tops. If one of the children mentions a train which doesn't match any of the rhythm types above, clap and chant the name and record the number of claps *with noteheads only*.

- Set the rhythms to music using E G and A. Record in any way that makes it clear which notes are to be played or sung.

- Make small stand-up cards for each train and its rhythm. Put them and some instruments in the music corner. Put two, three or four rhythms together and play an extended rhythm. Either one child can play and chant the lot, or allocate a train per child and let each come in with her or his train in the order specified by the card arrangement.

- Give one of the train names to each child in the class. (You'll probably have several children with the same train name but that doesn't matter.) Play one of the *rhythms* and ask the 'trains' which match the rhythm to stand up, turn round and sit down again.

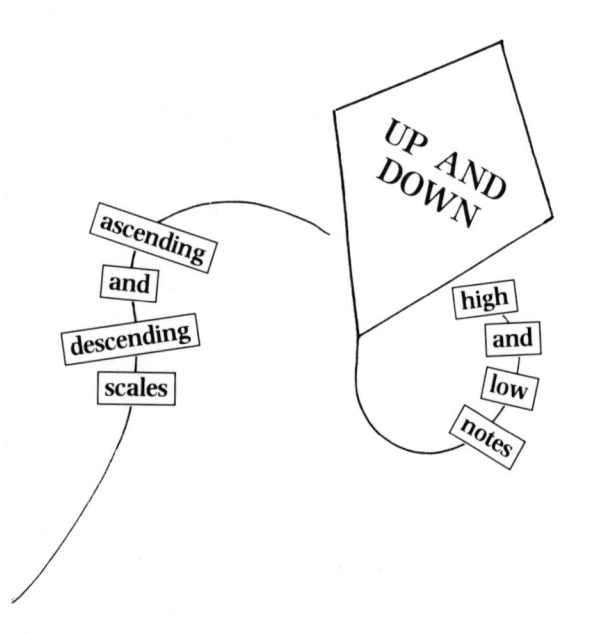

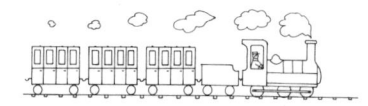

UP AND DOWN

- ascending and descending scales
- high and low notes

- Set out an octave of chimes, middle C to C above (or leave an octave of bars on a glockenspiel or xylophone, removing the unwanted bars). Ask someone to make the train sound as though it's climbing a hill – pay attention to speed. Now make it come down – fast. Can anyone make it sound as though it's travelling along a level track at the top of the hill? Now make it travel along a level track on low ground.

- Play the game behind a screen and ask the children to guess what the train is doing. They could draw a picture to show what is happening.

instruments to make and play

MARACAS OR SHAKERS

Some of the earliest maracas were made out of gourds. Dry seeds inside hardened fruit cases make a lovely rattling sound. Have a go at collecting or making some 'natural' shakers, e.g. poppy seed heads, pebbles and shells held in cupped hands, dried leaves on a twig.

Shakers are cheap and easy to make and a wide range of sounds can be produced by using a variety of *containers* and *fillings*. Young children can't manipulate large shakers so avoid washing-up liquid or large shampoo bottles. The following guidelines may be helpful.

- Use containers small enough to be held easily in small hands.
- Don't use breakable containers.
- Don't overfill containers.
- Use containers with clip-on or screw-on lids. Many a good music session has been marred by showers of rice descending on the players.
- Establish the firm rule of *no looking inside shakers during a playing session*.

Container suggestions

- yoghurt pots with clip-on lids
- pill containers with all labelling removed
- plastic herb or spice containers
- small plastic eggs (sweet containers)
- small shampoo bottles and other cosmetic containers
- plastic lemons
- small cardboard boxes – matchboxes
- tobacco tins

Filling suggestions

Beads, buttons, rice, sand, gravel, lentils, macaroni, beans, screwed-up bits of silver paper, liquid, etc.

Filling maracas can be a valuable experience in itself, involving counting and balancing. Things like buttons can be counted – try one, shake and listen, add another, shake and listen, etc. More fluid fillings can be measured in spoonfuls. Help the children to describe the sound of their shakers, e.g. *rustling, rattly, quiet, slithery*, etc. For practical reasons it's better not to mix fillings. If the children over-fill their containers, let them either start again or tip some back. *You can't make shakers without a certain amount of mess!* Put a sheet under the table where all the filling is taking place or you will be crunching lentils underfoot for weeks.

Decorating suggestions

Avoid decoration that will come off when the shaker is in use. It's a good idea to start by painting the container with one colour – use gloss or emulsion paint. Patterns can then either be painted or stuck on (self-adhesive stickers).

SLITHER BOXES

Slither boxes are long maracas. They aren't usually played quickly or rhythmically but are useful in sound effect work – waves, wind, etc. When tipped slowly from side to side they produce a sustained slithering sound. Long cardboard tubes (with the ends firmly sealed), fig, date or chocolate boxes, make good slither boxes. Sand, milk bottle tops and pins make effective fillings.

SANDPAPER BLOCKS

These are easy to make but lose some of their effect as the grains of sand are rubbed off the sandpaper. You will need some cuboid wooden bricks – of a size that can be easily held in small hands – and sandpaper. Stick a piece of sandpaper on the base of each brick and extend it a little way up each side. The finer grades of sandpaper are best. The blocks are played in pairs by being gently rubbed together.

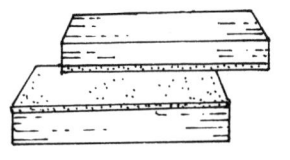

instruments to make and play

RASPS OR GUIROS

These are either notched *hollow tubes* or notched *solid cylinders*. The sound is produced by rubbing a stick over the notches. Plastic or bamboo tubes can sometimes be obtained from carpet shops. Cut into 20 cm lengths and cut notches along the length at intervals of about 2 cm. Corrugated cardboard stuck onto a length of timber can sound interesting if scraped gently. Reeded hardboard is another possibility. Try stroking a cheese grater with a lollipop stick or with the bristles of a toothbrush.

curricular links

RELATED THEMES: journeys • holidays • transport • freight • steam power • clockwork • bridges • tunnels

Language

Fill in a train and truck outline with letter *t*'s.

Collect words beginning with *tr* – *train/track/truck*.

Talk about the sound *ai* as in *railway* and *train*.

How many words can you make out of *railway carriage*?

Play *Listen and do*. Give each child a sheet on which is drawn the outline of an engine and two or three carriages or trucks. (Older children can draw their own.) Give oral instructions, e.g. *Draw a man in a red hat in the second carriage*, or *Draw five sacks of coal in the first truck*, and so on.

Play *I looked out of the train window and I saw. . . .* Each child repeats what he has said before and adds something of her or his own. This is best played in small groups. The game can be modified by asking that everything 'spotted' begins with *t* or *tr*, or that the first thing begins with *a*, the next with *b*, etc.

Read *High on a hill* (page 94) and talk about effect of distance on size. Show the children some aerial photos. *The giant jam sandwich* by John Vernon Lord contains some pictures of the countryside seen from above. Imagine you are in an aeroplane/high in a block of flats/on a cliff top/on a big wheel at the fair, and describe what you can see. Encourage comparisons, e.g. *The houses looked like matchboxes/The river looked like a piece of silver string/The people looked like ants*.

Talk about speed. Make a collection of things which travel fast. Try to arrange them in order of speed. Make a collection of 'fast' words and write them inside the outline of a rocket/a jaguar, etc. Make up stories about a race/a chase/an emergency/a creature being hunted/rushing to keep an appointment. Read them aloud using vocal speed for dramatic effect.

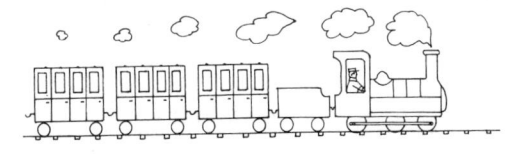

curricular links

Number work

Draw a train using geometric templates.

Construct a three-dimensional train using solid shapes. *Make it big.*

Use cereal or similar boxes to make a train with carriages or trucks. Stick the boxes to a board in such a way that objects can be put in and taken out. Label the trucks 1st, 2nd, 3rd, etc. Use the display to teach ordinal numbers, e.g. *Put Billy Blue-hat in the first carriage. Put four beads in the last truck.* The train can be used for computing, e.g. *Two more people get into the third carriage, how many people are there in the train now?/Four people get out, how many are left? Help nine people get into the train so that there is the same number of people in each carriage.*

Use railway lines to help with an understanding of straight/curved/parallel.

Help the children to draw a large map showing two towns, in between which is a river, a hill, marshland, a wood, a main road and a castle. Ask them to plan a route for a railway line, taking into consideration such things as construction difficulties, preservation of natural surroundings, length, consideration for people and wildlife. Measure the length of the finished stretch of railway line using string. Talk about scale measurements. Draw the map on squared paper and use grid references.

Make a train layout using a battery or electric train and use it to explore time. How many times can the train complete the circuit in three minutes? Add a few trucks and test again. Load up the trucks with marbles and test again. How many times can you write your name in the time it takes for the train to complete one circuit of the track? Ask the children to time how long it takes them to get to school. How long do they spend getting to and from school in a week?

Environmental studies

Make a study of trains. Extend it to include other forms of transport. Talk about freight. What is brought into the country, what is exported?

What makes trains move – steam/electricity/diesel fuel/batteries/clockwork? Make a collection of objects powered by one or more of these. Look at a clockwork mechanism. Make an electrical circuit.

Look at the various ways in which toy trucks are coupled together – magnets, hooks. Make a survey of shoe or coat fastenings.

Use construction toys to make bridges out of bricks and planks. Try to make a tunnel in the sandpit. How can the tunnel be strengthened? Talk about local bridges and tunnels. Look at pictures of famous bridges and tunnels.

Art and craft

Using a variety of collage materials, make a large frieze with a railway line as its main feature. Include on the picture things which produce a characteristic noise or sound, e.g. a school playground, a farmyard, a duckpond, a factory, an aerodrome, etc. Use the frieze to make a *sound picture* – mount a cut-out train on a stick and as the train is moved along the track add sound effects. Fade the sounds in and out as the train approaches and departs.

Drama and movement

Make lines of three or four children and play *Follow my leader*. Each 'train' copies its 'engine'.

Use PE equipment to make an exciting layout with bridges and tunnels and hills, and let the train(s) move around the room. Adapt speed to match route, e.g. slow down on hills, speed up on the straight. A small group can accompany with sound effects.

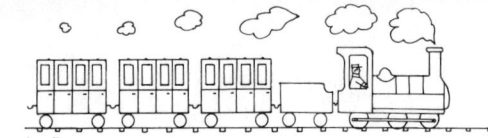

list of resources

STORIES

There's a train going by my window by Wendy Kesselman (Hodder and Stoughton)

'The little red engine goes to market', and 'Benjamin Bear stationmaster' in *Tell me a story* (Puffin)

'Huff and Puff' and 'The train that wouldn't stay on the lines' in *Time for a story* (Puffin)

The steam train crew by Andrew and Janet McLean (OUP)

Freight train by Donald Crews (Bodley Head)

Inter-city by Charles Keeping (Oxford)

Truck on the track by Janet Burroway and Janet Lord (Cape)

Polar express by C.V. Allsburg (Andersen)

The Railway Series by Rev. W. Awdry (Kaye and Ward Ltd)

The giant jam sandwich by John Vernon Lord (Piccolo)

Ivor the Engine stories by Oliver Postgate (Picture Lions)

The railway engine and the hairy brigands by Margaret Mahy (Dent)

Mandy and the train journey by Alison Coles (Hodder and Stoughton)

Topsy and Tim's train journey by Jean and Gareth Adamson (Blackie)

Whistle up the chimney by Nan Hunt (Hamish Hamilton)

SONGS

Appuskidu (Black)
   Morningtown ride

The jolly herring (Black)
   Casey Jones

Knock at the door (Ward Lock Educational)
   Let it rain (rhyme)
   Train is a-coming

POEMS

Over and over again (Beaver Books)
   You can go to sleep on a train
   Clickety-clack and clickety-click

The young Puffin book of verse (Puffin)
   Looe
   The porter

Seeing and doing (Methuen)
   Skimbleshanks the railway cat
   The holiday train
   The song of the engine
   The train to Glasgow
   From a railway carriage
   The engine driver
   The runaway train

MUSIC

'The little train of the Brazilian countryside' by Villa Lobos

Train sound effects on *Sound Effects No. 1* (BBC Cassettes)

'Skimbleshanks the railway cat' from *Cats* by Andrew Lloyd Webber

'Morningtown ride', and 'The runaway train' (*All Aboard* · BBC Cassettes)

'Journeys' – Sandra Kerr (*Macdonald 345*)

The 'Think again' and 'Swap shop' themes (*BBC Children's TV Themes* · BBC Cassettes)

'Coronation Scot' by Vivian Ellis (*Reginald Gardiner's Trains* LP produced by *Railway World*)

INFORMATION

Looking at trains by Cliff Lines (Wayland)

Trains Starters Series (Macdonald)

Going on a train by Althea (Dinosaur)

bells

speech rhymes
Deep bells, slow bells   *114*
Dring! Dring! Telephone   *114*

action rhymes
Ring the bell   *115*
Midnight   *116*

poem
Woodland fairies   *116*

songs
Dong! Dong! Dong! Dong!   *118*
Chime over the village   *120*
Lullaby   *122*
Follow the ringle-jingle bells   *124*
Pussy in the night   *125*

sound story
Father Christmas forgets   *126*

games and exercises   *130*

instruments to make and play
Plant-pot bells, tubular bells, wind chimes and gongs   *135*

curricular links   *136*

list of resources   *138*

speech rhymes

Deep bells, slow bells

Deep bells,
Slow bells,
Tolling low bells.

High bells,
Fast bells,
Tumbling past bells.

V.C.

Deep bells, Slow bells, Tol-ling low bells.
xylophone

High bells, Fast bells, Tumbling past bells, etc.
glockenspiel

1 Read the rhyme, making your voice match the two types of bell.

2 Talk about *deep bells* – Big Ben, town hall clocks, church bells, grandfather clocks. What about *high bells*? Play any bells, cymbals and gongs you have available and separate into the two categories.

3 Chant the first stanza together in deep, slow voices. Let the children make their own chanting 'tune' – they'll probably settle on a repeated low note. In the second stanza ask the children to make the words *tumble*. They probably won't attempt to match their tunes. *Maintain a unified rhythm*. Repeat several times.

4 Sing stanza 1 on a repeated middle C. Then sing stanza 2 to a descending scale (see left). Put the tunes and percussion instruments in the music corner. Try putting the tunes together.

Dring! Dring! Telephone

Dring! Dring!
  Telephone.
Dring! Dring!
  No-one home.
Dring! Dring!
  All alone.
Dring! Dring!
  Lonely phone.
Dring! Dring!
Dring! Dring!
Dring! Dring!
Dring! Dring!

BARBARA IRESON

1 Read the poem in a voice which expresses first anticipation, then disappointment, then sadness. The *Dring! Dring!*s should always sound the same. Savour the silence at the end of the rhyme.

2 Talk about telephones. Do the children like the ringing of a telephone? Ask for imitations of own telephones – you'll collect a surprising variety of ringing tones. Read the rhyme again, but instead of *speaking* the *Dring! Dring!*s, choose one child to imitate his or her phone – two rings each time. Next time ask all the children to be the phone. *Aim to sound like one phone*.

3 Make a collection of all the words in the rhyme with the *oa* sound. (Older children can compare spellings.) Speak each of the words, exaggerating the *oa* sound. What effect does this repeated *oa* sound have?

4 Clap and play the rhythm of *telephone*. Half the class can chant *telephone* and the rest can imitate

speech rhymes

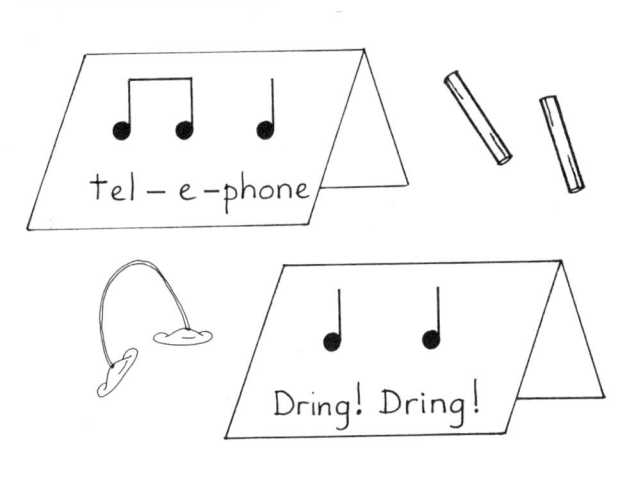

the rhythm with a telephone bell sound, *brr brr brrrr*. What other words or phrases in the rhyme have the same rhythm as *telephone*?

5 Clap and play the rhythm of *Dring! Dring!* Make up patterns using this rhythm and the telephone rhythm, e.g. *Dring! Dring!/Telephone/Dring! Dring!/Telephone/Dring! Dring!/Dring! Dring!/Telephone/Dring! Dring!*

6 Chant and play the two rhythms together.

action rhymes

Ring the bell

Ring the bell,
Ting-a-ling!
Knock at the door,
Rat-a-tat-tat.
Turn the knob,
Clickety-click.
Walk right in,
'How d'you do?'

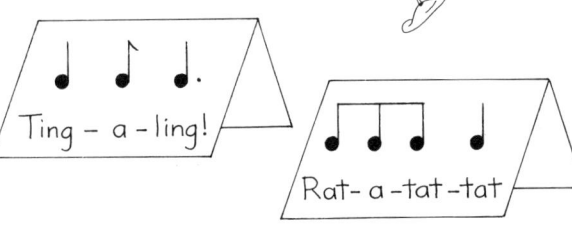

TRADITIONAL

1 Read the rhyme, making the sound effects in the even lines as realistic as possible. Demonstrate the actions:

line 2 Copying the rhythm of the words, press an imaginary bell in the centre of the palm of one hand with the forefinger of the other.
line 4 Knock the rhythm of the words in the air or on the floor or on the other hand.
line 6 Hold an imaginary handle with one hand and turn it first one way and then the other in time with the pulse of the words.
line 8 Shake hands with a partner, two firm shakes, one on *how*, one on *do*.

Chant together with the actions.

2 Choose an instrument for each sound effect – the *bell*, the *knock* and the *clicking knob* (italic lines). Accompany the chanting with the instruments. Alternatively, speak the sound effect and follow it with the instrumental sound.

3 Make and display rhythm cards for lines 2, 4 and 6. Encourage the children to practise them, chanting and playing on instruments, in the music corner.

action rhymes

Midnight

One for the priest with long black skirts,
Two for the choir with snow-white shirts.
Three for the pews so hard and long,
Four for the organ, loud and strong.
Five for the stained-glass windows bright,
Six for the candles' flickering light.
Seven for the flowers which smell so sweet,
Eight for the stone beneath your feet.
Nine for the Bible bound in gold,
Ten for the statues, smooth and cold.
Eleven for the bells in the high church tower,
Twelve loud chimes for the midnight hour.

V.C.

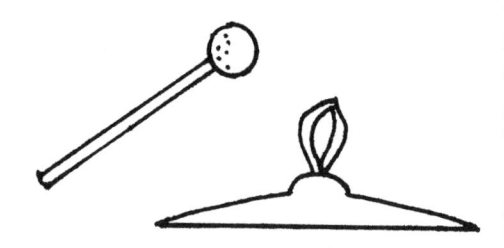

1 Ask the children to join in by speaking the number at the beginning of each line. They can pretend to pull a bell rope as they say the number. Accompany each number with a gentle cymbal chime. Speak against a background of quiet organ music (recorded).

2 Put a gong or suspended cymbal in the music corner next to a clock showing a time 'on the hour' (. . . o'clock). The children should strike the hour maintaining a steady, slow chime. Keeping changing the time.

Woodland fairies

1 Talk about the woodland sounds and imitate with voices and instruments. The wind can be whistled. Finger nails tapped against a table top make an effective rain sound. Try rubbing the bars of a glockenspiel with a wooden beater for the rippling stream. Indian bells or triangles can be used for the bluebells. Share out the sounds between the children and help each group to come in, quietly, at the appropriate place (that is, after the second line, continuing to the end of each verse). Everyone plays in the last verse.

2 Use the poem to develop gentle, quiet, body movements. Flutter, sway and spin with the wind, make dropping movements with hands and body in imitation of falling rain, travel in a smooth weaving pattern for the stream, and make flicking, spiky finger movements for the chiming bluebells. Use the sound effects practised in (1) to accompany the movement.

3 Place an assortment of instruments in the music corner and ask the children to make up some dancing music for the fairies. Work in twos or threes. Some can play while others dance.

poem

Woodland fairies

Woodland fairies, why do you lie
So still in the light of the moon?
   'How can we dance,' they said with a sigh,
   'We cannot dance without a tune,
   This midsummer evening in June.'

A light wind rustled the leaves on the trees
In the light of the silver moon.
   *'*Shshsh – shshsh*,' sang the murmuring breeze,
   'Now you can dance to my humming tune,
   This midsummer evening in June.'

The rain fell down from the starry sky
In the light of the silver moon.
   '*Pit-a-pat, pit-a-pat,*' it sang from on high,
   'Now you can dance to my drumming tune,
   This midsummer evening in June.'

The stream ran sparkling out of the wood
In the light of the silver moon.
   '*Tra-la-la*,' it rippled as sweet as it could,
   'Now you can dance to our ringing tune,
   This midsummer evening in June.'

Each bluebell nodded its pretty bowed head
In the light of the silver moon.
   '*Ting-a-ling, ting-a-ling*,' each bluebell rang,
   'Now you can dance to our ringing tune,
   This midsummer evening in June.'

The fairies started to dance and sing
In the light of the silver moon.
   *'*Shshsh, pit-a-pat, tra-la-la, ting-a-ling*,
   The wind and the rain, the stream and the flowers,
   They all joined in with the magic tune,
   That midsummer evening in June.

ROSE NEEDHAM

* or gentle whistle

songs

Dong! Dong! Dong! Dong!

V.C.

Line 1 Dm

D
Chimes
Dong!   Dong!   Dong!   Dong!

Cymbal

Line 2

F   E   F   D
Chimes
List - en   to   the   church   bells'   song.

Line 3

D
Chimes
Dong!   Dong!   Dong!   Dong!

Cymbal

Line 4

A   G   A   F
Chimes
Tol - ling   on   and   on   and   on.

118

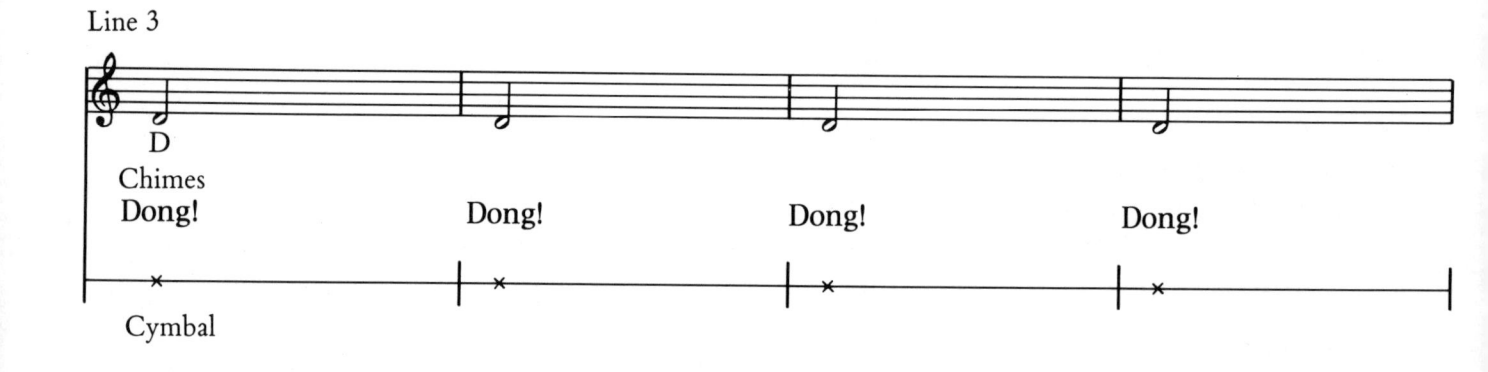

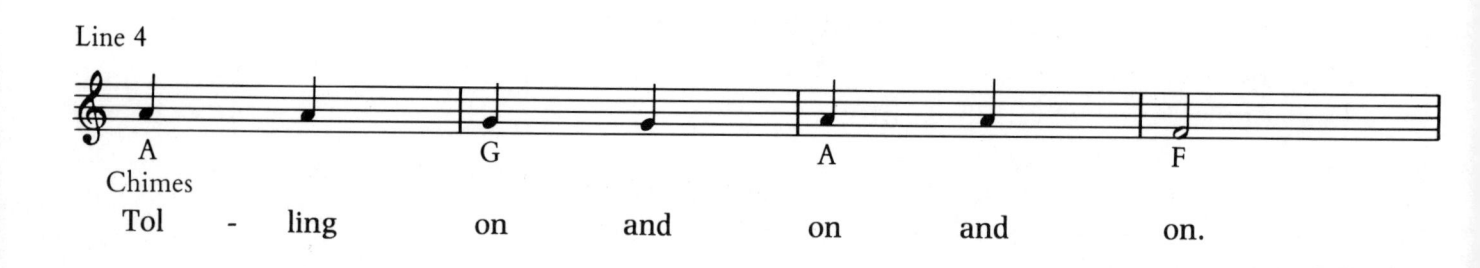

songs

Line 5

D
Chimes
Dong!   Dong!   Dong!   Dong!

Cymbal

1 Sing the song to the children and talk about church bells. What's the difference between a tolling bell and a pealing bell? Is there a church with bells (real or recorded) near the school? A visit to a church with a bell tower could be rewarding. On what occasions are church bells rung? Sing the song again and ask the children to pull an imaginary bell rope on all the *Dong!*s. Make it a *big* movement – let the body bend forwards then raise the hands above the head, lean back and pull down again. Accompany the *Dong!*s with the note D on as many tuned percussion instruments as you can. These long notes are minims (see page 131).

2 When the children know the song, talk about the tune. What's special about all the *Dong!*s? Play the tune of line 2 and compare it with the tune of line 4. Play them together. Help the children to sing the *Dong!*s on the note D while the tune to line 2 is played. Now play the tune of line 4 to an accompaniment of four sung *Dong!*s. *Play the three tunes together on percussion instruments.* Put the three sets of chimes (bars) in the music corner so that all the children can have a go. Encourage them to sing as they play.

3 Try to *sing* the three tunes together (accompanied by instruments). Start off a *Dong!* group. When it's well established, bring in the line 2 group. If each of the two groups is holding its tune well, bring in the line 4 group. Encourage quiet singing and ask the children to listen to each other. Record their efforts and play back. *Don't expect instant success* – with practice you'll be surprised how effectively your young children can harmonise, and they will be delighted at their cleverness.

D
Dong! Dong! Dong! Dong!

D E F
Listen to the church bells' song.

F G A
Tolling on and on and on.

songs

Chime over the village

TUNE 'AUPRÈS DE MA BLONDE'
WORDS V.C.

Capo 5th fret and play chords in brackets

Xylophone

Glockenspiel

Chime over the village, Chime a-cross the bus-y town.
Chime o-ver the ci-ty, O-ver hill and down. Bells ring out at
Christ-mas For ba-by Jesus' birth. Bells ring out at New Year for

120

songs

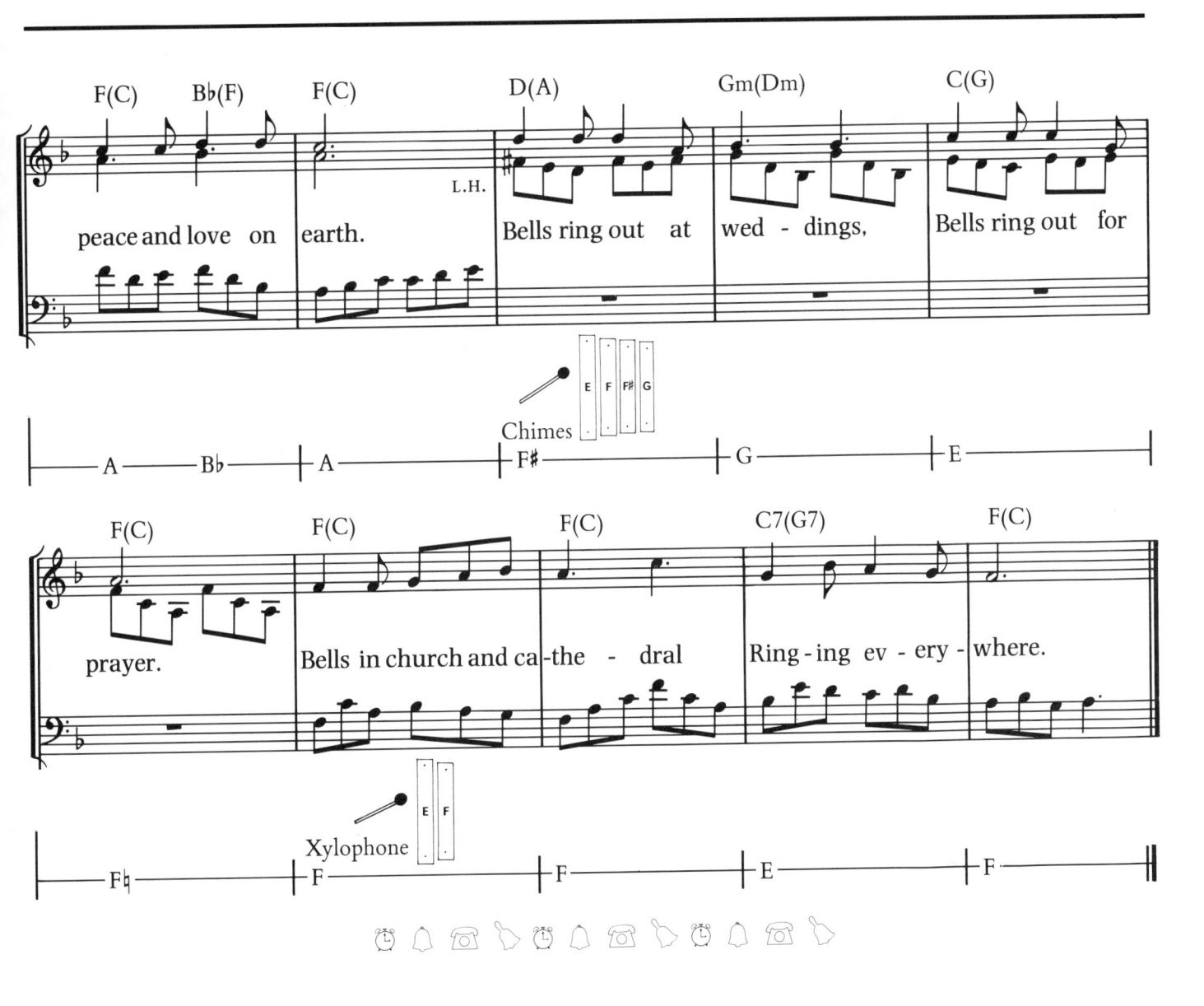

[Sheet music with lyrics:]

...peace and love on earth. Bells ring out at weddings, Bells ring out for prayer. Bells in church and cathedral Ringing everywhere.

This old French marching tune lends itself to the theme of ringing bells.

1 Accompany the first word in each of the first four lines with a gentle tap on a large cymbal.

2 Try the suggested accompaniment for xylophone, glockenspiel and chimes. This song makes an unusual and joyful contribution to a programme of Christmas music and the time spent helping three children to master the tuned percussion accompaniment is time well spent.

3 Ask the children to clap every time they sing the word *bells*, or instead of clapping, tap triangles or Indian bells.

4 Play the piano accompaniment, or get someone to play it for you, and ask the children what they think about it.

121

songs

Set out the octave of C major.

C B A G F E D C

Play a *descending* octave slowly. Ask the children to sing with you to *la*. Draw the tune in the air and on paper or the blackboard. Put an octave of chimes in the music corner and ask the children to play the descending scale. Remember that the peal starts on the high note C (that is, the smaller of the two notes C). Arrange the bars as shown left. Some children might find it strange to play from right to left, but with practice it will begin to feel more natural.

Try singing any of the following phrases to the descending octave, or to the 'Church bells' tune', as it will probably become known:

Happy birthday baby Jesus

Ring the bells to greet the new year

Praise the Lord for flowers and sunshine

Bless the happy bride and bridegroom

Easter is a time of gladness

Encourage the children to make up their own tunes of celebration.

Lullaby

This song sounds lovely sung by lots of young voices with just a quiet piano or guitar accompaniment. A delicate tap of Indian bells on the three *Twinkles* sounds pretty. Try 'splitting' the song between a group and two soloists. Choose a child with a true, high voice to sing the two *Twinkle* lines, and another child (or a few children) with 'lower' voices to sing the last two lines. The lines in italic can be sung by the rest of your children, or have one child sing it all the way through as a solo and repeat with everyone.

Lullaby

PAULINE APPS

Capo 2nd fret and play chords in brackets

Bright stars little stars shining in the sky, Shine shine your bright light on Beth-le-hem to-night. Twin-kle bright-ly, twin-kle bright-ly, Twin-kle up on high. Bright stars little stars shining in the sky. Sleep ba-by sleep, sing a lul-la-by, Sleep ba-by sleep, Je-sus do not cry.

songs

Follow the ringle-jingle bells
• singing game •

v.c.

Follow the ringle-jingle bells, Jingle bells, jingle bells.
Follow the ringle-jingle bells Round and round the village.

Who shall take the jingle bells,
Jingle bells, jingle bells.
Who shall take the jingle bells
In and out the houses?

I shall take the jingle bells,
Jingle bells, jingle bells.
I shall take the jingle bells
In and out the houses.

Follow the ringle-jingle bells,
Jingle bells, jingle bells.
Follow the ringle-jingle bells
Round and round the village.

Form a large circle (or two or three smaller ones). One child in the circle holds a set of hand jingles. In the first verse everyone skips 'round the village' in time with the music. Don't hold hands. Encourage the child with the jingles to shake them rhythmically. This is quite tricky and not all the children will be able to do it. However, the motion of their bodies will cause the jingles to ring.

At the end of verse 1, everyone stops, leaving room for the child with the jingles to skip in and out of the 'houses'. Everyone sings verse 2 as the jingle bearer weaves in and out. At the end of the verse the skipper stops and hands the jingles to the nearest child. In verse 3 the new jingle bearer continues skipping in and out – he or she can sing this verse as a solo. In verse 4 the soloist joins the circle and everyone skips round again. And so on . . .

Instead of standing 'free' in verses 2 and 3, older children can form arches with their hands and arms. This will help with the spacing.

Pussy in the night

• singing game •

v.c.

Pus-sy in the night, Pus-sy in the night,
Pus-sy ring your lit-tle bell, Pus-sy in the night.

Glockenspiel, chimes, etc.   Four times

Puss puss puss puss – ding-a-ling
Puss puss puss puss – ding-a-ling
Puss puss puss puss – ding-a-ling

Pussy dance with me,
Pussy dance with me,
Pussy come inside the house,
Pussy dance with me,

This singing game describes calling in a cat at night. Make a large circle (or several smaller circles). One child – the cat's owner – stands in the centre of the circle, blindfolded. As the first verse is sung, a bell is passed round the circle from hand to hand. Whoever is holding the bell on the last word of the first verse becomes the nocturnal cat. In between verses the owner calls *Puss puss puss* and the 'cat' must ring the bell once. On hearing the bell, the owner moves towards the sound. She or he is allowed to call three times, then must touch the person whom she or he thinks is the cat. If the guess is correct the united couple take the centre of the ring and dance round together as the rest of the children sing the second verse. (All the children can dance at this point, either in pairs or in a circle.) If the owner makes the wrong choice, the game starts again with a different child in the centre. Why not substitute the name of one of the children's cats for the word *Pussy*? Try the simple percussion accompaniment.

sound story

Father Christmas forgets
by Veronica Clark

'Grand evening,' said Father Christmas to no-one in particular, as he pulled on his fur-lined boots. 'Clear sky, lots of stars, good moon and no wind. Perfect.' As he dragged the huge sack of toys over to the sleigh he sang his special Christmas Eve song.

Chimes

San - ta's sleigh rides through the night Under-neath the stars so bright. Ding - a - ling - a - ling the sleigh bells chime,____ Tel - ling ev' - ry - one it's Christ - mas time.

The six reindeer, impatient to be off, tossed their heads and pawed the frosty ground with their hooves. 'Right, me dearios,' said Father Christmas, tying his red hat firmly under his chin, 'let's be off.' He tugged at the reins and clicked with his tongue. The reindeer started to move across the hard-packed snow, slowly at first, then faster and faster, until the sleigh was skimming across the frozen ground [1]. As the reindeer took off,

sound story

the pounding of the hooves stopped. The sleigh tilted backwards and soared gracefully up into the black sky. Higher and higher it flew until Father Christmas' house and stables looked like dots against the white snow.

Father Christmas liked this part of the evening. He had a few hours of flying before the present delivery began. He leaned back against his warm cushions and burst into song again.

Repeat song

He sang it right through before he realised that something was wrong. Puzzled, he sang it again.

Repeat song

He stopped. There was something missing. Usually, when he got to the *Ding-a-ling-a-ling* bit the reindeer joined in by shaking their harnesses. Tonight, although the reindeer were shaking their heads around like mad, no sound was coming from their harnesses.

'Oh thunderclouds and foot-rot,' groaned Father Christmas. 'Oh snowstorms and peasoupers. I've forgotten the sleighbells.' Then he remembered – he had taken the bells off the harness because they needed polishing, and in the hustle and bustle of packing, he had left them on the kitchen table. 'Christmas Eve won't be the same without the sleighbells,' sighed Father Christmas.

The rest of the journey passed in silence. Even the reindeer looked miserable. When they reached the first houses it was a not very jolly Father Christmas who set off down the chimneys with his bulging sack of toys.

In one of the houses a fire was still glowing in the grate and a piece of Christmas cake had been left out on the table, so Father Christmas sat down in an armchair for a short rest. He was just brushing a few crumbs off his beard when a little voice from the doorway said, 'Excuse me.'

'Well, well, well,' said Father Christmas. 'Well, well, well. And who might you be?'

'I'm Sonja', said the little girl who stood there, 'and I know I shouldn't have stayed awake to see you', she continued, 'but

sound story

you see my mummy had a new baby today and I thought you might not know about it, and if you didn't know then you wouldn't leave him a present, and that would be a shame because it's his first Christmas...'. She paused to take a breath.

'That was a long sentence for such a little girl,' said Father Christmas, his eyes twinkling. 'What do you think your baby brother would like?'

'Well, he's very little,' said Sonja, 'but I think he might like a rattle.'

'Right,' said Father Christmas. 'Now you get back to your nice warm bed, close your eyes, and before you can say "Jack Frost" it will be Christmas morning.' Sonja smiled, waved and disappeared as quietly as she had come.

Father Christmas gathered up the last crumbs and went back to his sleigh. He always carried extra baby presents with him, for although he was usually well-informed about new arrivals, there were always a few last-minute babies he didn't know about.

It was when he was rummaging through the sack of baby toys that Father Christmas had his good idea. As you know, babies like noisy toys: toys which bang and rattle and squeak and grunt and jingle. 'If', thought Father Christmas, 'if I sort out all the baby toys with bells, I could tie them to the harnesses and the sleigh would sound Christmassy again.' Pausing only to pop back to Sonja's house to leave a rattle by her brother's cot, Father Christmas squeezed and rattled all the toys in his sack until he had found all the jingly ones 2. The reindeer did look rather comical with balls and rattles and fluffy rabbits dangling from their antlers, but when they shook their heads they made a very jolly ringing sound.

'That's better,' chuckled Father Christmas as he climbed back into his sleigh. He jerked the reins and clicked with his tongue and the sleigh began to move 1, 2.

Hours later, as dawn was streaking the sky, a tired but happy Father Christmas headed for home. He had lost count of the chimneys he had been up and down but he was satisfied that no one had been forgotten – not even the newest of babies. As

sound story

the sun rose red in the east, the sleigh began its slow descent towards the snowy fields round Father Christmas' house. The reindeer, thinking of the warm straw and oats waiting for them in their stable, tossed their heads. Father Christmas smiled and slowly sang his song again. This time, the reindeer joined in.

Repeat song

Apart from the reindeer's hooves [1], the only sound effects required are those of the improvised jingle bells [2].

For hoof sounds use coconut shells, woodblocks, claves, jar lids, etc. Aim for a muffled effect as the reindeer are galloping over snow. Start off slowly, increase the speed, then cut out the sound as the animals take off.

When the children are familiar with the story, play the following sound discrimination game:

> Collect as many 'noisy' toys as possible – ask the children to bring them from home. Put them in a sack and let the children (without looking) put their hands into the sack and squeeze, rattle, etc. the first toy they find. Describe the sound – ringing, squeaking, grunting, etc. Guess the toy. Sort out into sets according to their sound.

Next time the story is told, put about ten of the toys (half of them *ringing* toys) into the sack and, at the point in the story when Father Christmas hunts for toys to tie onto the harnesses, let one of the children act out the scene. As the toys which ring are located, they can be handed out and used to accompany the sleigh when Father Christmas takes off from Sonja's house. Use them also to accompany the song at the end of the story.

Use cymbals, Indian bells, triangles, glockenspiels, metallophones and chime bars to accompany the following passage:

> *The moon shone round and white.*
>
> *The stars in their millions twinkled in the black sky.*
>
> *Far below, the snow glistened on hills and tree tops.*
>
> *At midnight, church bells rang out to celebrate the birth of Jesus*

games and exercises

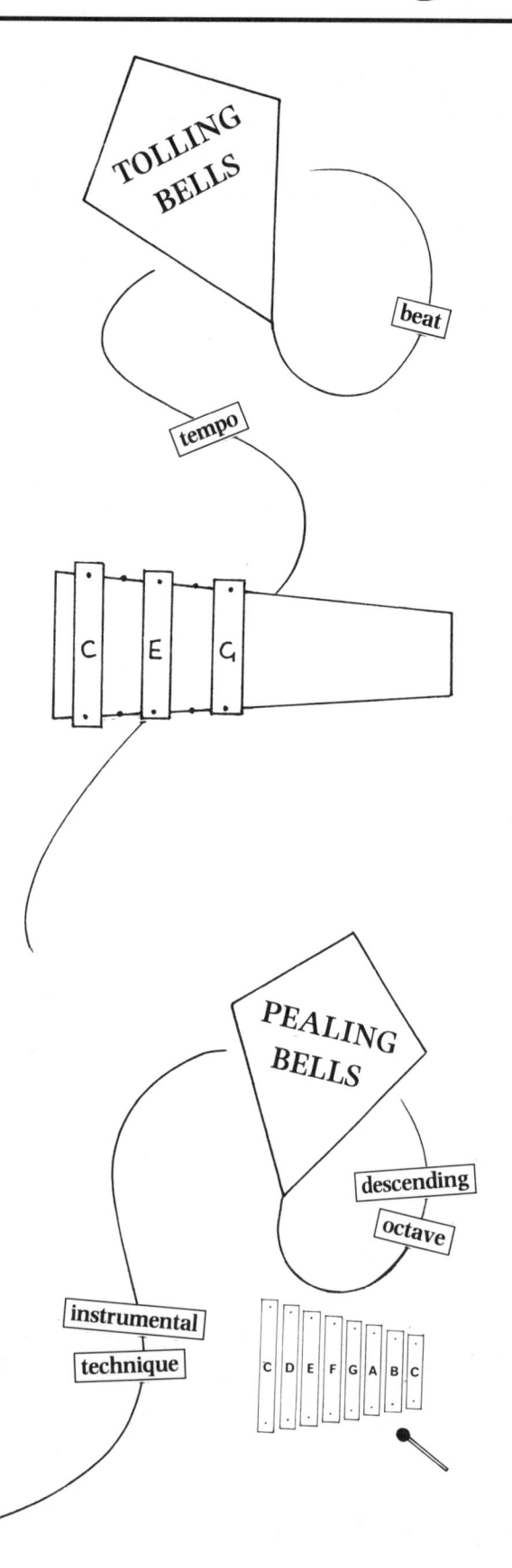

TOLLING BELLS

beat · *tempo*

- Give each child a *non-tuned chiming instrument* – triangles, Indian bells, gongs, cymbals. If there aren't enough to go round, ask those without instruments to *mime* the striking of a cymbal. Establish a regular beat (or toll) on a large cymbal and invite the children to join in when they are ready.

- Try the same exercise but this time use *tuned chiming percussion instruments* – chimes, glockenspiels, metallophones. Isolate all the notes C, high and low. Children without an instrument can *mime* the tapping of a chime bar.

- Instead of playing *the same note*, play the notes which make up the chord of C and allocate one child to each note or bar (Use all the low C's, all the E's, and all the G's.) Remove the other bars.

- *Vary the speed or tempo* of the tolling. Always remind the children to listen carefully before joining in.

- Instead of playing instruments, ask the children to *sing 'dong'* in time and on a given note. Vary the notes. Some children will find it hard to 'pick up' the pitch of the note from a chime bar. *Try with closed eyes.*

PEALING BELLS

descending · *octave* · *instrumental technique*

- Prepare an octave of chime bars, C to C'. Play a slow descending peal and talk about it. Is the tune going up or down? What does it sound like? Draw the shape of the melody in the air. Invite children to play the peal.

- Prepare an octave (C to the C above) on as many tuned percussion instruments as you can lay hands on. Allocate a child to each instrument. Ask them to try to play the peal of bells *together* – they should sound like one big bell. Conduct clearly.

- As above, but ask the children to come in with their peals *one after the other* without a break. Have the children heard church bells pealing at Christmas or for weddings?

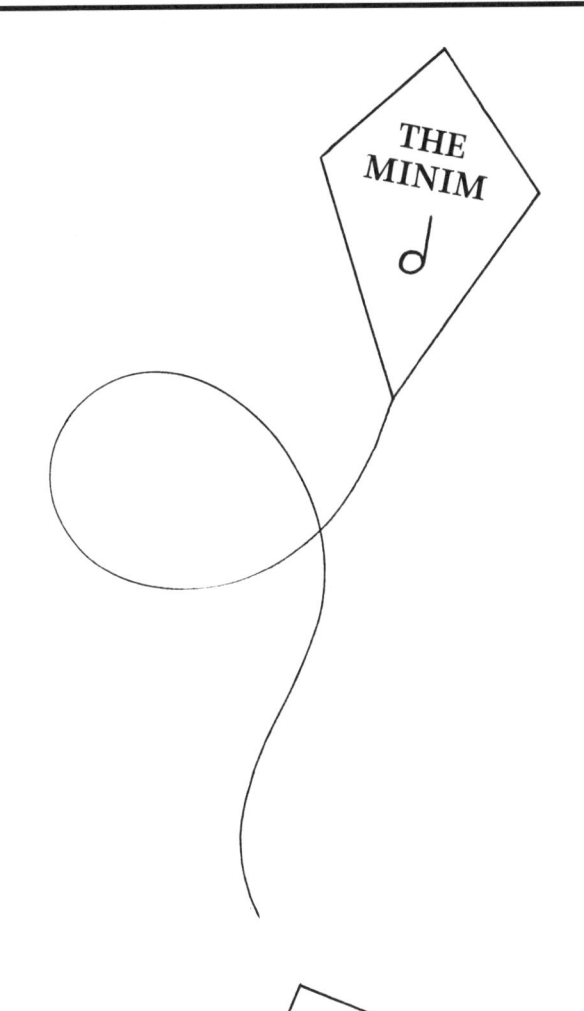

games and exercises

THE MINIM ♩

- The sustained sound made by chiming instruments makes it possible to play long notes. So far, the children have met and played and sung *crotchets* and *quaver pairs*. The *minim* lasts for *two beats* and looks like an empty crochet ♩.

- Play a steady beat on the tambour and, over the beat, sing a series of *dong!*s on D, each *dong!* lasting for two beats. Stop. Tell the children to listen carefully and count how many beats accompany one *dong!* Play and sing again. Having got the answer *two*, show the children what a minim looks like (the strokes represent beats):

/ / / / / / / /
♩   ♩   ♩   ♩

- Ask the children to sing the *dong!*s on D. Point to the minims as they are sung.

- Invite someone to try to play minim D's on a cymbal, a chime bar or a glockenspiel.

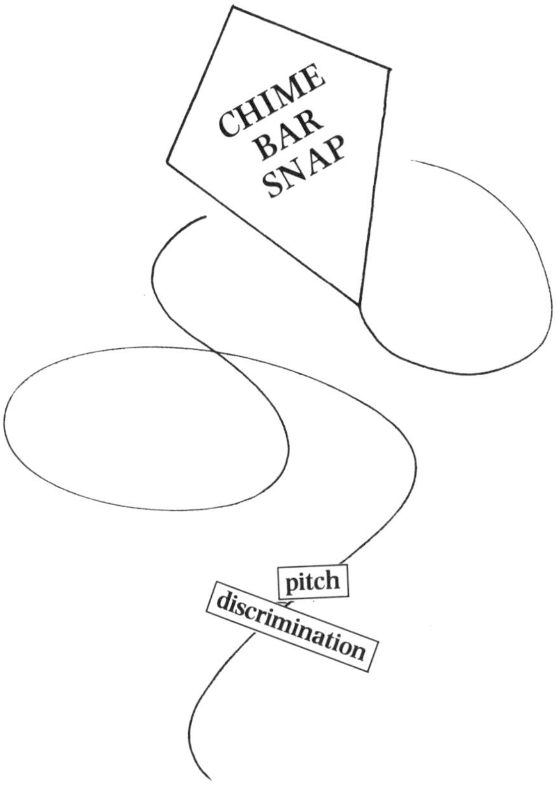

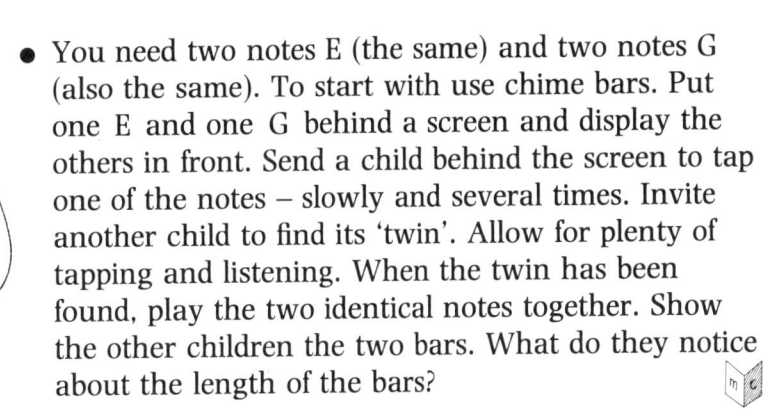

CHIME BAR SNAP

pitch discrimination

- You need two notes E (the same) and two notes G (also the same). To start with use chime bars. Put one E and one G behind a screen and display the others in front. Send a child behind the screen to tap one of the notes – slowly and several times. Invite another child to find its 'twin'. Allow for plenty of tapping and listening. When the twin has been found, play the two identical notes together. Show the other children the two bars. What do they notice about the length of the bars?

- Play again but use two different tuned percussion instruments. Put the two chimes behind the screen and a glockenspiel or xylophone (all superfluous bars removed) in front.

- Increase the number of notes to three (E G and A) and later to four (C E G and A).

games and exercises

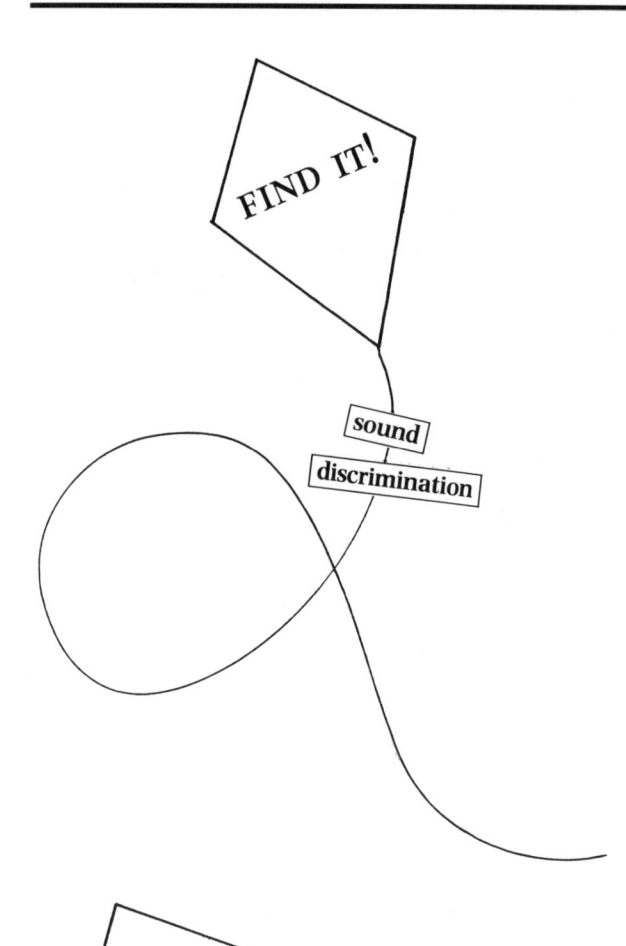

FIND IT!
sound discrimination

- Place two or three *untuned* chiming instruments behind a screen. Play and talk about each one before concealing it. Place identical instruments in front of the screen. Send a child behind the screen to play one of the instruments. Ask another to find its twin in front. The instrument should be identified by name. Hold both instruments up so that the children can *see* as well as *hear* the similarity.

- Extend the game by playing two of the concealed instruments one after the other. Can anyone imitate the sequence? Extend to three instruments.

- Another variation is for a short rhythmic pattern to be played on *one* instrument behind the screen – this makes the task twice as hard. First the correct instrument has to be chosen, then the exact rhythmic sound reproduced. Younger children will simply tap two or three or four notes, older infants may make up a rhythmic pattern of more complexity – their name rhythm, for example, or the rhythm of the instrument being played.

WHAT'S THE TIME?
aural accuracy

- You need two cymbals (clocks) and a screen. (Two identical chime bars or two triangles will do.) From behind a screen one child strikes an 'o'clock' time. Another child listens and copies. The rest of the children count with the second player to see that the 'answer' is correct.

- You need one cymbal (or chime bar or triangle) and a clock with movable hands. One child strikes an 'o'clock' time, another moves the hands of the clock to show what time it is. The game can be played in reverse – clock time first, chimes second.

- If you have a clock in the classroom, ask the children to keep their eyes open for the 'o'clock' times. The first child to come and tell you that the clock is showing an 'o'clock' time can strike the hour on a gong or cymbal.

games and exercises

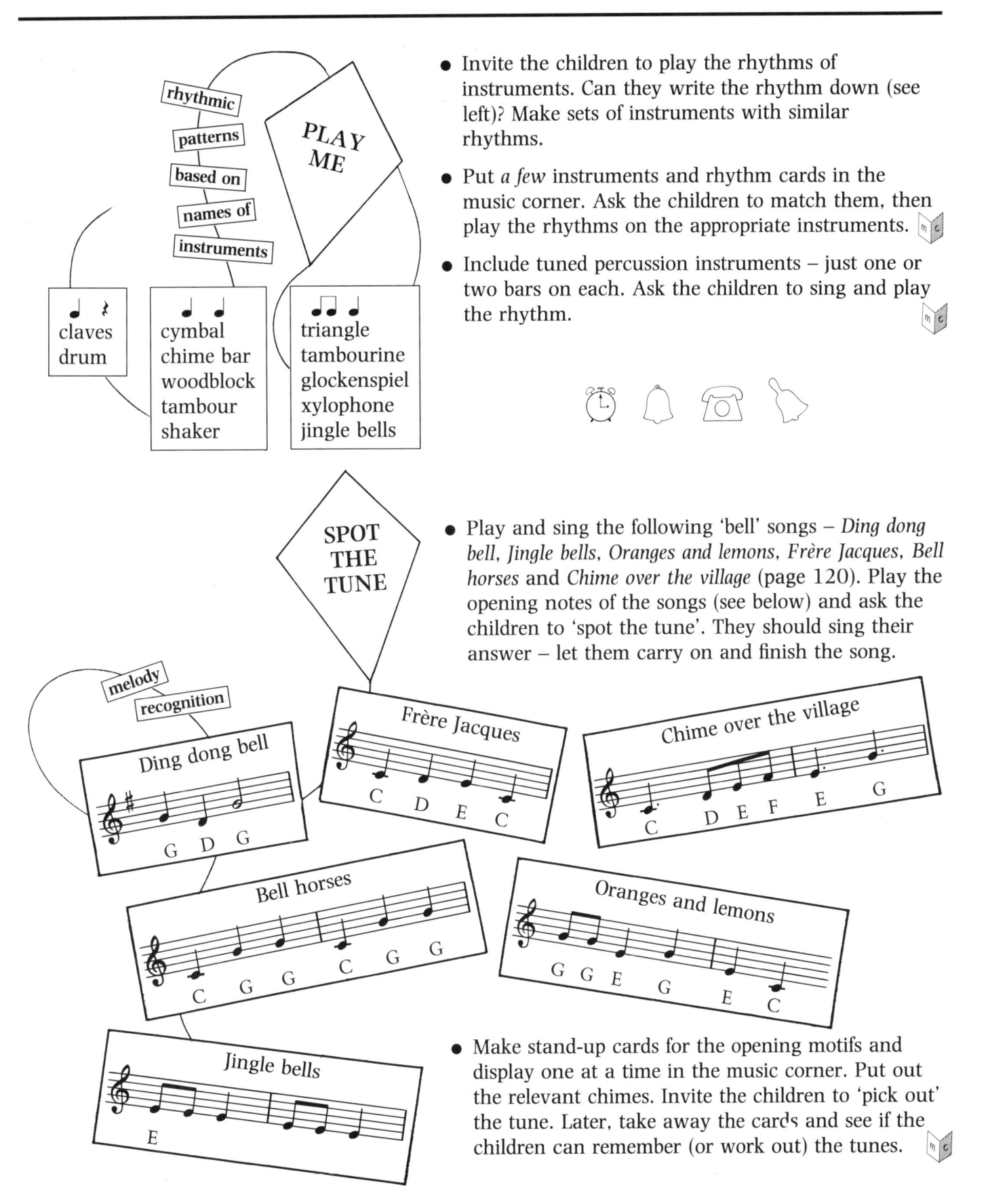

- Invite the children to play the rhythms of instruments. Can they write the rhythm down (see left)? Make sets of instruments with similar rhythms.

- Put *a few* instruments and rhythm cards in the music corner. Ask the children to match them, then play the rhythms on the appropriate instruments.

- Include tuned percussion instruments – just one or two bars on each. Ask the children to sing and play the rhythm.

PLAY ME

rhythmic patterns based on names of instruments

claves / drum

cymbal / chime bar / woodblock / tambour / shaker

triangle / tambourine / glockenspiel / xylophone / jingle bells

SPOT THE TUNE

melody recognition

- Play and sing the following 'bell' songs – *Ding dong bell*, *Jingle bells*, *Oranges and lemons*, *Frère Jacques*, *Bell horses* and *Chime over the village* (page 120). Play the opening notes of the songs (see below) and ask the children to 'spot the tune'. They should sing their answer – let them carry on and finish the song.

Ding dong bell — G D G

Frère Jacques — C D E C

Chime over the village — C D E F E G

Bell horses — C G G C G G

Oranges and lemons — G G E G E C

Jingle bells — E

- Make stand-up cards for the opening motifs and display one at a time in the music corner. Put out the relevant chimes. Invite the children to 'pick out' the tune. Later, take away the cards and see if the children can remember (or work out) the tunes.

133

games and exercises

VOLUME FLAGS

crescendo

I can play the cymbal

diminuendo

I can play the chimes

THUNDER CLOUDS AND FOOT-ROT

melodic composition

○ ○ ○ ○ ○ ○
Thunder clouds and foot-rot

○ ○ ○ ○ ○ ○
Snow-storms and pea-soupers

- Get out a cymbal, a large tambour and a chime bar – plus a beater for each. Ask the children to experiment with each instrument so that the sound gets gradually louder and louder. Try getting quieter and quieter.

- Show the children the musical signs for getting louder ———————, and getting quieter ———————. Make a card for each. Distribute instruments to the children (any instruments which will show a variation of volume) and ask them to play a steady beat, not too loud, not too quiet. Hold up one of the cards. The children should adapt their playing accordingly.

- Make *volume flags*. Write *I can play the . . . . . .* on both sides, but adapt the writing to fit the dimensions of the triangular-shaped flag. Stick the flags in potato halves or plasticine and place in the music corner near their instrument. The children should play the instrument according to the way the flag is pointing, getting either louder or quieter. The voices, chanting or singing (singing for the tuned percussion), should also reflect the flag's message. This is quite a tricky exercise. Allow plenty of time to practise.

- In the sound story *Father Christmas forgets*, Father Christmas, on realising he has forgotten the harness bells, exclaims *Thunderclouds and foot-rot* and, later, *Snowstorms and peasoupers*. Practise chanting and clapping the two 'grumbles'.

- Put out the chimes C E G and A. Set the grumbles to music. Sing and play. Remind the children that they don't have to use all the notes. To help with the recording of the music, prepare a worksheet. The notes of the tune are written in the rings above the words.

- Ask the children to make up their own grumbles, e.g. *lumpy custard, wet playtimes, shouting teachers, fights in the playground*, etc. Set them to music.

instruments to make and play

Make a collection of school instruments which *ring* or *chime*. This will include triangles, Indian bells, cymbals, gongs, jingle bells and the tuned percussion instruments. With the exception of the xylophone, the vibrating part of these instruments is likely to be made out of metal. Find words to describe the sound of each instrument.

Whereas it's difficult to make a tuned percussion instrument like a glockenspiel, there are several simple instruments which can be made by the children which will sound attractive and which will help the children to understand the relationship between pitch and length.

PLANT-POT BELLS

Earthenware plant-pots make good bells. Any crack in the pottery will spoil the tone. Collect plant-pots of various sizes which are in a good condition. Suspend from a rack – a dressing-up clothes frame might be suitable. Secure the rope or cord to the inside of the pot by tying the end to a large bead or washer or, if the rope is quite thick, with a large knot. Make sure the pots are suspended at a height suitable for the children. They should be level with their chest. Experiment with a variety of beaters but take care not to hit the pots too hard or they will crack.

Talk about the sound each pot produces. Are they the same? Relate the pitch of each note to the size of its pot. Arrange the pots in order of pitch, the deepest on the left. The deepest note should come from the largest pot, but variations of thickness may affect the pitch. The pots should get smaller as the notes get higher. Do any two pots sound the same? Match the notes with xylophone notes. Pick out some tune fragments.

TUBULAR BELLS

Collect lengths of metal tubing – most hard metals produce an interesting sound. Try copper, steel and aluminium tubing. Drill a hole through the top of each tube. Polish the metal tubing with metal polish and rub with wax polish. Suspend with either string or fuse wire. The pitch of tubing can be raised by shortening its length. It can be lowered by cutting a small notch in the centre of the tube. Let the children see you do this. Provide the children with a selection of beaters. Which tube and beater produces the clearest ringing sound? Let the children brush the tubes against each other.

WIND CHIMES

Make a collection of manufactured wind chimes. Chimes made out of shells, brass, bamboo, stone, all sound attractive. Make your own wind chimes. Frames can be made out of coat hangers, lampshade frames, small hoops, cardboard plates (stick two or three together for extra strength) and upturned plastic pots. Avoid brittle plastic as it will split when pierced. You can suspend bamboo, cane, cardboard tubes, dowelling, coconut shells, walnut shells, 'lucky' stones (stones with holes), buttons, coins, nails, knitting needles (minus points), keys, bones, lids, shells, cutlery. Delicate objects can be *stuck* to the string, and small objects threaded in bunches or rows.

Talk about the materials used – their colour, texture, length, size, structure (solid or hollow), smell, strength, weight, and suspend the chimes near a door to catch the breeze.

GONGS

The lids of round sweet or biscuit tins make quite a pleasant sound when tapped. Drill a pair of holes about 4 cm apart near the perimeter and suspend the lid with cord or string. Use the gong for clock games or to give messages, e.g. a gong *roll* means stand still, a *single tap* means put your hands on your head and listen. A musical message is more effective than a verbal instruction. Unfortunately the novelty soon wears off!

curricular links

RELATED THEMES: Christmas • churches • fairies and magic • communications • warnings • signals • celebrations

Language

Draw a large outline of a bell and fill with letter b's.

Collect words ending with/containing the sound *ell*.

Talk about household and other bells and collect describing words. Write the words inside a cut-out shape of the item they are describing, and display, e.g.

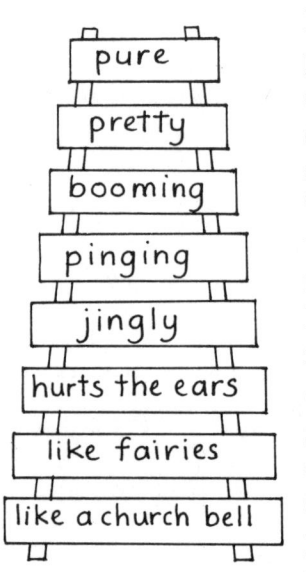

harsh

pure
pretty
booming
pinging
jingly
hurts the ears
like fairies
like a church bell

Play your tuned percussion instruments and find words to describe the various sounds they produce. Tap or rub in different ways to produce a range of sounds. Prepare a worksheet for each child showing a bird's-eye view of a glockenspiel with eight or more bars. Write a describing word or phrase in each bar, trying to match the length of the word to the length of the bar. As a reading exercise, ask the children to 'play' (with pencils) each word as it is said by the teacher.

Use two telephones to improvise a good/bad news conversation.

Make a set of picture cards, each one depicting a bell – *alarm, front door, telephone, fire bell,* etc. Shuffle. Start off a story, e.g. *When Flora got up, little did she realise what an exciting day it was going to be. She was on her way downstairs when she heard . . .*'. At this point, pick out a bell card at random and incorporate the bell into the story. Add a few more sentences, pause at a suitable point and pick out another card. And so on. Bring the story to a conclusion after about six bells. Ask your children to make a comic-strip account of the story, one frame per bell. Story suggestions *My magic bell/The morning the alarm bell didn't go off/Good news/Bad news.*

Prepare four cards labelled *queen, witch, robot, monster*. Prepare four more on different coloured card labelled *telephone, Big Ben, church bells, siren*. Label four more on yet another colour labelled *Christmas party, fire, battle* and *wedding*. Without looking, take a card from each group and ask the children either to help you make up a story incorporating the three things, or to make up stories on their own. If you are making up a class story it's a good idea for the teacher to act as scribe. The final version can be typed or written out later, photocopied and distributed. Leave spaces for individual illustrations.

Number work

Make a symmetrical bell using folded paper.

Use plastic templates to make pictures of a grandfather clock or a church.

Using a gong or cymbal, strike an 'o'clock' time and ask the children to record it either by drawing in the hands on a clock outline, or by moving the hands of a model clock.

Time the duration of the peal of either a kitchen timer or an alarm clock. Try various methods – sand timers, counting (*one – ticker – two – ticker – three*, etc.), stopwatch. As high numbers are

curricular links

likely to be involved, devise a tally system, for example put one bead in a pot every count of ten.

Show the children how to put the bars on a xylophone, starting with the longest (lowest). Check the final result with an ear test, i.e. play the notes and see if they *sound* right. Give each child a sheet on which is the outline of a xylophone frame. On another sheet prepare the outlines of eight bars (mixed up). Ask the children to cut out the bars, arrange them in order of size on the frame beginning with the longest, and stick in position.

Collect three bells of differing weights. Using a balance, arrange them in order of weight. 'Weigh' each bell using a variety of units. Record the results.

Talk about *minims* (two-beat notes). Draw three minims on the board and work out how many beats they are worth (two-times table): 2 + 2 + 2 or 3(2) or 2 × 3. Children who understand the note values of the crotchet and the quaver could make up sums incorporating several different notes, e.g. ♩ + ♩ = 3 crotchets or ♩ + ♩ + ♫ + ♩ = 4 crotchets.

Environmental studies

Before the era of telephone, radio and television, bells were often harbingers of good and bad news. Bells were used to guide travellers on land and sea. Use three or four chiming instruments to send messages – cymbal means *stand up*, chime bar means *sit down*, jingles means *close your eyes*, etc. Or, using just one instrument, pass messages using a variety of different taps or shakes, e.g. a long shake on the jingles means *line up at the door*, five short shakes means *sit on the floor*, etc.

Visit a local church, the older the better. Study the building, windows, organ, graves, bell tower and churchyard. Look at the times of the services. What is the history of the church?

Visit local fire, police and ambulance stations. Find out about their communications systems.

Take apart and look at a telephone bell unit, an alarm clock, a kitchen timer, a bicycle bell.

Talk about sound waves and vibrations. Sprinkle talcum powder on top of a large cymbal. Tap the cymbal and watch the powder dance. Feel the vibrating rim of the cymbal. Pinch it. What happens to the sound? Experiment with other instruments.

Art and craft

Cut bell shapes out of textured wallpaper. Draw round them on foil and cut out. Stick the foil bell over the wallpaper bell and gently rub the pattern through.

Cut two identical bell frames out of black paper. Stick coloured tissue paper across the bell-shaped hole in the middle of one of the frames until the shape is filled. Mount the second frame on top of the first to hide the edges of the tissue paper. Dry. Trim and display on a window.

Make bell mobiles out of bottle caps, plastic pots, etc. Either spray silver/gold or cover with foil.

Make a bell shape out of string stuck onto a wooden block and use it for printing.

Drama and movement

Use your chiming instruments to develop a range of movement: *rubbed glockenspiel bars* – rippling, flowing, weaving, floating / *jingle bells* – wobbling, shaking, shivering, trembling / *cymbal* – strong, growing, shrinking / *triangle and Indian bells* – sparking, flicking, darting, shooting. Help the children to create characters and situations from the sounds. Build up movement sequences based on stories suggested by the children.

list of resources

STORIES
The doorbell rang by Pat Hutchins (The Bodley Head)
Sunshine by Jan Ormerod (Kestrel Books)
When Willie went to the wedding by Judith Kerr (Picture Lions)
'Thorn Rose' – *The Brothers Grimm* illustrated by Errol Le Cain (Faber)
The little fire engine by Grahame Greene (Picture Puffins)
The clown of God by Tomie De Paola (Methuen)
Clocks and more clocks by Pat Hutchins (Picture Puffins)
What's the time Mr Wolf? by Colin Hawkins (Picture Lions)
Dick Whittington by Catherine Storr (Methuen Children's Books)
'The twelve dancing princesses' – *The Brothers Grimm* illustrated by Errol Le Cain (Picture Lions)

SONGS
Sing hey diddle diddle (Black)
    Ding dong bell
    Hickory dickory dock
    Oranges and lemons
    Ride a cock-horse
    Upon Paul's steeple

POEMS
Over and over again (Beaver Books)
    Bells are ringing loud and clear
    What a noisy house
    Jingle bells
The book of a thousand poems (Bell and Hyman)
    The bells of London
    The New Year
    Bluebells
    Song
    Silver bells
    Fairy music
    Jack Frost in the garden
    Chimes
    Who's that ringing at the front door bell?

MUSIC
'Fossils' from *The Carnival of Animals* by Saint-Saëns
'Dance of the Sugar Plum Fairy' from *The Nutcracker Suite* by Tchaikovsky
'Little bells' from *Wand of Youth Number 2* by Edward Elgar
The Submerged Cathedral by Debussy
1812 Overture by Tchaikovsky
'Anitra's Dance' in *Peer Gynt* by Grieg
The Toy Symphony by Mozart
Music for Strings, Percussion and Celesta by Bartók
Danse Macabre by Saint-Saëns
'Crazy dazy' by Dick Mills (*The Soundhouse* · BBC Radiophonic Workshop)
The 'Dr Who', 'Playschool' and 'Willo the Wisp' themes (*BBC Children's TV Themes* · BBC Cassettes)
André Previn's Guide to Music Vol. 2 Percussion (EMI)
Bells on *Sound Effects No. 1* (BBC Cassettes)

INFORMATION
Feasts and festivals by Catherine Storr illustrated by Jenny Rhodes (Patrick Hardy Books)
Fighting fires by Althea (Dinosaur)
The fire service (People who help us) by Irene Dodds (Ladybird)
Child Education Special, Nos. 38, 44 and 50

OTHERS
'Hang on the bell Nellie' (song) in *Okki-tokki-unga* (Black)
'Frère Jacques' (song round) in *Flying around* (Black)
'Snowdrop bells' (song) in *Harlequin* (Black)
'Oh the Ning Nang Nong' in *Poems for 9-year-olds and under* (Puffin)
'Bells' in *Moments* (National Christian Education Council)

in town

speech rhymes
Flicker-flicker-flack   *140*
Look out!   *140*
Red lorry, yellow lorry   *141*
Peanuts!   *141*

action rhymes
The flats are high   *142*
Emergency!   *142*
I pedalled past the quacking ducks   *143*
Watch out, heavy load   *143*

poems
Sing a song of people   *144*
Ace!   *144*

songs
Stroll along   *145*
Fog   *146*
Good boy Jim   *148*
Listen   *150*
Out for a walk   *151*

sound story
No sugar for breakfast   *152*

games and exercises

instruments to make and play
Outdoor sound effects   *157*

curricular links

list of resources

speech rhymes

Flicker-flicker-flack

Flicker-flicker-flack,
Flicker-flicker-flack,
The wipers on the car go
Flicker-flicker-flack,
The rain goes flick,
The rain goes flack,
The wipers on the car go
Flicker-flicker-flack.

JAN BETTS

1 Talk about windscreens and wipers. What is the function of each? Imitate the movement of wipers. Read the rhyme.

2 Help the children to move their forearms and hands in time with the pulse of the rhyme. The windscreen wipers keep moving all the time, even when the car stops at traffic lights. The children should keep their arms moving even at the end of the lines when the words stop. Accompany with light taps on claves.

3 Experiment to find a sound which describes rain hitting a car body. Play it as a continuous background to the speaking, with the claves (wipers) sustaining the pulse.

4 Another time, clap, tap, shake the rhythm of the first line. Talk about the rhythm. Put the rhythm card and a selection of instruments (ones which make the children think of wipers) in the music corner.

Look out!

Look out! Look out!
A *lorry is coming!
Look out! Look out!
A *lorry is coming!
LOOK OUT!

PAUL EDMONDS

* car/bus/bike/taxi, etc.

1 Read the rhyme and talk about road safety – the need to keep a constant look-out.

2 Let the children chant the *Look outs*. Shout the final LOOK OUT! Try again with a different vehicle (see footnote).

3 Chant the whole rhyme together, aiming for a gradual crescendo – as though a lorry is approaching and drawing level with the person trying to cross the road.

4 Let a small group or a soloist make a lorry sound as an accompaniment to the chanting. Have you got a shaker which sounds like an engine?

speech rhymes

Red lorry, yellow lorry

Red lorry,
Yellow lorry,
Red lorry,
Yellow lorry.

This is a popular tongue twister. Change the colour, change the vehicle – *gold Rolls, silver Rolls,* or *green pantechnicon, black pantechnicon*. What makes some words harder to say than others? Make a collection of vehicle tongue twisters, illustrate and stick in a scrapbook. Try clapping their rhythms.

Peanuts!

Peanuts!
Two bags for five!
They brush your teeth,
They curl your hair,
They make you feel a millionaire!
Peanuts!
Two bags for five!

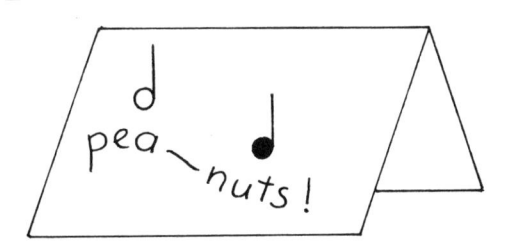

This is an old American street cry – two bags of peanuts for five cents.

1 Practise chanting the cry in unison. The *ea* sound in *peanuts* should be extended to last two beats. Drop the pitch on *nuts*. In time a sort of tune will evolve – this is to be encouraged. Lines 3, 4 and 5 should rattle along without a break.

2 Try again with a solo voice taking lines 3, 4 and 5.

3 Divide the class into two, and give one half the first two lines, and the other half lines 3, 4 and 5. Start off group 1 and when it has 'got going' bring in the second group so that all the children are chanting together.

4 Make up some modern street cries. Chant them in sequence/together.

5 Talk about street vendors/newspaper sellers/market stalls.

lovely tomatoes   Evening News
ripe juicy mangoes
green bananas

action rhymes

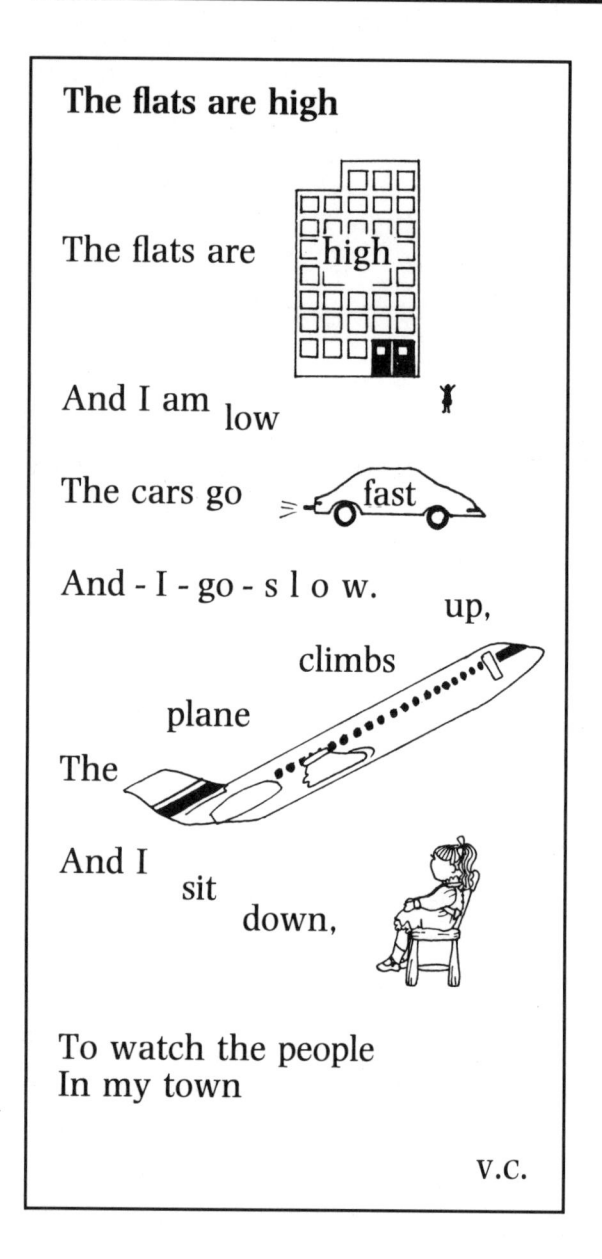

The flats are high

The flats are high

And I am low

The cars go fast

And - I - go - s l o w.

The plane climbs up,

And I sit down,

To watch the people
In my town

V.C.

line 1 Stretch both arms high.
line 2 Place flattened hand near to floor.
line 3 Whiz a hand to and fro in front of face.
line 4 Move voice and feet slowly.
line 5 Imitate the take-off flight of a plane with index finger, and stand up.
line 6 Sit down again.
lines 7 and 8 Look slowly around, maybe putting one hand up to eyes.

Practise chanting with the actions. Let voices reflect the meaning of the words, e.g. say *The cars go fast* quickly and the next line slowly. In line 5 the voice should rise, only to sink again on the word *down* in line 6. Experiment to find instrumental sounds for *high* and *low*, *climbs up* and *sit down*.

Emergency!

Whaa-aa!
Let me pass.
Emergency!
There's been a crash

V.C.

1 Chant as quickly as possible. Repeat several times. Rapidly open and close the fingers of both hands in imitation of flashing lights.

2 Form three groups. One group makes the sound of a siren, another chants *Let me pass, let me pass*, and a third group chants *Emergency!*

action rhymes

> **I pedalled past the quacking ducks**
>
> I pedalled past the quacking ducks,
> I pedalled past the hen,
> I pedalled through a puddle,
> Then I paddled back again.
>
> CAROLINE FREEMAN SAYER

Read the rhyme then talk about bicycles and tricycles, stabilisers, etc. Where it is safe to cycle, what's it like to go fast, fall off? Why did the cyclist *paddle* back through the puddle?

1 Make a fast pedalling movement with the hands as lines 1 to 3 are spoken. In the last line slap alternate hands slowly on alternate knees as though splashing through a puddle.

2 Find something which makes a pedalling sound – a guiro or shaker or vocal squeak – and something to make a splashing sound in line 4.

3 Add a few quiet quacks and clucks.

4 Try speaking the rhyme whilst lying on backs and pedalling in the air.

> **Watch out, heavy load**
>
> Watch out,
> Heavy load,
> Keep your distance,
> Clear the road.
> Flashing lights
> On either side
> Say I'm slow
> And long and wide
>
> V.C.

This slow rhyme contrasts with 'Emergency!'. Talk about heavy loads – they are sometimes escorted by police cars. The loads are often massive machines used for construction.

1 Chant to a regular slow pulse and accompany with a slow rotating movement of the arms at the side.

2 Add a quick high sound – triangles, glockenspiel – for the flashing lights.

3 Group about sixteen children into the shape of a large vehicle, and provide pretend police cars, one on each side and at the front and back, as an escort. The cars and heavy load move slowly round the room, maintaining the same speed and spacing, while the rest of the class chants the words. If you are working with a small number of children, ask the 'vehicle' to chant too.

143

poems

> ### Sing a song of people
>
> Sing a song of people
> Walking fast or slow;
> People in the city
> Up and down they go.
>
> People walking singly,
> People in a crowd.
> People saying nothing,
> People talking loud.
> People laughing, smiling,
> Grumpy people too,
> People who just hurry
> And never look at you.
>
> LOIS LENSKI

1 This is part of a poem describing people in a city. Read it and talk about the various types of walkers. Collect the children's observations about people en masse – at football matches, in a supermarket, in a bus or tube.

2 Divide the children into two groups: a 'quick' group and a 'slow' group. Ask the 'quick' group to 'walk' their hands *quickly* on their thighs while the 'slow' group should 'walk' their hands *slowly* on their thighs. *Don't attempt to conform to a fixed fast or slow beat – each child should 'walk' independently.* Try the exercise from a kneeling position 'walking' hands on the floor in front, or stand up and walk on the spot. If you have room, move round the classroom. The 'slow' children can stop and chat with each other, but the 'quick' walkers should keep moving without paying attention to anyone or anything. Swap over.

> ### Ace!
>
> Some say the world's
> A hopeless case:
> A speck of dust
> In all that space.
> It's certainly a scruffy place.
> Just one hope
> For the human race
> That I can see:
> ME –
> I'M ACE!
>
> KIT WRIGHT

This short poem will provoke a lot of discussion. Ask each child to tell you (write down) what is *ace* about him or herself.

1 Bring about ten children to the front of the class. Ask the children each to think of a monotonous sound they can make with their bodies or voices. *It must be quiet and it must stay the same.* Listen to all the sounds to check that your instructions have been understood and then bring them in one by one until everyone is humming or tapping or singing (on one note). Choose another child, an extrovert, to be the ACE. He or she can improvise a lively tune (singing *la la* or *tumpty tum*), over the drone of sound.

2 Try with instruments. Children with tuned percussion should play just one note. It will require a lot of skill to play an unchanging trill on the triangle, or a quiet sustained shake on a maraca. Allow time for practice and don't involve too many children. The 'individual' or ACE can be presented with a piano, glockenspiel, metallophone or drum and allowed to do what she or he likes with it. Tape and play back for comment.

though
Stroll along
• singing game •

Stroll a-long, stroll a-long, Stroll a-long the bou-le-vard.*

Stroll a-long, stroll a-long, Stroll a-long with me.

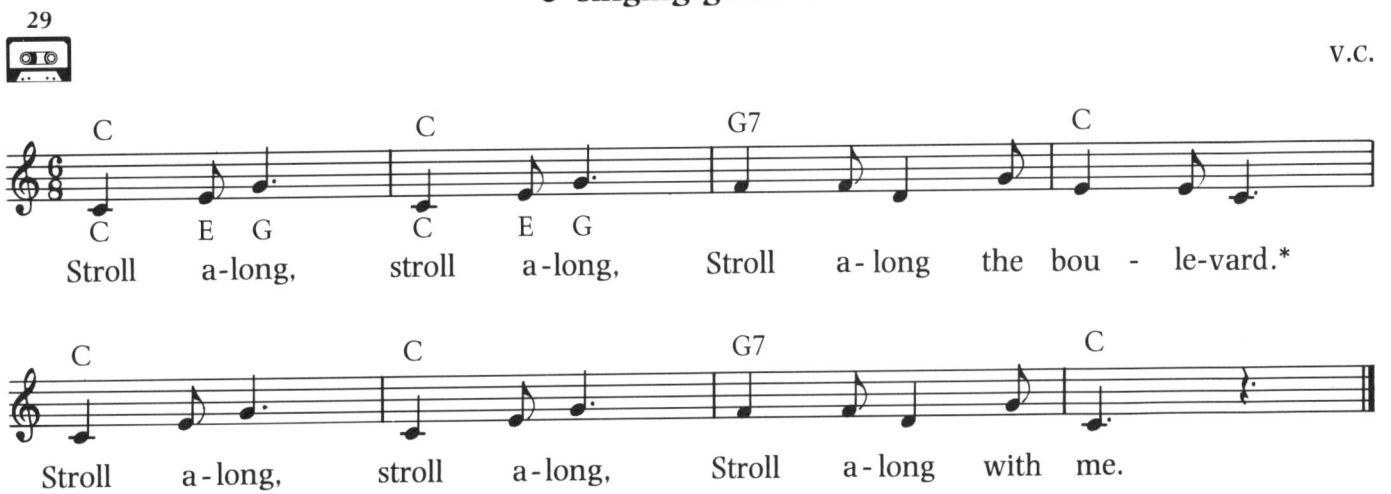

Tuned percussion
Ostinato 1

Ostinato 2

March along, march along,
March along the boulevard.
March along, march along,
March along with me.

Huff and puff, huff and puff,
Huff along the boulevard.
Huff and puff, huff and puff,
Huff along with me.

Skip along, skip along
Skip along the boulevard.
Skip along, skip along
Skip along with me.

Sprint along, sprint along,
Sprint along the boulevard.
Sprint along, sprint along,
Sprint along with me.

* avenue, alleyway, promenade, playground

songs

1 Children like this song because of the contrast in speed between the slow huffing and puffing in verse 4 and the wild sprint in verse 5. Start off in a leisurely fashion, making the strolling fit in with a lazy beat. The second verse needs to be crisp and quite fast. Straighten backs, swing arms, etc. The tempo won't change much in verse 3, but the piano playing should be lighter and the children can attempt to skip in time. You may prefer to 'gallop' along. Younger children find the sideways slip-step easier than a skip. The children enjoy exaggerating their state of collapse in verse 4. This is fine as long as they listen to the beat and make their actions match it. Don't expect the sprinting to conform to the speed of the singing – it will become a wild 'letting-off-steam' race round the room. Start again with the strolling, but this time ask the children to hold hands with a partner. Use a tambour to mark the beat. In the skipping verse, tap the skipping *rhythm*.

2 Talk about each verse and its *tempo* (speed). Add some more verses – stride along, creep along, etc. The game can be played in the classroom. Children are surprisingly adept at marching, running, etc. in and out of the tables and chairs, and it's a good exercise in controlled movement. Or play in a sitting position, slapping hands on knees (feet on floor if you're on chairs) in time with the singing.

3 By using just one of the verses (1, 2 or 3) the game can be made cumulative. One child starts off strolling round the room. She or he chooses a partner at the end of the verse and the pair stroll round as the verse is sung again. Then the two children split up and each chooses a new partner, and so on until everyone is strolling. When everyone has a partner, carry on singing to the end of the song.

4 The accompaniment is simple. Encourage the players to use two beaters. Each ostinato pattern has to be played four times per verse. Choose one untuned percussion instrument per verse to play the beat or rhythm – a lazy-sounding instrument for verse 1, a military sound for verse 2, and so on.

Fog

Capo 5th fret and play chords in brackets

SCUNTHORPE AND DISTRICT TEACHERS' CENTRE BOOK

When the fog comes down___ On the dull grey town,___ The
(rain)

songs

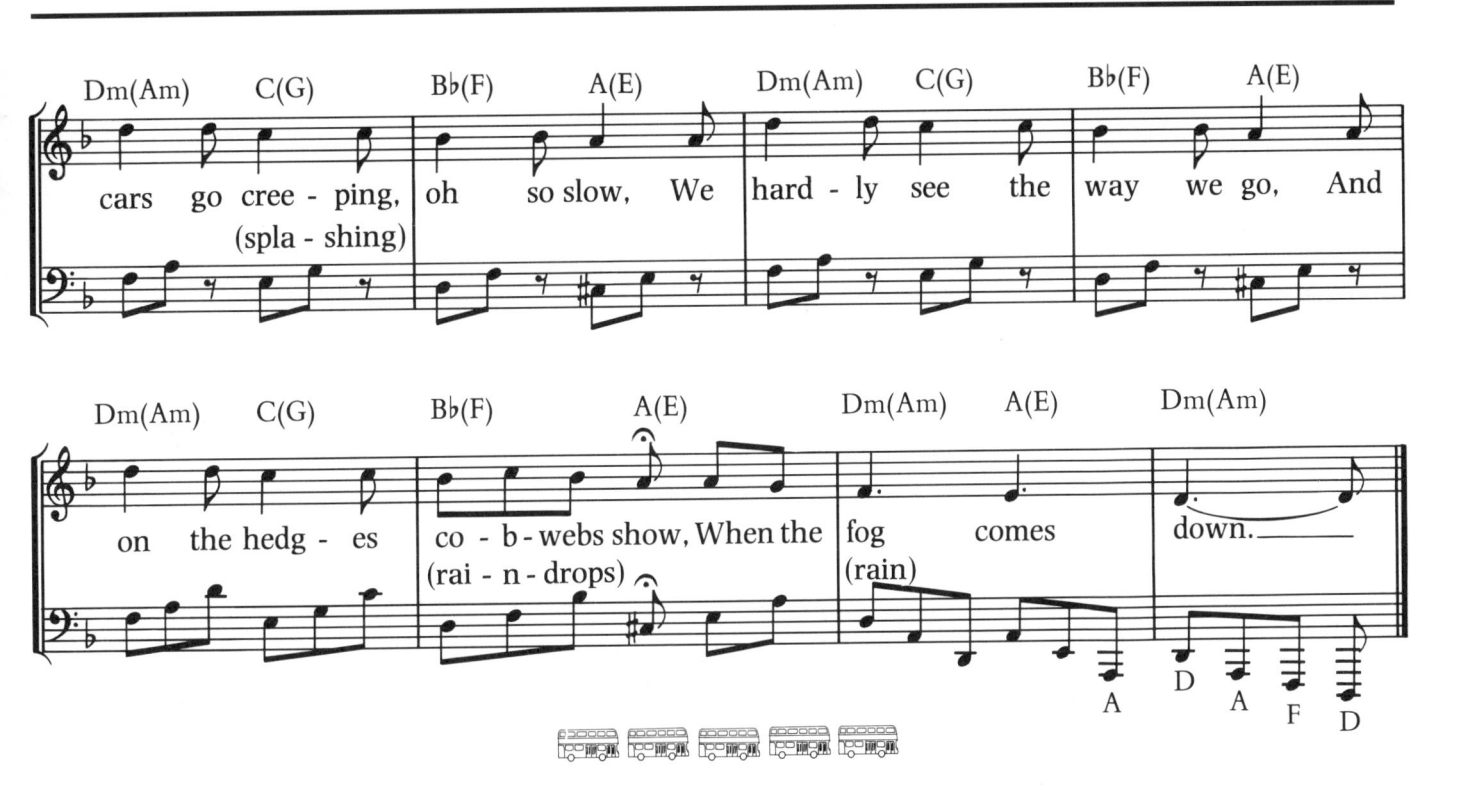

[Musical notation with lyrics:]

cars go cree-ping, (spla-shing) oh so slow, We hard-ly see the way we go, And on the hedg-es co-b-webs show, (rai-n-drops) When the fog (rain) comes down.

1 Talk about fog (mist, smog, haze). What's a *pea-souper*? Why is fog dangerous for drivers and pedestrians? Fog makes outlines fuzzy and soft – let the children experiment to produce muffled sounds, e.g. slippers on carpet · talking with mouth full · talking with a cup to mouth · hailstones on grass · horse galloping on turf · knocking at door wearing gloves · a quarrel heard from beneath bedclothes · sneeze in a hanky · singing with a toffee in mouth. Talk about the contrasts, e.g. high-heels on concrete, speaking through a loudhailer, hailstones on a glass windowpane, etc.

2 ACCOMPANIMENT The ostinato F E D can be played throughout. What sort of beater should be used? A cymbal tapped with a large, soft beater (or two) makes a pleasant muffled sound. Either try a gentle roll throughout the fog verse, or tap on the words *fog, dull, cars, hardly, on* and *fog* in the last line. For the rain verse, experiment to find the most effective way to produce a *continuous* rain sound – fingernails on tin lid, shaker, rice moved from side to side of large tambour, slither box, etc. What instrument makes a splashing sound?

3 This song is in a *minor key* and sounds sad. Put the bars D E F G A in the music corner and ask the children to pick out the tune to *When the fog comes down*. Put out A B♭ C' D' and see if anyone can play the middle section – that is, lines 3, 4 and 5. You may find your children singing a bit flat. You can't do much about it apart from opening windows, sitting up straight or standing up. You could sing it one tone higher in E minor (see chords in brackets). The ostinato would then be G F♯ and E.

See *Curricular links* (Page 159) for art and movement ideas relating to fog.

songs

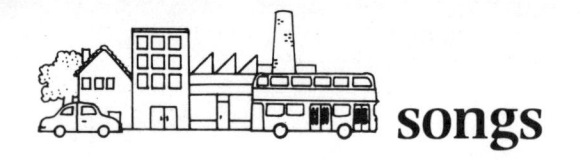

Good boy Jim

• singing game •

31

Capo 5th fret and play chords in brackets

v.c.

Chorus Jim-my was stan-ding and wat-ching and wai-ting to cross the road, cross the road. Gran-ny was stan-ding and wat-ching and wai-ting for him to come to tea. *Verse 1* He looked to the left, he looked to the right. He looked and he list-ened with all his might. But just as he was go-ing to cross, A-long came a car. *Verse 4* looked to the left, he

V.2 (motor bike.)
V.3 (lorry.)

looked to the right. He looked and he list-ened, no-thing in sight. He

148

songs

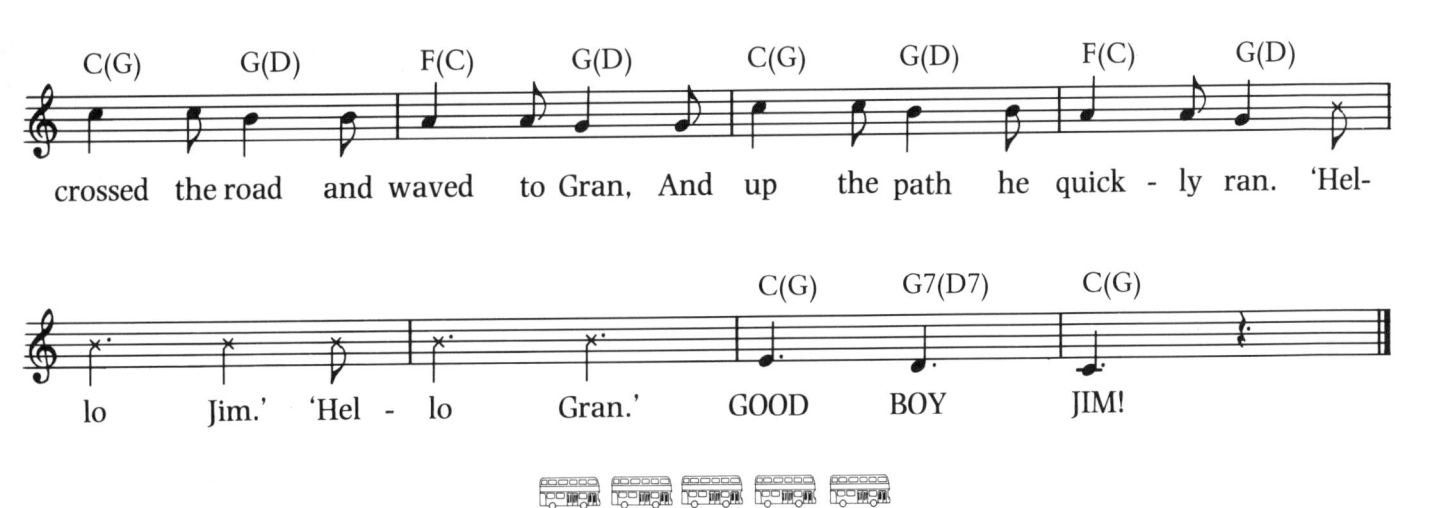

[Musical notation with chords: C(G) G(D) F(C) G(D) C(G) G(D) F(C) G(D)]

crossed the road and waved to Gran, And up the path he quick-ly ran. 'Hel-

[Musical notation with chords: C(G) G7(D7) C(G)]

lo Jim.' 'Hel-lo Gran.' GOOD BOY JIM!

This song/game was written originally to teach young children to cross the road safely. Choose one child to be Jimmy (you can change the name to that of the child), and another child to be Gran. Decide what vehicles are going to come along the road and practise their sounds. Discuss speed (likely to be in a 30 mph zone, therefore shouldn't be much variation). Choose a child for each vehicle (or pair of children for larger vehicles) and line them up a little distance away, in order. The rest of the children can form two lines to mark the sides of the road. Sit down leaving a space for Jim to cross. The chorus is easy to pick up (one child can sing the echo *cross the road*), and the children won't take long to learn the rest. The pauses allow for Jimmy to look left and right and to listen. The two actors sing their own words at the end, with a loud GOOD BOY JIM! from the assembled company to conclude.

Listen

• sound effects song •

WORDS AND MELODY V.C.
ACCOMPANIMENT JOHN PURCELL

Chorus When you go for a walk in the park, Listen, listen.
Close your eyes and you'll hear in the dark, When you listen, listen.
Verse The rustling of leaves in the trees above, (sound effect of rustling leaves) The rustling of leaves in the trees above, I can see them in my mind.

The splash of puddles as I stamp along,
   (*sound effect of feet in puddle*)
The splash of puddles as I stamp along,
I can see them in my mind.

The sigh of wind in the flowers and grass,
   (*sound effect of sighing wind*)
The sigh of wind in the flowers and grass,
I can see them in my mind.

Note: Add more verses and sounds, e.g. the crunch of leaves, the cries of children, the roar of traffic, the squeak of swings, etc.

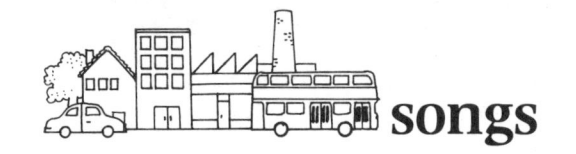

Out for a walk

• singing game •

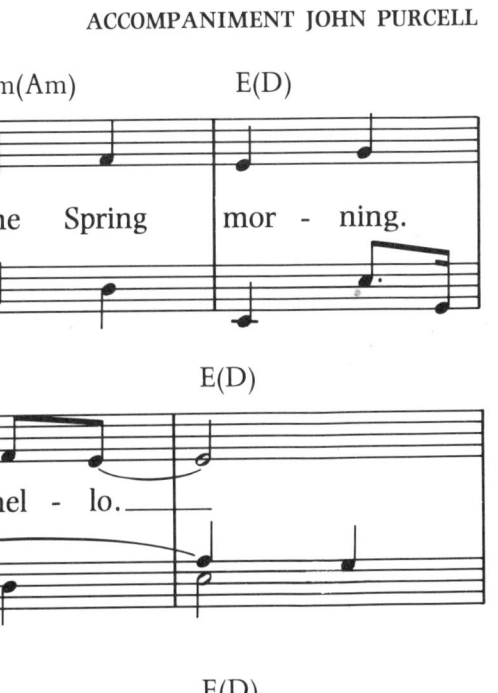

WORDS AND MELODY V.C.
ACCOMPANIMENT JOHN PURCELL

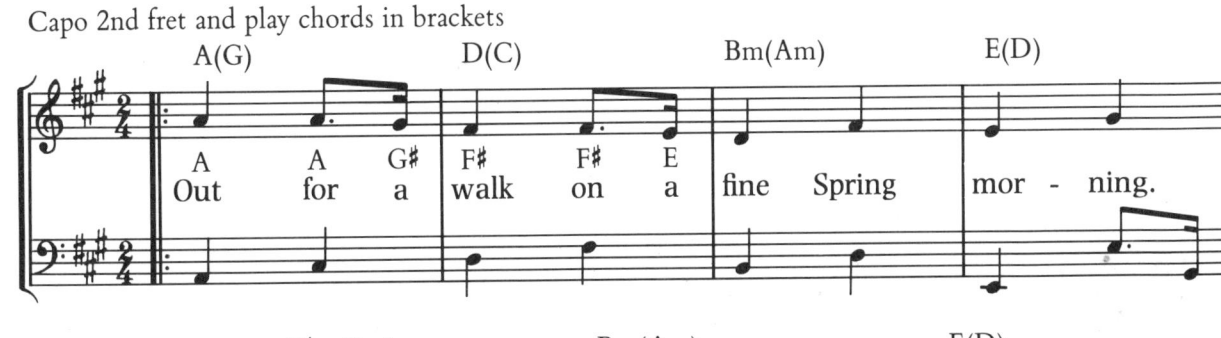

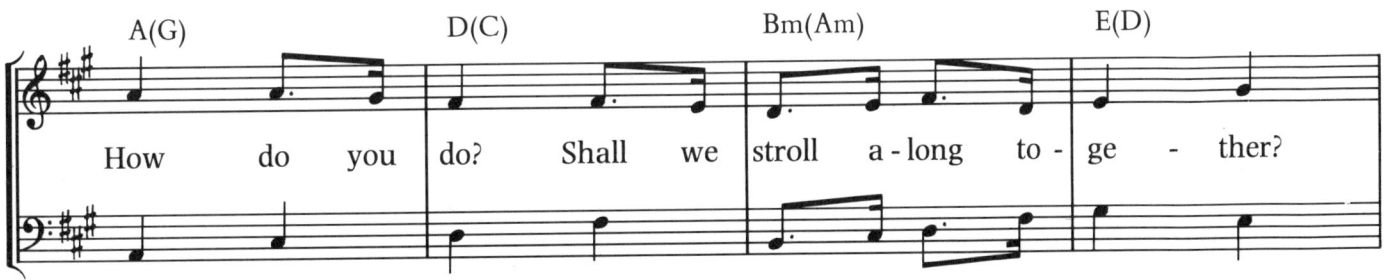

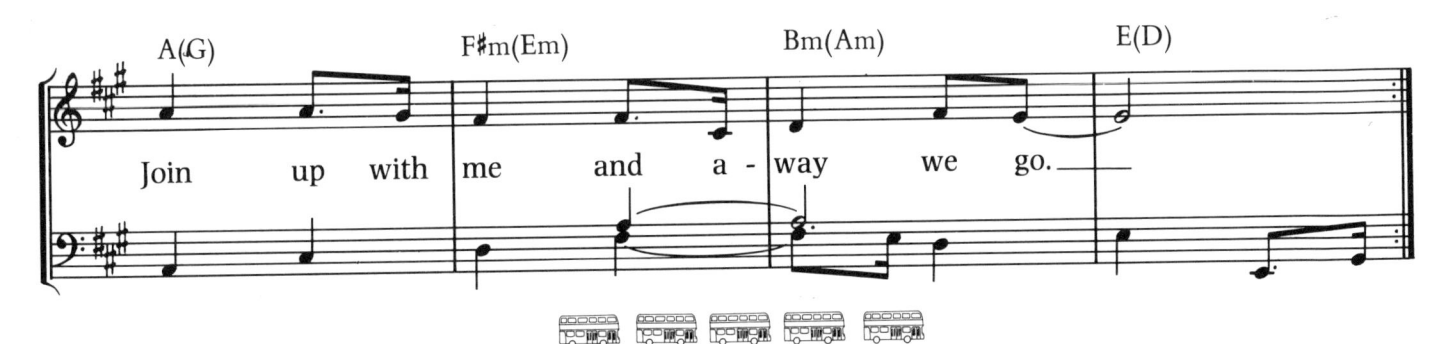

Capo 2nd fret and play chords in brackets

Out for a walk on a fine Spring mor-ning.
Look, there's a friend, let's say hel-lo.
How do you do? Shall we stroll a-long to-ge-ther?
Join up with me and a-way we go.

Sing and clap a few times until the children know the song well. Practise walking round the room in time with the fast beat (eight beats/line).
Line 1 The children walk round independently.
Line 2 They spot a friend (arrange partners beforehand or the song will grind to a halt here), and move to join him or her.
Line 3 Shake hands in time with the music.
Line 4 Hold hands or link arms, and stroll off together.

sound story

No sugar for breakfast

by Veronica Clark

Carly was not in a good mood. In fact she was feeling absolutely beastly. It all started when her mum stopped her having sugar on her cornflakes. Then she knocked the milk bottle over, and then she dropped marmalade down the front of her tracksuit.

After breakfast mum told Carly to get ready to go to the library. Carly said she'd rather stay in and watch telly but mum didn't even answer. Worse still, she made Carly put on a really babyish bobble cap, because, she said, there was a cold wind. Carly pulled the hat down over her face so she couldn't see.

As they walked down the street Carly dragged on her mum's hand and waited to be told off. Instead mum said, in quite a pleasant voice, 'I know a good game.' Carly didn't say anything. Her mum went on, 'Pretend that you're blind and I'm leading you.' Carly still said nothing, but she pulled the hat down even further and rolled up the edge to make it thicker. 'Slow down, we're nearly at the road', said mum.

'I know', said Carly.

'How?' said mum.

'I can hear the traffic. There's a motorbike coming' [1]. Sure enough, when Carly's mum looked down the road she could see a motorbike coming towards them. It roared past and disappeared up the road.

'Who's a smarty pants then,' said mum. Holding Carly's hand firmly, she led her across the road, telling her when to step down and up.

'I know where we are now,' said Carly.

'Where?' said mum.

'We're near the road works on the corner.'

'And I know how you know,' said mum as they walked past the pneumatic drill [2]. Carly put her hands over her ears.

'I'm blind and deaf,' she announced, then tripped over a paving stone. Her mum picked her up, rubbed her knee and held her hand again. Carly gave a little skip.

sound story

As they approached the park, Carly could feel and hear dry leaves crunching under her feet ⃞3. 'We're nearly at the park,' she said.

'You're very good,' said her mum. 'Are you sure you're not peeping?'

''Course I'm not,' said Carly, 'I'm just absolutely and utterly fantastic.' In the park Carly heard a panting and scampering noise ⃞4. 'Is that a dog?' she asked.

'Yes,' said mum, 'and there's something else coming along the path.'

Carly listened. 'Bicycle?' said Carly.

'No.'

'Ummm... I know,' yelled Carly, 'Someone on roller boots.' ⃞5

Carly and her mum went through the park hand in hand, and Carly listened and told her mum about all the things that were going on around them. She heard an aeroplane high up in the sky ⃞6. She heard the town hall clock strike 10 o'clock ⃞7. They walked past the gardener who was sweeping up leaves and burning them on a bonfire ⃞8. A lady in clicketty high-heeled shoes ran past ⃞9.

As Carly and her mum reached the other end of the park, they could hear the rumble of traffic in the town centre. Engines revved, horns blared and brakes squealed ⃞10. 'I like the park sounds better,' said Carly.

'So do I,' said mum.

Carly rubbed her eyes through her hat. They were hot and itchy. 'Mum, can I take my hat off now?'

''Course you can. Anyway, we're nearly at the road again, so you ought to look where you're going.'

Carly pulled off her hat with a flourish. 'Crumbs, it's ever so bright,' she said, blinking.

As they walked into the precinct, a woman walked by. She was led by a big labrador dog wearing a special harness. 'That woman really is blind,' said Carly's mum. Carly didn't say anything. She thought of the game she and her mum had played in the park. It had been fun, but only for a bit.

sound story

Get into the habit of asking your class to stop what it is doing and to listen to the sounds of the school. Talk about the sounds and analyse them: are the footsteps fast or slow, are they made by a child or an adult?

Read the story without sound effects. At the end, ask the children how many sounds they can remember. Does anyone know a blind person? Find out about guide dogs.

Add vocal sound effects, taking care with entrances and endings. The motorbike, for example, should sound quiet to begin with, roar past and fade away.

Experiment to find the best sounds for the story. Rig up a screen so that listeners cannot see anything and perform a 'radio play' for another class. Can the audience guess how the various sound effects were made?

story sounds	body sounds	instrumental or other sounds
1 motorbike	listen to a few vocal imitations and select the best	a 'noisy' **maraca**, e.g. filled with drawing pins
2 pneumatic drill	machine-gun-type stutter	another loud **maraca**
3 dry leaves	champing noises with mouth	**milk bottle tops** in plastic bag 'walked on' with hands, Velcro shoe fastenings or just hands on **crinkly paper**
4 panting and scampering +	panting, and fingernails scratching head or nylon material	fingernails on **carpet**, or real **dry leaves**
5 roller boots	a loud purring	use the real things: put them on a pair of hands and spin the wheels
6 aeroplane	hum	
7 clock	ten resonant *doi-ing*'s	**cymbal** or **gong** and felt beater – slow and steady
8 leaves +	swishing noises for the sound of brushing, and quick, light mouth clicks for the fire	**scrubbing brush** on paper and **crackly paper** for fire
9 high heels	clicks at back of mouth	**woodblock** or **claves** – fast
10 traffic +	assorted engines, horns and squealing brakes made with the voice	real **horns**, otherwise vocal sounds

+ sounds which can be made by several children

games and exercises

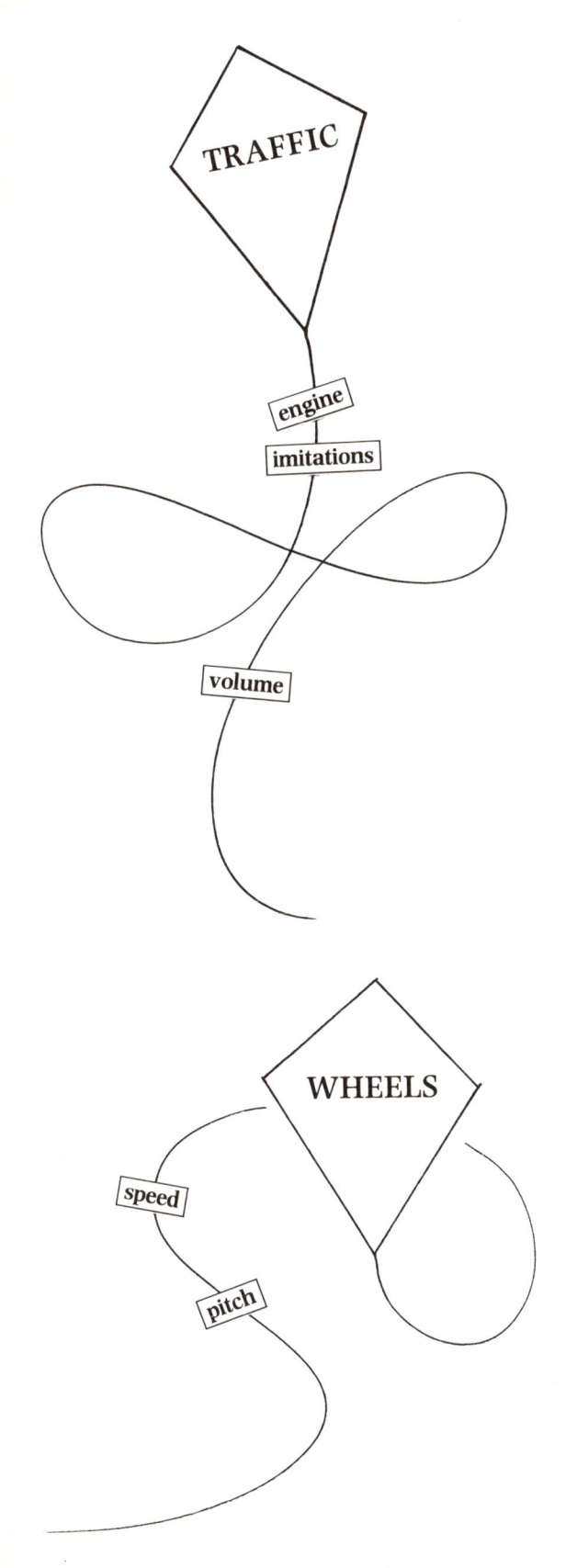

TRAFFIC
- engine
- imitations
- volume

- *Talk about traffic* – how many different kinds of road vehicle can the children name? Talk about them – number of wheels, function, size, etc. Play a tape of traffic and individual vehicle sounds (*Sound Effects No. 1*, BBC Cassettes). Imitate engine sounds, horns, squealing brakes, sirens, indicators, etc. Tape vocal imitations and talk about them. Make up a story incorporating the oral traffic sounds.

- Tell the children they are waiting to cross a busy road. A motorbike approaches (quiet vocal roar getting gradually louder and louder), it draws level and passes (maximum volume) and disappears in a cloud of exhaust fumes (fade engine-sound to nothing). Try with other vehicles.

- Show the children the musical symbols for getting louder ———————— and getting quieter ————————. Draw each on a piece of stiff card. Instigate a massed, but not too loud, engine noise. Show one of the cards and see what happens.

- Sing *Good boy Jim* (see page 148) with the appropriate sound effects. Don't forget to make the engine sounds reflect distance and movement.

WHEELS
- speed
- pitch

- Pretend to start a car and make the appropriate engine sounds – engine turning over, spluttering, springing into life, revving and settling down to a steady cruising speed.

- Pretend that the hands are the car wheels. As the car moves off, move the hands round and round each other in a rolypoly action, increasing the speed as the imaginary car moves off.

- Take the car on a longer journey and include lots of speed variations – slowing down at corners, stopping at traffic lights, going fast on the motorway, etc. *The engine notes should rise with increased speed, and drop with decreased speed.* The wheels (hands) should vary their speed of rotation according to the speed of the car.

155

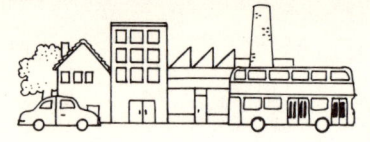

games and exercises

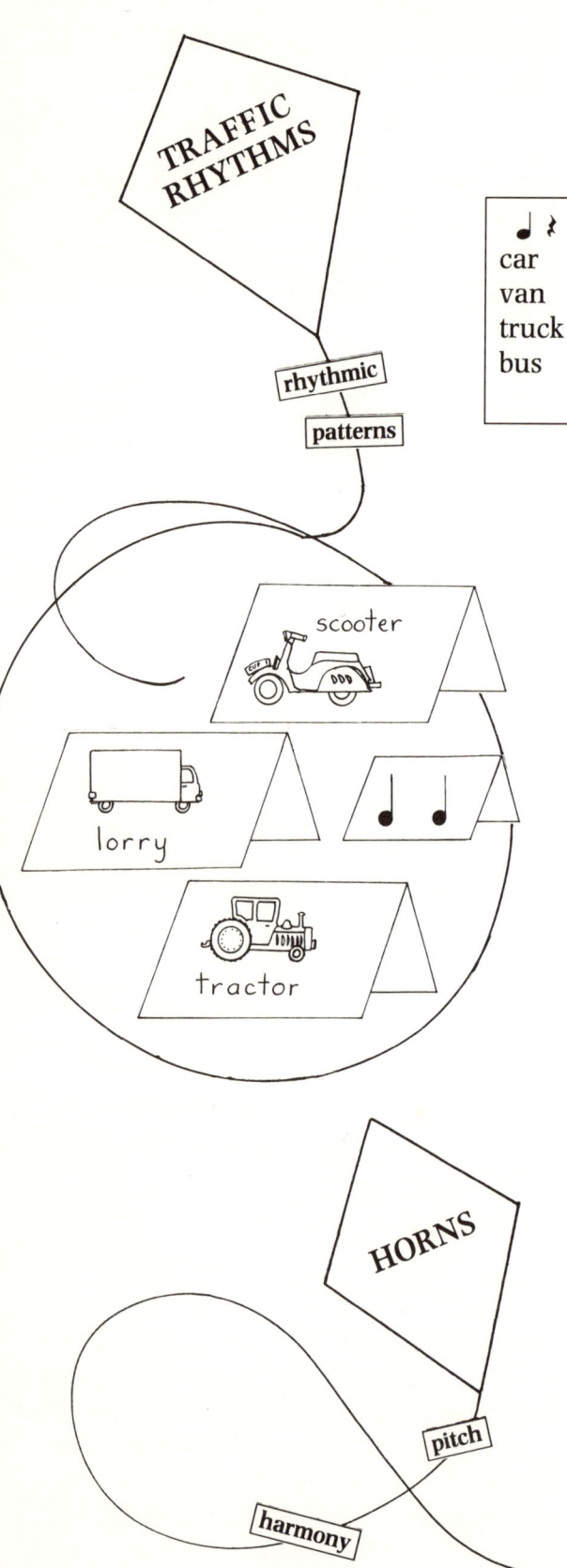

TRAFFIC RHYTHMS — *rhythmic patterns*

- Collect names of vehicles and chant, clap and play their rhythms. Count the number of notes in the rhythms. Try to identify the *rhythm pattern* of each vehicle – see below.

| car
van
truck
bus | tractor
lorry
scooter
bus | bicycle
ambulance
tricycle
motorbike
J C B | double-decker | fire engine |

- Prepare a labelled *set ring* for each rhythm group. Get the children to help you to make illustrated and labelled cards, one for each vehicle, or use models. Ask the children to put the cards or models in their rhythm sets.

- Let the children put two or three or four vehicle pictures in a row, and chant and play their rhythms. Can they write down these extended patterns – put a *bar line* between each vehicle rhythm, e.g.

  J C B | van | double-decker | bus ||

- Make up simple tunes for each rhythm using E and G. Play and sing. Record.

- Older, more experienced children can make up tunes using more notes, e.g. E G A or C E G or C E G A.

HORNS — *pitch, harmony*

- Invite car horn imitations. Talk about high horns, deep horns, slow beeps, fast beeps, long beeps, short beeps. Pretend there's a traffic jam – ask the children each to blow their horns. Why do cars have horns? Talk about misuse of car horns.

- Play a repeated, regular note C on the recorder. Ask the children to join in singing *beep* (or *parp*) on the same note. Try again, this time with the note E. Then try with G. Keep changing the note.

instruments to make and play

OUTDOOR SOUND EFFECTS

This topic about traffic and park sounds is suitable for helping the children to make realistic sound effects. There are several skills involved in producing sound effects, all of which are relevant to musical training. First the child must listen to the sound she or he wants to copy, then analyse it and finally experiment with it until a fair imitation can be produced.

The children should have available a wide range of materials – musical instruments, odds and ends, their own bodies, and maybe even the real thing – nothing can reproduce the sound of a bicycle bell better than a bicycle bell.

Below are a few suggestions for some basic, simple sound effects. Don't just think about the *timbre* or sound quality – pay attention too to duration, speed and volume. Use the sound effects to play guessing games – maybe behind a screen. Help the children to develop a keen ear for detail, e.g. *Make the sound of a horse galloping on turf*, or *Yes, it's rain, but tell me more about it. What do you think the rain is falling on? Is it a shower or heavy rain?* And so on. Help the children to make their own *Out of doors* lotto game. Provide sheets of A4 paper divided into six or eight rectangles – older children can make their own by folding – and ask them to draw pictures of things whose sounds they can reproduce or copy. Drawings done in pencil or black felt-tip pen can be photocopied so that groups of children can play. There is no element of competition in these listening lotto games – the children simply place a counter on (or colour or cross off) each picture as they hear its sound. Games which centre around one basic sound, *cars*, for example, can be most valuable in that they demand not only a discerning ear but a clever drawing hand. The pictures could include *a car starting off*, *a car braking to avoid something*, *a car speeding along the motorway*, and *a car stopping*.

Footsteps Think about and imitate feet on gravel, feet on concrete, feet on grass, feet on leaves, feet in water.

Horses' hooves Clip together small coconut shell halves or yoghurt pots or coffee jar lids. If the horse is walking on grass, place a thick piece of material on a table top and clip the pots or shells down on it.

Birdsong Most children enjoy whistling, but they are unlikely to produce a realistic bird sound. However, let them experiment – you may have a burgeoning Percy Edwards in your class! A wet cork rubbed on the side of a glass milk bottle sounds good. Use the voice for seagulls. The children will enjoy the bird whistles you fill with water and blow.

Animal sounds Try with voices. Sheep, cow or pig noises can be made with toyshop novelties which are shaped like cylinders and make a sound when tipped up.

Machinery Some children can produce wonderful, often very wet, engine sounds. Stand well back and ask for demonstrations. Small quantities of gravel or buttons or beads, put in a tin or large plastic pot and shaken rhythmically, sound like a noisy engine. Rasps and guiros produce winding and grinding sounds. Use woodblocks and claves for hammering or knocking. Keep a collection of metal pieces for jangling noises.

Rain Random or regular tapping of fingernails on a hollow surface, empty box or table top, is effective. Dripping sounds are best imitated with oral clicks.

Waves Put a small quantity of rice in the lid of a large biscuit tin or in a large tambour, and slide it slowly from side to side. Shoeboxes can be useful here. Roll a few pebbles around in a plastic tub for a shingle sound.

curricular links

RELATED THEMES: traffic • road safety • vehicles • machines • wheels • police/ambulance service/road maintenance/refuse collection • weather • maps/plans • road signs • shopping • parks • garages and petrol • playgrounds

Language

Talk about the sound *ow* as in *town, down*. What happens to the sound in *slow* and *low*?

A lot of the vocabulary used in this topic begins with the lettter *w*. Make up sentences using *wet, windy, weather, windscreen, wipers, walk*, etc.

Make a study of road signs and notices – most will be written in capital letters, e.g. GO, STOP.

What can you see from your bedroom/kitchen?

Read the poem 'Disobedience' by A.A. Milne, in *When we were very young*, in which James James Morrison Morrison loses his mother. Have any of your children ever got lost? Talk about it, write about it.

Imagine that one of the swings or a roundabout in your local playground is magic – what happens, where do you go?

Make up a scarey fog story with derelict buildings, creaking doors and cobwebs.

Write about *The day it rained black/red/gold*, or *The day it rained lemonade/soap powder*.

Talk about strangers, litter, dogs in towns (with special reference to parks), effect of noise and pollution from vehicles.

Carly in *No Sugar for breakfast* was in a bad mood. Why? Ask the children to draw a picture of themselves (small) with a huge, black cloud coming from their heads, and in the cloud write or draw all the things that put them in a bad mood. In a golden cloud, depict or write about things that make them happy.

Number work

Collect the house numbers of the children in your class. Are they odd or even? Ask the children to find out, if possible, how many houses there are in their road. How are the houses numbered? Draw a road with houses on each side and number.

Make a car survey – Who has or hasn't a car? What kind of car? What colour is it? Where was it made? Talk about car registration numbers.

Children like wheels – how many wheels has a bicycle/tricycle/car/lorry/aeroplane? Collect model vehicles and study the wheels. Have a competition to find the model with the most wheels. How many wheels have two tricycles? 2(3) = 6, etc.

Collect information about seating in a bus. How many are allowed upstairs (maximum) and downstairs?

Is there a lift in your local supermarket? If so ask the children to find out its maximum load.

Talk about one kilogram in relation to fruit and vegetables – if possible go out on a shopping expedition and buy them at your local shops or market. How many apples/potatoes/onions, etc. balance one kilogram?

Environmental studies

This topic could inspire several class visits into the locality. A visit to a supermarket is rich in

curricular links

possibilities – weighing, buying, comparing prices, making surveys (how many people use the lift during a 15-minute period/how many men, women, children enter or leave the shop during a 5-minute period, etc.)

A nearby park can be a good focus for study. Playgrounds might inspire the children to look at the structure of the equipment.

Invite the local police, fire brigade or ambulance service to visit you (with vehicles). Involve parents where possible.

If there are any road works in your area, go out and watch the work in progress. The children will be amazed to see what goes on under a road.

What happens to your litter? Visit your local tip and find out.

Art and craft

Make a city-skyline frieze using tall rectangles, or use painted or covered boxes for a 3-dimensional effect. A night-time frieze looks effective if the buildings are black with gold or yellow windows. Stick cars on a road at the bottom with glowing front and back lights (gold, silver and red foil). Fix up some Christmas tree lights for street lamps.

Show the children *Rosie's walk* by Pat Hutchins. Make a large television out of a cardboard carton and paint or draw Rosie's walk on a long strip of paper. Pass it through the screen and add a commentary. The children can make up their own television stories.

Make a foggy picture – paint a picture of a street scene, then, when it is dry, stick a piece of grey tissue over it. Or cover a sheet of paper with a grey wash and paint over it while it is still damp – this will give everything a blurred effect.

Movement and drama

Practise making strong, precise shapes. Now try soft, relaxed, rounded shapes. Relate to weather conditions – in clear sunlight everything looks clear, but fog softens the outlines of objects. Use a *triangle* to suggest sunshine and a *soft beater* on a *cymbal*, for fog. Start off with, for example, the shape of a lamp-post to the accompaniment of a trilling triangle. Fade and start a soft roll on the cymbal. As the fog descends the children should slowly 'muffle' their shape. Try a tree shape, a crane, a policewoman on traffic duty, a dustbin.

No sugar for breakfast (page 152) describes how a blindfolded Carly was led across the park by her mother. Make an obstacle course in the hall using PE equipment. The children get into pairs, one pretends to be blind (eyes closed or blindfolded), the other is the leader. First ask the children to lead each other round the hall without touching anything. Then let the 'blind' people feel the obstacles and guess what they are.

Ask one child at a time to feel the outline of an imaginary car/lamp-post/roundabout.

Imitate the movements of a range of vehicles and machines – cranes, pneumatic drills, diggers, motorbikes, scooters. Match speed to machine. Play the guessing game, *What am I?*

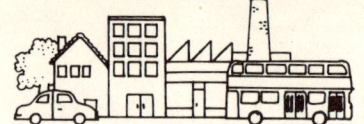

list of resources

POEMS
This little Puffin (Puffin)
   The policeman
   Here comes a big red bus
   Tall shop in the town
   As I was walking down the street
   The wheels of the bus go round and round
The young Puffin book of verse (Puffin)
   The window cleaner
   General store
Seeing and doing (Methuen)
   Adventure
   The park
When we were very young (Methuen)
   Disobedience
   Lines and squares
Others
   'Snowy morning' in *Listening · Sense and Nonsense* (Macdonald)
   'The town' in *Moments* (NCEC)
   'Roller skating' in *Harlequin* (Black) (song)
   'Lollipop man' in *Flying around* (Black) (song)
   Going out · poems and photographs selected by Shona McKellar

SONGS
Knock at the door (Ward Lock)
   My motor is humming (rhyme)
   Old John Muddlecombe (rhyme)
   One wheel on a barrow (rhyme)
   Two fat gentlemen (rhyme)
   Daisy
   Our milkman (rhyme)
   Marching in our wellingtons (rhyme)
Sing hey diddle diddle (Black)
   Dr Foster went to Gloucester
   Yankee Doodle
Dancing rhymes (Ladybird)
   O have you seen the muffin man
   Sally go round the moon
   Round and round the village

STORIES
The shopping basket by John Burningham (OUP)
At the shops by L.A. Ivory (Burke)
In the street by L.A. Ivory (Burke)
Lost and found by Camilla Jessel (Methuen Chatter Books)
The wind blew and *Rosie's walk* by Pat Hutchins (Picture Puffins)
Meg's car and *Mog in the fog* by Helen Nicoll and Jan Pienkowski (Picture Puffins)
Teddy Bear postman/coalman/baker/dustman by Phoebe and Selby Worthington (Warne)
Going shopping by Sarah Garland (The Bodley Head)
The bears' bicycle by Emilie Warren McLeod (Andre Deutsch)
Ben's Box (pop-up) by Michael Foreman (Hodder and Stoughton)
Having a picnic by Sarah Garland (Picture Puffin)
When we went to the park by Shirley Hughes (Walker Books)
What Sadie sang by Eve Rice (The Bodley Head)
'Pip goes to the country', 'Marmaduke in a jam' and 'The boy who ran away' from *Tell me another story* (Puffin)

MUSIC
Cockaigne (In London Town) Overture by Edward Elgar
'The flight of the bumble-bee' by Rimsky-Korsakof
'Catch the wind' by Dick Mills (*The Soundhouse* · BBC Radiophonic Workshop)
'Wiper flop', 'Come to the shops' and 'Wheels keep turning' (*Sing a Song of Playschool* · BBC Cassettes)
'Journeys' – Sandra Kerr (*Macdonald 345*)
Sounds around the town on *Sound Effects No. 1* (BBC Cassettes)

INFORMATION
The shopkeeper by Anne Stewart (Hamilton)
Slam bang (first words) by John Burningham (Walker Books)
Rain (book without words) by Peter Spier (Collins)
Building a house by Althea (Dinosaur Books)
Making a road by Althea (Dinosaur Books)
Cars and trucks by Graham Thompson (Macdonald)